ANGEL PATRIOTS

Angel Patriots

The Crash of United Flight 93 and the Myth of America

Alexander T. Riley

NEW YORK UNIVERSITY PRESS

New York and London

NEW YORK UNIVERSITY PRESS
www.nyupress.org

References to Internet websites (URLs) were accurate at the time of writing.
Neither the author nor New York University Press is responsible for URLs
that may have expired or changed since the manuscript was prepared.

LIBRARY OF CONGRESS CATALOGING-IN-PUBLICATION DATA
Riley, Alexander.
Angel patriots : the crash of United Flight 93 and the myth of America / Alexander T. Riley.
pages cm
Includes bibliographical references and index.
ISBN 978-1-4798-7047-9 (cl : alk. paper) — ISBN 978-1-4798-6845-2 (pb : alk. paper)
1. United Airlines Flight 93 Hijacking Incident, 2001. 2. Terrorism—Social aspects—United
States. 3. Memorialization—United States. 4. Myth—Social aspects. I. Title.
HV6432.R547 2015
974.8'79044—dc23
2014040547

New York University Press books are printed on acid-free paper,
and their binding materials are chosen for strength and durability.
We strive to use environmentally responsible suppliers and materials
to the greatest extent possible in publishing our books.

Manufactured in the United States of America

10 9 8 7 6 5 4 3 2 1

Also available as an ebook

CONTENTS

ACKNOWLEDGMENTS

This book could not have been written without the tremendous help I received from people and institutions in and around Shanksville and from others elsewhere in the world.

Barbara Black, Joanne Hanley, Donna Glessner, and others at the U.S. National Park Service made precious time in their busy schedules to talk with me, and Barbara allowed me to look about and take photos freely in the archives at the Park Service Somerset office. I am greatly in their debt.

Hundreds of visitors to the temporary memorial and the Flight 93 Chapel shared some of their experiences of the memorials with me, and many others did so nonverbally as I observed them—I hope inconspicuously—as they interacted with the memorials. All deserve my profound thanks.

Paul Murdoch, the lead architect of the permanent memorial design, gave me gracious, detailed explanations of the ideas behind his group's design and allowed me to use one of their images in this book. I am exceedingly grateful for his help.

Many academic colleagues who heard various papers based on this research asked helpful questions and suggested additional reading material. Above all, I should mention the faculty and graduate students in the Cultural Sociology program at Yale and the Department of Sociology at the University of North Carolina, Greensboro. A number of members of the faculty at the University of Évora in Portugal were able, thanks to their location outside of American culture, to give me insights into the phenomena under investigation I did not encounter in the United States. Thanks to all.

I am also grateful to my wife Esmeralda and daughter Valeria for surrounding me with the moral cocoon necessary for engaging in the extended and lonely work that writing a book can sometimes be. I love you both very much.

The book is dedicated to the memory of Alphonse Mascherino, the late founder and chaplain of the Flight 93 Memorial Chapel. Father Al, as he was generally known (though, because he told me it was a name he was given in his youth and I found it endearing, I usually called him Father Fonzie), was tremendously supportive on every level of my work at the chapel, talking with me at great length about the history of the site and allowing my family to stay at the guesthouse free of charge, dropping off secret care packages of Progresso soup and soda on the front porch to ensure that we were nourished, even offering to make available at the chapel copies of an early article I wrote on Flight 93 memorialization. He was the most fascinating of interview subjects, but he quickly became much more than that. He was my friend. I had greatly hoped to give him a copy of this book and hear his opinion of my work. Although I was aware that he had been dealing with a difficult cancer diagnosis and recovery for the past several years, and although I knew he was not a young man (his unbelievable energy level notwithstanding), it was stunning to learn of his death as I was completing the book. Perhaps I had come to believe, based on the evidence of his tireless work at the chapel, that he was superhuman. Alas, despite his vitality and charisma and joyous spirit, he was mortal and we have lost him. I only wish I felt that I had sufficiently reminded him of my gratitude for all the care he extended to me and to my family and of how much he meant to us while I had the chance to do so. May his memory and his spirit live on in the chapel. *Requiescat in pace.*

1

Flight 93 and 9/11

American Mythology in the Making

It is something of a cliché to say that things as awful as the 9/11 attacks are beyond description. One book on the topic puts it this way: "September 11 is precisely the kind of event that defies representation."[1] In the moment, this certainly seemed to be so for many who fully understood the reaction of CNN reporter Aaron Brown on witnessing the collapse of the North Tower of the World Trade Center: "Good Lord . . . [six-second pause, which, on live air, seemed an eternity] there are no words." And yet it is not so. There are always words, and there are always representations. Even to say "there are no words" is to produce words that inevitably spin a web of meaning and interpretation (in this case, stunned horror) around the event described by these words. Like any other events that would acquire meaning, the attacks of 9/11 and the specific portion of those events that constituted the crash of United Flight 93—the fourth hijacked plane in the day's terrorist attack and the only one that did not hit its intended target, crashing instead in a field in southwest Pennsylvania—call for representation in order to exist in the human world. Without it, they would not be. No events speak for themselves, and no historical memory descends to us from the heavens, however much we might cloak such decision making in the language of the acts of God or nature that is culturally imperative for us. Events become events, and then events of a particular moral tenor, with a particular cast of characters, relationships, and meanings, only when we use the tools of our culture to make them into such things. The most basic of those tools are the stories we tell about who we are and the symbols and characters that make them up. These stories are like the air we breathe, so self-evident to us that we have trouble clearly articulating their plots and characters to listeners not already as saturated in them as we are. Humans have been telling themselves such stories, and fitting events into the frameworks provided by those stories, for a very long time, and the basic ways in which the process works have changed relatively little since the beginning.

But if the ways in which human societies have done this interpretive work have not much changed, the ways in which we study that cultural work certainly have. In the past century, new human and cultural sciences have emerged to do this work that had traditionally been the purview of the humanities alone. After their simultaneous birth more than a century ago, the twin disciplines of anthropology and sociology have drifted from their initial intellectual Pangaea into two distinct and alien continents, speaking only occasionally and in the very broadest of terms to one another. Though sometimes housed, as at the university where I am employed, in a dual department, they have nonetheless generally been almost completely torn from the close kinship that bound them early on. A central idea justifying the separation is the axiomatic claim that premodern and modern peoples are differentiated by fundamental sets of characteristics, and the study of the two kinds of human therefore require different theoretical and methodological principles. This way of thinking has been productive in at least one sense: it has led to the creation of many specialized journals and academic posts for the slew of Ph.D.s who adhere to and reproduce it in their work. But it is not quite so evident that it has given us a better understanding of how humans use the stories of their cultures to make sense of catastrophic events like the crash of Flight 93.

Émile Durkheim and his nephew Marcel Mauss, who between them made an unmatched contribution to the creation of the modern disciplines of sociology and anthropology, made it clear in their work that they rejected the idea that the cultures of so-called primitive people work according to fundamentally different principles than those at work in our own. Though they recognized that modernity had brought essential changes in structures of social organization and technology, they found that the evidence showed that there are deep rules about the working of human culture that are basically unaltered by such changes. At the root of human meaning, both primitive and modern, are sets of collectively held beliefs, the symbols and stories that express them, particular practices that celebrate and reinvigorate them, and moral ties to communities committed to maintaining them. Durkheim and

Mauss argued that religion, which in their terms is the omnipresent human phenomenon of creating sacred things, is the broadest of the fields in which these human meaning-making processes sprout and grow, and mythology is one of the most important cultural forms upon which religion relies for narrating the meaning of the life of a people to its members.

Although I am indebted to many other thinkers in this book,[2] it is this basic intellectual framework created by Durkheim and Mauss nearly a century ago that serves as the central analytical lens in the study. The premise of the book is that, just as contemporary societies still have religions, they also still have mythologies which must be attended to by the student of modern Western society. The Greek word "mythos" (μῦθος) has a number of meanings. One of the oldest, dating to well before the time when Aristotle used the term as a central element in his theory of tragedy, is basically equivalent to the modern English "story," and with approximately the same deft connotational dodging of the epistemological distinction between truth and falsity. "Mythos," from which "myth" is derived, thus refers simply to narratives about something that might be true or might not, and there is nothing in the definition of the term to indicate the necessity of one or the other side in the game of truth. The action in this definition of myth is not in the truth or falsity; it is in the story itself and the way it moves people, the way it provides them with sustenance they need to make their everyday lives bearable, i.e., sensible. For man is the sensible animal, the animal that cannot simply live, as the other animals do, eating and being eaten, growing and then declining, reproducing and then perishing. Beyond these basic elements of life, he requires a story to explain why the world is as it is, how it came to be that way, and, generally, why that is a good thing. He yearns for a conception of his place in the chaos of events and entities that parade before his senses, and not just of his place, but of the place of his people as well.

A fair amount of what most of us know about many things, including the last flight of United 93, is adequately and accurately classified as mythological. But the myth of the last journey and violent end of United 93 is not a classic creation myth of the kind described by the historian of religion Mircea Eliade when he defines myth as something that "relates an event that took place in primordial times, the fabulous time of 'beginnings' ... [when] thanks to the exploits of Supernatural Beings, a reality came to exist, whether the totality of reality, the Cosmos, or only a fragment of it: an island, a plant species, a human behavior, an institution."[3] It does not seem to speak of origins or of the shadowy time when humans and gods simultaneously walked the earth and interacted. Yet it is nonetheless completely reliant for its meaning on myths that have to do with the creation and the most fundamental meanings of the American nation and people. The myth to which Flight 93 is most intimately related reenacts, in history but also outside history in the static time of the sacred, the foundational myth of heroic and selfless sacrifice that undergirds the entire system of beliefs and practices of the people for whom the narrative of Flight 93 is intended. A structure of conservative imitation and repetition undergirds myth: when a people recount myths and describe their importance, they say, "As our ancestors did in the ancient times, so do we today."[4] The myth is a model, however symbolic, that directs the actions of the people in normal times. In this book, I will argue that the mythology of Flight 93 serves a similar purpose for Americans today.

In his study of popular mythologies of French culture circa 1960, Roland Barthes presents myth in a way that would be recognizable to many contemporary readers: it is in Barthes's view essentially a distortion of reality. Though it "hides nothing,"[5] it disconnects entities from their histories, turning them into complex and potentially misleading signs. In the example typically cited from the book, Barthes argues that a photo of a black colonial soldier saluting on a French magazine cover communicates a racist and reactionary French nationalism by obfuscating the soldier's lived experience as a colonial subject of an imperialist power. The racial minority identity of the soldier is placed into a simplified narrative through the action of his salute and the French military uniform on his back, and this is a narrative of the willing participation of the oppressed victim in the colonialist mystifications of the nation that oppresses him that may very well have little or nothing to do with his reality. Such myths, Barthes argued, are politically regressive, in their very essence the tools of conservative political powers, and they should be relentlessly decoded and explained (and thereby defanged) by critical intellectuals like Barthes himself. Here is a reading of myth frequently encountered today in the humanities and social sciences, dominated as they are by those on the cultural and political left eager to deconstruct and criticize what they see as the ideological work of the political right.

But while Barthes was certainly correct that some myth does just the kind of work he described in the image of the black colonial soldier, his vision needs to be refined. For he was himself a member of a particular social group (Parisian intellectuals of the left) with a shared culture and its own set of well-developed mythologies. One of the most important of these myths of the Parisian Marxist and quasi-Marxist left portrayed the enemies of the left alone as the purveyors of myths, that is, as dependent on obfuscation, lies, and untruths for the pursuit of their political goals. But our side, the French leftists told themselves, has no mythology because it does not need one. Truth is its currency and the substance of its analyses and theories about the world. If only all would be as committed to rational, scientific analysis of the situation as the intellectuals of the left are, the Enlightenment-inspired leftist myth goes, then myth would lose its power and quickly disappear from the human world.

In his later work, in the wake of the traumatic consequences of the May 1968 rebellion in France, Barthes began to recognize the limits of a one-sided deconstruction of myth and at least contemplated the idea of assembling a collection of the mythologies of his own tribe. He came to accept the fact that myths have provided meaning in every human society of which we know anything. In all existing societies, myths continue to exist. And, as the chapters of this book to follow will show, they have done much of the work to provide the meaning of Flight 93 to the contemporary, rather large tribe known as Americans.

American culture is sustained by mythologies, and mythologies are inevitably about something simultaneously more and less than the truth. Our mythologies tell us, for example, that the American boys on the beaches at Normandy single-handedly saved the world from fascism, but they omit the essential contribution Soviet boys in the streets of Stalingrad made to that accomplishment. They also fail to refer to what the United States did before the war to help drag an economically crushed Germany into madness or after the war to quickly replace old colonial chains with new ones in places such as the backward southeast Asian nation that would later come to haunt the American imaginary for the next generation. We embrace mythologies that tell us we are in our souls a Puritan, ascetic people, and as a requirement of this belief we ignore the inconvenient fact that we purportedly puritanical and ascetic Americans are more likely to be obese than to pay federal income tax.[6] That these myths are so easily shown to be based on a limited array of factual material takes nothing away from the emotional and narrative force they exert, and, if our goal is to understand the force of myth, we perhaps do well to bracket debunking for a later time and place. If it is demonstrably obvious that our myths are not truth, it is equally obvious that they are powerful, though precisely how this power is generated is not so self-evident.

In a study of the cultural power of film, Edgar Morin makes a startling comparison of the relationship of, on the one hand, primitive man and his double, who travels from the land of the dead to our living world and back in dream-time, and, on the other, contemporary man and the equally hypnotic, hallucinatory photographic and filmed images that crowd our waking and dream lives.[7] Our modern mythologies, he argues, are almost always mass-mediated mythologies, and this is profoundly true of the myths of 9/11. David Friend describes watching the Twin Towers fall live on huge television monitors mounted at Times Square, both a direct witness of sorts—there in the city, only miles from the event—and yet as thoroughly screened from it by the technological medium as were almost all the others around the world who saw the nightmare take place on their television sets hundreds or thousands of miles away from the smoking remains of the World Trade Center.[8] Friend reminds us that the bad guys in our mythologies also recognize the role of media in our cultural imaginations, and they mobilize that fact in their own efforts to intervene in those myths. When the Afghan opposition leader Ahmad Shah Massoud was killed in the week before 9/11 by terrorists, they were able to get close enough to perform the deed by posing as TV reporters—the bomb was hidden in their camera.

Almost exactly 40 years ago, the sociologist and scholar of religion Robert Bellah delivered a series of lectures at Hebrew Union College/ Jewish Institute of Religion in Cincinnati, Ohio, that provide a powerful conceptual lens through which to view the events of the 9/11 attack and their mythologization. The title of the book that came of these lectures was *The Broken Covenant*, and the task Bellah set for himself was formidable. He wanted to offer an analysis of the American character as a whole, and particularly of its internal contradictions and conflicts that were, at the time of his writing, threatening to tear the country apart. It was the turbulent "end of the sixties" and Bellah, along with a great many others, understood that the country was in a "time of trial at least as severe as those of the Revolution and the Civil War."[9] The two sides in the Second American Civil War of the mid-1960s to early 1970s, that is, the antiwar, free-love radicals and Nixon's Silent Majority, managed in their frenzied struggle to obscure deep truths that Bellah endeavored to excavate and reinvigorate. These truths do reside in American tradition, as the conservatives claimed, but what the conservatives pointed to are, according to Bellah, not those traditional truths. American history is filled with injustice and oppression, just as the radicals claimed, but the tools of criticism alone cannot build the new society they desired. The answer requires an acknowledgement of the indispensability of myth in the life of a people, and a subsequent effort to use reason, not in its technical but in its transcendent, "ecstatic" form, to burn away the intolerable obfuscations of American myth and build a new set of myths consonant both with tradition and recognition of tradition's flaws.[10] Bellah thus turned to a deeply historical investigation of the American origin myth, of the mythological structures that portray Americans as a chosen people, and of myths that touch upon questions of nativism, cultural pluralism, salvation, and success in order to show how much then current events owed in their structures of meaning to these mythic traditions.

I too believe we can only deeply understand the contemporary cultural landscape, its meaningful events and its euphorias and conflicts, by reference to the American myths that undergird it. In the myth of Flight 93, we find evidence of deeper myths of America. We can discern a number of components in the myth of Flight 93, details about both the myth itself and its heroes. This myth is articulated in the public performances and media spaces where we tell ourselves stories about who we are. It is told in news coverage of the crash, in books and films about the flight and its passengers, and, perhaps most centrally, in the Flight 93 Memorial Chapel and the Flight 93 National Memorial at the crash site in Shanksville.

Flight 93 and American Civil Religion

In 1966, just a few years before his lectures on the broken covenant in American society, Bellah wrote the seminal essay "Civil Religion in America." The term "civil religion" was not of his coinage, but came from the 18th-century philosopher Jean-Jacques Rousseau. In the turbulent years preceding the French Revolution, Rousseau had argued that French Catholicism, and Christianity generally, would have to be radically reworked, if not completely dismantled, in the transition from a feudal monarchy to a rational, democratic republic. All that remained in his revision of religion were the elementary building blocks in belief and ritual necessary for undergirding a moral and democratic social order. The doctrine of religious tolerance, belief in the existence of God and the world to come, and the posthumous rewarding of virtue and punishment of evil performed in this mortal realm were the entirety of Rousseau's prescribed civil religion.[11] Bellah filled in important historical and cultural detail. Whatever simplistic visions of wholly secularized modern states might have us think, the realms of religion and politics share a concern for ultimate things and this means they are thrust into inevitable contact, and sometimes conflict, with one another. In primitive societies, the two realms are fully fused and there is no distinction between the sacred and the ruling order. The divine kingships of the Bronze Age monarchies of the second millennium B.C.E. provide the model for the emerging fields of politics and religion and the relationship between the two. The historic world religions announce a growing separation of the two realms, but deep interconnections nonetheless remain. Constitutions are frequently historically rooted in religious moral frameworks, albeit in occluded ways. At the experiential level, religion continues to inform the occupational work of legislators and citizens in at least informal and implicit ways. Nevertheless, the trend in the modern world seems to be toward increasing distancing of religion and the state, except in some extraordinary cases. In some but not all societies, there emerge sets of beliefs and ritual practices that are connected to the past, present, and future of the society and framed transcendentally. Symbols, cultural narratives, and meaning structures that have their origins in religious vocabularies come to be mobilized in the political realm, but without an explicit and exclusive fusion with either the state or any existing church or religious doctrine. This Bellah calls civil religion.

In societies where church and state emerge as competing parties for dominance, no civil religion exists. In Mexico, for example, one finds a dominant Roman Catholicism, Mexicanized by massive syncretism, and a nationalist ideology fundamentally informed by the militantly anti-clerical politics of the Mexican Revolution in an uneasy truce, separated and competing for different parts of the Mexican soul. In the United States, things work differently. Here, to be sure, there is a church, or rather churches, and many of them, all neatly separated from the state, and there is a secular American nationalism, based in a liberal consti-tutional perspective that sees in the Constitution a central right to be free from state-sponsored religion. But there is also a civil religion, a set of cultural symbols and narratives that unites a conviction concerning the special purpose of the American democracy with a belief in super-natural forces and actors guiding that political project.

There is however no *Christian* civil religion in America, despite the fact that a very large majority of Americans identify as Christian. The American civil religion that Bellah describes is not oriented around Jesus Christ, but rather around the Judeo-Christian lawgiver God described in the Old Testament. This is likewise not the Yahweh of the tribal Middle Eastern people of Israel, but instead the Supreme Judge of the Universe named in the Declaration of Independence, who may have first emerged as the God of the Israelites but who is now distinctly the God of the Americans, having chosen us to carry forward his proj-ects on Earth in the contemporary era. Scholars of the religiosity of the Founders have presented them as largely Deist, that is, believers in a God who assembled the world, created the universal laws that keep it running, and then retreated to allow us, his stewards, to administer it. But the God of the American civil religion is not a Deist God either. The Supreme Judge does not only judge, though he certainly does that; he also desires that his people make the morally correct choices and do his work in this world. Narrative structures and symbols from Old Testament stories frequently find themselves adapted to events in American history under the civil religion. As the Israelites were chosen by their God and helped in their escape from bondage in Egypt, the Americans too were chosen by theirs, who aided them in their exodus from Europe. Both peoples, after hard journeys, were eventually led to a Promised Land. Both peoples sinned against their God and were required to make bloody sacrifice in recompense. The great wars and struggles of American history are frequently framed under this aegis: Revolution, then (and especially) Civil War, then world wars, all are episodes of the Chosen People being given the opportunity to conquer their own sinful nature in order to earn their place in their God's favor. The civil religion also has its feasts: Memorial Day, Veterans Day, Presidents' Day, the Fourth of July, all drenched in the dual symbolism of patriotism and supernatural election. In contrast to the secular patriotism of the liberal constitutional state and the secularly framed rights of the Constitution, here we have a vision of America as a republic under God, with the Declaration of Independence and its invocation of divine providence as its holy writ. Bellah argues that American culture, like all other cultures, requires narratives of heroes and gods and tremendous deeds and holy ground and other such things, and we have a particular framework of such narratives that manages to tie nation and supernatural neatly together.

Deliberately rejecting what he saw as a totalizing secularism increasingly dominant in the intellectual classes, Bellah was an advocate of the civil religion, not merely its analyst. He feared that the trend was away from the sense of community and collective moral responsibility it entailed and toward a drifting, radically individualist, deritualized, morally decentered vision of the relationship of citizen to state that could only bring disaster. No more the moral mission of the people as a whole, and instead a corrosive overemphasis on an unattainable total freedom from others and the liberty to do whatever one wants. One does not have to look far to find the evidence of this position today on both the libertarian right ("I may hoard as much wealth and property as I can legally amass, and those dying in the street may make no claim on my charity") and the hyperindividualist cultural left ("I may do absolutely anything and everything I wish short of physically harming others in the expression of personal identity, and any claims by institutions on my moral responsibilities are by their very nature illegitimate and offensive"). One can also distressingly easily find evidence in the contemporary American landscape of far-right-wing versions of the civil religion that push it to extremes Bellah imagined but never endorsed.

When political figures of national prominence such as the Minnesota congresswoman Michele Bachmann, who presented herself as a contestant in the Republican nominating process for the 2012 presidential election, describe their belief, which for Bachmann is apparently rooted in the Christian legal education she received at the Oral Roberts University Law School, that the source of all law is God, that the Constitution is a holy covenant between God and the chosen people that cannot legitimately be altered, and that the Founders of this country fervently desired to seamlessly unite church and state, we see not only the results of a half century of right-wing institution building, but also another twisted path away from Bellah's vision. He hoped for a morally productive American civil religion that would serve as the cultural glue to hold us together while not suppressing the political and cultural diversity that are central features of our society. Bellah felt strongly that "[t]he split between rational and mythic discourse which has characterized our recent cultural history is dangerous for it impoverishes both modes of thought," and his work was intended as an effort to help put the two back into contact with one another.[12] I have the same ambition in this book.

Flight 93, 9/11, and Cultural Conflict in America

One of the first questions a book on this topic that purports to see in it a powerful statement about the basic nature of American culture must answer is: *Why Flight 93?* Why is it so important in cultural terms? Indeed, was it not the case that United Flight 93 was relatively overlooked in the events of that day, overshadowed by the fates of the three other planes that were enlisted with it as part of this grand attack? As Martin Amis put it, Flight 93's story "would normally have been one of the stories of the year," but it was unarguably what he calls starkly and with ominous simplicity "the second plane," United Flight 175, "galvanized with malice, and wholly alien" that so many around the world watched fly and then, astonishingly, seemingly disappear into the South Tower of the World Trade Center at 9:03 a.m. Eastern Standard Time—it was this plane and not Flight 93 that came to symbolize the day and its horrific events.[13] It was not only the devastating nature of Flight 175's terminus, nor the fact that the human and property destruction was so terrible in New York City, that made Flight 93 shrink in the collective mind. There were other cultural myths that contributed to this. In a segment of the National Geographic special *Inside 9-11*, we see a narrative driven by artists and aspirant artists, foreign-born and native New Yorker amateur filmmakers who were, prior to the 9/11 attacks, obsessed with filming and photographing the city and who therefore chanced to film parts of the attacks on that day as part of their quotidian work toward an artistic career. The firm subtext is that New York, bustling magnet for artists and creative spirits of all sorts, was necessarily the centerpiece of the attacks. After all, the assumed question would have it, where were the filmmakers and photographers in Shanksville who would have captured the crash of Flight 93 and its aftermath in full detail if that tiny Pennsylvanian village had a real claim to be considered a main player in the story?

And yet, the meaning of Flight 93 in the midst of the broader meanings of 9/11 is at the very heart of some of the most important American cultural processes and debates. I hope to impress upon the reader in the chapters to follow not only that we should properly talk about the myth of Flight 93, but that we should also talk of the myth of America, and of the relationship between the two.

One of the most basic reasons I wrote this book is simple to recount: so far as I was able to tell, there existed no other books that described in the crash of Flight 93 what I see there. The volume of writing, a good deal of it compelling, on the attack on the World Trade Center is daunting and probably more than sufficient. Books on Flight 93 existed when I began to consider writing this one, but all of them were doing quite other things than what I hope to do here. Among those other books are biographical accounts of the people on the plane, narratives of loss by the families and friends of those people, and studied and not-so-studied attempts to discern what might have happened on Flight 93 in the last 30 minutes or so of its journey on September 11, 2001. There are even books that claim Flight 93 did not crash at all or that the planned memorial to the plane is in fact not a memorial to the passengers of the plane, but a gigantic mosque intended as a celebration of the efforts of the hijackers. I will discuss a good number of these other books in chapters to come, for they contribute, in their various ways, to the myth of Flight 93. I could however find no books that described the process by which we have pieced together meaning and myth from the crash of this plane, and I came to believe such a book might be good to have, and that I might be the person to write it.

As I was writing, however, and visiting and revisiting the sites, and talking to visitors to the sites, and reading and rereading the books and seeing the films and videos over and over again, it became clear to me that it was not simply a hole in the literature I was trying to fill. I was also seemingly inevitably being led to speak to much larger questions about the state of American culture today. This began as a book about an event, a plane crashing into a field as a failed piece of a terrorist attack on the country, and the process by which that event was narrated by culture and an effort was made to mythologize and commemorate it. But unexpectedly, because of the specific nature of the event, to be sure, but also for other reasons having to do with the manner in which cultural narratives emerge—that is, because telling a story about an event requires delving into the depths of a whole set of more basic stories about who we are and why we are that way—it has, seemingly of its own volition, become a book about America.

Two years before this writing, I gave a talk at a series of annual faculty lectures at the university where I am employed that was centered on the topic of the fourth chapter of this book, the Flight 93 Memorial Chapel. In the talk, I endeavored mightily to emphasize the complexity of the cultural meanings churning around at the chapel, among its congregants and in the beliefs of its founder, and I made an especially strong effort to describe my own conflicted, even confused reaction to the chapel: at once wary of some of the cultural politics I saw potentially lurking in the symbolism and ritual there, but also frankly and unapologetically drawn in and moved by the warmth and emotional power of the celebrations every year at the commemoration ceremonies and by my evolving friendship with the pastor, Alphonse Mascherino. The evidence that my efforts at a certain kind of objectivity were not good enough, or were perhaps simply irrelevant, was clear in the first comments addressed to me by my gathered colleagues at the presentation's conclusion. Virtually everyone was focused on the perceived dangers of what was going on at the chapel, and in Flight 93 cultural memory work more generally, and tried to get me to talk about something I was adamant not to talk about, as I saw it as well outside the purview of my office. In short, many of my colleagues wanted me to offer advice on how to mobilize a political and cultural counterstrike against the folks at the chapel and others with similar beliefs. As one, then another went on emotionally charged diatribes against the "Tea Baggers" (the term actually used by one respondent) that were only weakly masked as questions about my research, I tried to hide my disappointment in this simplistic and stock "culture war" reading of what is going on around Flight 93. I had hoped to get some help in understanding the phenomenon as an anthropologist of the cultural imaginary. And yet, disheartening as I admit I find it when scholars follow their first instincts into the mire of political denunciation, it is nonetheless an unavoidable fact that the cultural work around Flight 93 necessarily touches upon important points of conflict in American culture. But did my colleagues not know that the mythology of Flight 93 had been powerful enough even to reach intellectuals with rationalist and critical leftist credentials just like their own? The well-known sociologist and activist Todd Gitlin wrote in the wake of 9/11 about how he "took inspiration from the patriotic activists who seem to have brought down Flight 93 over Pennsylvania and saved the White House or the Capitol[, . . .] who hadn't waited for authorities to define their patriotism for them [and] . . . were not satisfied with symbolic displays."[14] Clearly, and although I will show in the pages to come that there is much of a culturally conservative nature in Flight 93 memorialization, it was not only the members of the Tea Party who had been impressed by the cultural narrative that was emerging about Flight 93.

In *The Broken Covenant*, Bellah asked hard questions about American culture at a time of great social upheaval and conflict about the meanings of that culture. He wrote the book in 1971, at the tail end of the cataclysmic events of the 1960s. The American civil religion, which had served to culturally glue together the various elements of American society for generations, albeit with moments of unmistakable tension, now seemed in grave danger of collapsing altogether in the midst of the frightening centralization of power in the hands of small groups of social elites, the same elites who had been challenged by the 1960s counterculture and who had by the time Bellah wrote largely succeeded in routing that formidable if inchoate challenge. I wrote these pages largely between 2010 and 2012, in the midst of another crisis of comparable proportions. Indeed, we may still be struggling amid the same upheaval that concerned Bellah 40 years ago, as cultural revolutions are not rapid events and the core of his analysis regarding the instabilities of American society remains true. A cultural discourse that unites a utilitarian morality of individualist self-interest (which, it bears repeating, can be found both on the conservative and libertarian right and on the cultural left) and a remorseless capitalist economy continue to provide the *Zeitgeist* in which we live. The economic crisis of 2008 revealed that Bellah's fears of the possible consequences of such a situation are, or should be, our own. In the 1960s, the countercultural response to the brokenness of the dominant American culture at least challenged the dominant cultural ideology, even if it offered few real possibilities for addressing and healing the most malignant tumors on the body social. In our moment of the crisis, on the other hand, what purports to be the countercultural response to the rapacious greed and lack of concern for any but self that have brought us low constitutes little more than a return to the more xenophobic, nativist, and irrational aspects of historical American culture and fails to provide any real criticism of the narrow-minded self-interest that is the primary cause of the dire circumstances we face. The Tea Party purports to reject illegitimate hierarchy and to defend democratic principle, but its most forceful rhetorical ammunition has been pointed not at the excesses of 21st-century capitalism and the right's systematic destruction of all post–Great Depression legislation designed to reign in dangerous speculation but instead at populations who have been the historical targets of the dominant American culture. According to the Tea Party, it is outsiders and immigrants, whether Mexican or Arab, who are undermining American society, not the mostly white and U.S.-born criminals on Wall Street and in Washington who have presided over the last 30 years of intensified class stratification and weakening of democracy. The Occupy movement emerged in recent years to attempt to provide a critical voice from the left on the American political status quo, but at this writing it seems to have mostly dissipated in the wake of a coordinated police crackdown.

So we are in a particularly contentious moment in American culture, which is at nearly all times frightfully conflict-ridden, and 9/11 is a particularly difficult issue for an intellectual to treat if he wants to do something other than stroke the egos of members of one group or another aligned at battle stations in our cultural debates. One of my teachers, the

sociologist and media scholar Michael Schudson, described a problem
he faced when he entertained the project of writing a book about Watergate that strikes me in all its essentials as much like the one I encountered as I was working on this book:[15]

> One friend counseled that the subject was too volatile and too important
> to use simply to illustrate something else. Watergate was too important,
> the legacy of Richard Nixon too dangerous . . . to diminish the political
> significance of the subject by using it for academic purposes. . . . I shared
> the mainstream position that Watergate represented a threat to constitu-
> tional government and that constitutional government is precious, so I
> was sympathetic to the view that Watergate should not be trivialized. . . .
> But I came to see the constitutionalist position I held as one perspective
> among several and that the place of Watergate in our memory lies not
> with one interpretation or another exclusively but with the play of lead-
> ing interpretations against one another.[15]

Schudson's vision of the ultimate meaning of Watergate as something
that transcended his own deeply held partisan stance on it, which was
itself an unavoidable and indeed positive consequence of committed cit-
izenship, and pointed toward a larger cultural process of making meaning out of differing interpretive strategies and conflicts, resonates profoundly with my own sense of the object that I describe here. I cannot
avoid having the stance I have, but I want to try as much as I can to avoid
hypostatizing my interpretation and instead look at the play and conflict of warring interpretations. This effort is aided, I believe, by my own
natural sympathy with the position of the contrarian and the fact that
differing contexts force such a creature to take up differing perspectives.
In my work life, my automatic tendency is to keep my critical guard up
against the widespread consensus, in the social sciences and humanities worlds I inhabit at least, of a position on 9/11 that refuses a priori
almost all patriotic sentiment and invokes a peculiar kind of ideological
self-righteousness in angrily denouncing in advance any critical analysis
of Islam's role in making 9/11 possible. Outside the university, I tend to
adapt just as readily a critical response to the broad consensus in the
country that 9/11 reveals America as an innocent victim and those who
attacked her as the pure, unadulterated agents of Evil with a capital "E."

At the ten-year anniversary of 9/11, the late journalist Christopher Hitchens wrote an essay for *Slate* magazine reflecting on the attacks that was bluntly titled "Simply Evil." In the piece, Hitchens argued that, while the job of intellectuals is usually to bring complexity to topics too easily simplified by the public, 9/11 is the exception to the rule: this was an event of world historical significance that is simply and effectively understood as an act of evil perpetrated on innocent victims. To be sure, Hitchens was sparring here with foes he took on frequently on 9/11 over the years, i.e., those on both right and left who have pronounced the United States politically responsible for bringing on the attack, or blamed parties other than al-Qaeda for the acts, or indeed even glorified the attack as a manifestation of anticapitalist, anti-imperialist Third World struggle, rather than engaging arguments like the one I will make here. Nonetheless, it needs to be said that his reading of the event is too simplistic. Not that the events of 9/11 cannot or ought not be understood in the terms he provides, but the events of that day, their meanings, their ramifications, the memories they inspire, the commemorations they produce, and which in turn produce them, are nearly infinitely complex. The construction even of the narrative Hitchens took as self-evident is the result of the actions of many actors and the meanings of many narratives and texts, and holds together, when and for whom it does so, for reasons of great sociological intricacy. No story is self-evident, ever. Hitchens surely knew this, but here gave in to the temptation to willingly join sides in the cultural struggle rather than attempt to describe how that struggle produces the object "Flight 93" itself as a piece of our collective memory. We are not of course required to pick only one or the other of these two tasks. Both hats can be worn by the same person, but he must be careful to take the one off before he sets about doing the work of the person that wears the other, and he would likely do well never to forget the fact of his ownership of both hats.

Remembering Flight 93's Journey from Newark to Shanksville on September 11, 2001: What Do We Really Know?

However much myths depend on elements that are separable from facts, the myth of Flight 93 must, in the end, have some relationship to things that actually happened aboard the plane. What do we know about those empirical things on which the myths are built? A rigorous sociological discussion of how knowledge is made requires considerable caution about easy claims concerning "objective facts," and I will not purport here to be presenting a God's-eye view of what happened so much as simply trying to limit to the extent possible the attachment of moral and aesthetic labels to factual elements of the events of that day, which is a difficult enough goal. The business of separating pure facts from elaborated narrative and myth is much harder than we generally reckon.

There are no eyewitness accounts of what happened on Flight 93, and there was no archive to consult other than the one constituted in the immediate aftermath by the wreckage of the plane itself. There are however the typical original sources in most plane crashes. We have a flight data recorder, which captured electronic systems settings and instructions during the flight and therefore tells us a good deal about how fast the airplane was going, when and by how much it changed altitude, and when and how it changed direction. There is also a cockpit voice recorder, which operated on a 30-minute loop and so gives us data from the flight's last half hour, from approximately 9:32 to the time of the crash at 10:03. This recording stretches over all but approximately the first four minutes of the period between the start of the hijacking and the crash. The voice recording salvaged in the wreckage was, as is often the case, murky and unclear. The technology for such recorders on many planes is often dated,[16] and the tumultuous nature of what seems to have taken place on Flight 93 produced equally chaotic sounds that are often less than easy to understand. Perhaps the most relevant fact about the transcript of the cockpit voice recording is that the best that could be done with many of the human utterances captured in the recording was the single word "Unintelligible," which appears more than any other single phrase. There is also the 9/11 Commission Report, which, as we are frequently reminded by conspiracy theorists and other critics of the established narrative of the crash, is a document that must be placed in a political context wherein motivations for bias cannot be wholly discounted and which inevitably suffers from the limitations and blinders typical of institutional bodies created to write such documents.[17] Jere Longman's book *Among the Heroes* is a journalistic attempt to tell the story based largely on interviews with officials and family members of passengers. It is admirable in its effort to reconstruct the events on the plane, and we can perhaps mine it for some factual details. As I will describe later, however, it ends up in some conspicuous ways as firmly rooted in the camp of hagiography as in that of history insofar as it too often uncritically relies on the very same deep American cultural narratives that serve as the base for the myth of Flight 93. It is precisely those narratives that must be analytically examined if we wish to understand why the myth has the contours and the power that it does.

United 93 left Newark Airport, bound for San Francisco, at 8:42 a.m., nearly a full three quarters of an hour later than its scheduled takeoff time of 8:00. By the time the plane had been in the air for 20 minutes, American Flights 11 and 175 had already crashed into the World Trade Center and the FAA and other authorities were aware that a plan involving multiple hijackings was underway. While the aviation and military authorities scrambled for a response to the unfolding disaster, things went routinely on Flight 93 until the flight crew received a cockpit message at 9:24 warning them to beware of cockpit intrusion. Only minutes later, at approximately 9:28, the hijackers acted. Two brief radio transmissions from the plane at this time, which were recorded by air traffic control, conveyed the sounds of a physical struggle and the captain or first officer giving the alert "Mayday!" and shouting at someone, "Get out of here!" Shortly after the assault on the cockpit, the hijackers apparently cleared the passengers out of the first class section and forced them toward the back of the aircraft, a fact relayed in several of the phone calls that were later made from the plane.

The four hijackers were all seated in first class: Ziad Jarrah, who flew the plane after the hijack, was in 1B; Ahmed Alnami and Saeed Alghamdi were side by side in 3C and 3D, across the aisle from Jarrah; and Ahmed Alhaznawi was in 6B, behind him. While the other three hijacked planes had five-man hijacker teams, terrorist manpower was reduced on Flight 93. It is believed that a fifth hijacker, Mohammad Al Qahtani, intended for Flight 93's team was prevented from participating in the mission by being refused entry to the U.S. the month before the attack, although the case has become complicated since May 2008, when charges against him were abruptly dropped by the Pentagon due to severe treatment he had received at Guantanamo. Although Al Qahtani has recanted his confession to involvement in the 9/11 plot, and it looks unlikely that he will be prosecuted due to the abuse to which he was subjected as part of the interrogation regimen, independent sources have corroborated his culpability.[18]

At 9:32, after assuming control of the plane, Jarrah made a radio announcement, intended to go to the passengers but sent inadvertently to air traffic control, stating in broken English that there was a bomb on board and urging passengers to stay seated: "Here the captain, please sit down keep remaining seating. We have a bomb on board. So sit." This is the first utterance that appears on the official transcript of the cockpit voice recorder, and from this moment the plane has just over another half hour in the air. At 9:39, a second announcement came from Jarrah, this one too overheard by air traffic control officials. He reiterated that there was a bomb on the airplane and attempted to falsely inform passengers (it is not certain that they heard either message) that they were returning to the airport.

Beginning almost immediately after the hijackers took over the cockpit, passengers began to make phone calls, using the seatback phones and, later, when the plane was at a much lower altitude, their own cell phones. They called friends and loved ones on the ground, attempting to relay the information that the plane had been hijacked to authorities.[19] There were calls from passengers and crew aboard the other three hijacked planes as well, and one call from a passenger, Brian David Sweeney, aboard United Flight 175 even suggests there was some consideration by passengers on that plane of an attempt to take back the cockpit.[20] The total number of calls from the other three planes was, however, low, despite the fact that, with the exception of United 175, which crashed only about 15 minutes after hijack, the other planes were in the air roughly the same period of time as Flight 93 after hijack.[21]

At least 37 phone calls[22] were made from Flight 93, all but two of them[23] made using the seatback phones near the rear of the plane, but at least ten of these terminated immediately upon connection or were misdials, and numerous others lasted only a few seconds before disconnection. Approximately 15 of these 37 calls lasted more than ten seconds and contained substantive communication between the person calling and another speaker; a still smaller number of the calls contained details of the events on the plane beyond the very most basic. The following passengers and crew members are identified as having placed at least one of these substantive phone calls and having actually spoken to people or left messages on machines from the plane: Lauren Grandcolas, Mark Bingham, Joseph DeLuca, Linda Gronlund, Jeremy Glick, Todd Beamer, Sandra Bradshaw, Thomas Burnett, CeeCee Lyles, Marion Britton, Honor Wainio, Waleska Martinez, and Edward Felt. According to the 9/11 Commission Report, in at least five of those calls, information was communicated to passengers concerning the attacks in New York City, and five different calls described the intent of passengers to attempt to take back the aircraft.[24]

Most of the 13 passengers and crew members who made calls made only one. Grandcolas left a message of less than a minute in length on her home answering machine for her husband, telling him they were "having a little problem on the plane."[25] DeLuca spoke to his parents for about two minutes, informing them that the plane had been hijacked. Gronlund, DeLuca's partner, spoke to her sister for just over a minute, informing her of the whereabouts of her will.[26] Felt called 911 only minutes before the plane crashed, using a cell phone from a bathroom in the back of the plane while the counterattack to take back the cockpit was going on at the plane's front end. He reported the hijacking in what the operator who spoke with him described as a highly emotionally agitated state. Britton spoke to a friend for nearly four minutes, telling him that the hijackers had "slit the . . . throats" of two people on the plane.[27] Wainio spoke with her stepmother for some four and a half minutes, ending the call with "They're getting ready to break into the cockpit. I have to go. I love you. Goodbye."[28] Crew member Lyles left a short message on the voice mail of her husband in which she told him of the hijacking and asked him to give her love to her children.[29] Fellow crew member Bradshaw made two calls, the first of approximately six minutes to United Airlines, the second of roughly eight minutes to her husband, whom she told of plans to "throw water on [the hijackers] and try to take back the aircraft."[30]

The longest and most substantive phone calls were made by the four young men on the plane who subsequently became the central figures in the construction of the hero myth of Flight 93: Todd Beamer, Mark Bingham, Thomas Burnett Jr., and Jeremy Glick. Beamer, Bingham, and Glick each made one substantive call. Bingham, after getting disconnected on his first attempt, reached his uncle's residence at 9:37 a.m.; his mother was staying there to help her brother and his wife care for the four children she had carried for the couple as a surrogate mother.[31] During a conversation of just under three minutes, he told his aunt that he was calling to say he loved them in case he never saw any of them again, then told his mother the plane had been hijacked by three men who claimed they had a bomb. He said he was calling from the seatback Airfone and, apparently aware of the outlandish nature of the story he was relating, asked her, "You believe me, don't you, Mom?" He then spoke with someone on the plane in whispered tones for about half a minute, and reiterated both his statement about the Airfone and the question to his mother. Before any more substantive information could be communicated, the call terminated.[32] Bingham apparently subsequently attempted to call back twice, at 9:41; the first time the connection was broken immediately, and the second time he misdialed the number and terminated the call after a few seconds. His mother called his voice messaging service twice subsequent to their short conversation and left messages, advising her son to try to take back the plane given what was going on in New York City at the time. He never heard those messages.

Glick and Beamer made their calls, the first to his wife, the second to a Verizon operator, at 9:37 and 9:44, respectively, and both calls lasted the duration of the time the plane had left in the air. Glick got through on the first try, but Beamer apparently unsuccessfully tried a toll-free number and a residence in New Jersey that may have been his own before dialing zero and reaching the operator. Beamer gave the Verizon operator, Lisa Jefferson, a detailed account of what had happened to that point: a team of three men had hijacked the plane and two of them were in the cockpit, apparently flying the plane, while a third, who apparently had a bomb strapped to his waist with a red belt, was standing guard over the cockpit in the first class section. The hijackers had knives, Beamer reported, and the pilot and copilot were laying, apparently either dead or wounded, on the floor in first class.[33] Beamer asked Jefferson if she knew if the hijackers sought ransom.[34] At some point in the conversation, Beamer indicated that the plane was flying erratically, and, according to Jefferson, his voice grew emotional for the first time in the call: "Oh my God, we're going down! We're going down! Jesus help us!"[35] The plane resumed a steady flight pattern, and Beamer told Jefferson it was "coming back up."[36] He asked Jefferson to pray the

Lord's Prayer with him, which Jefferson did.[37] According to Longman,[38] Beamer then recited the 23rd Psalm,[39] but, curiously, Jefferson does not describe this in her published account of their conversation. Beamer then asked her to communicate his love to his family in the event he did not survive and gave Jefferson his home phone number. Jefferson offered to call and patch him through to his wife, but he averred, desirous not to alarm her, given the fact that she was expecting their third child in January 2002.[40] The plane began to fly erratically again, and Jefferson could hear cries and screams from the background. Beamer finally told her that "a few of us passengers are getting together . . . to jump the guy with the bomb."[41] Jefferson asked if he was sure this was the right thing to do, and Beamer replied, "I'm going to have to go out on faith, because at this point, I don't have much of a choice."[42] She told him she supported his decision, and she reports that they then continued to speak in the hope that the plane could be saved.[43] He subsequently turned away from the phone to ask someone else if they were ready, then said, "Okay, let's roll!"[44] These were the last words Jefferson reports hearing him utter.

Using one of the seatback phones, Glick told his wife that "some bad men," in his estimation "three Iranian guys," had put on red headbands, told the other passengers they had a bomb, and forcibly commandeered the plane.[45] According to his wife, she and Glick then repeated "I love you" to one another "for four or five minutes."[46] Glick then expressed a fear that he might not survive the incident and told his wife to "promise me you're going to be happy" and for their daughter Emmy "to know how much I love her."[47] At some point in the conversation, Lyz Glick's parents had retrieved a cell phone and called 911, and Glick's wife then attempted to relay information back and forth between her husband and the 911 attendant. During this two-phone interplay, Glick said he believed the plane had turned and was headed south, somewhere near Pittsburgh in a rural area.[48] He asked her if it was true that other planes had crashed into the World Trade Center, apparently having heard this from another passenger. In her own published account of the conversation, his wife reports telling him the towers were "on fire."[49] Longman claims that the collapse of the South Tower, which took place at 9:59 a.m., happened during the course of their conversation and that Glick's wife told him "they knocked it down,"[50] but her account differs;

she denies knowing about the collapse of the first tower during the conversation.[51] She does recount telling her husband about the news of American Flight 77's crash into the Pentagon, which happened at 9:37 and was being reported live in national media within five minutes of that time. Shortly after this announcement, she recalls him telling her, "Okay, I'm going to take a vote. . . . There's three other guys as big as me and we're thinking of attacking the guy with the bomb. What do you think?" She asked him if the hijackers were armed, and he replied that he had seen knives, in addition to the purported bomb.[52] He reiterated that he was going to attempt to overtake the bomb-wielding hijacker, and his wife supported this decision. He then told her that he was going to momentarily put the phone down and then return to it when the deed was accomplished.[53] Glick's wife handed the phone to her father, who heard volleys of screams, then silence.

Tom Burnett made several calls to his wife, Deena, using either his own cell phone or the seatback phone.[54] Certainty is difficult to attain regarding all the calls from the plane, but especially with respect to Burnett's calls, as different sources provide significantly different accounts of the facts. According to an FBI interview with Burnett's wife, the number of calls was somewhere between three and five (although the report itself describes only four discrete calls). She later described precisely four calls in the biography of her husband she published in 2006. However, during the trial of Zacarias Moussaoui, a convicted coconspirator in the 9/11 attacks who was prevented from participating by his arrest in mid-August 2001, the official call records produced showed only three calls. Burnett's wife provides a timeline of the calls in her book, and it appears that it is what she cites as the fourth and final call that is not included in the Moussaoui trial records. In the first call, which took place just after 9:30 a.m. and lasted less than half a minute, Burnett told her the plane had been hijacked, that a passenger had been "knifed," and that the hijackers were wielding a gun and a bomb. He asked her to call authorities using her cell phone while he held the line, but she told him it was not charged, so he said, "Okay, I'll call you back."[55] Seven minutes later,[56] Burnett called a second time. During this call, which lasted just over a minute, he told her that the hijackers were in the cockpit and the injured man he had mentioned earlier was dead. His wife told him that two planes had been flown into the World Trade Center, and Burnett responded, "It's a suicide mission," which he then communicated to other passengers. He asked her what kinds of planes were being used, how many were involved, and who was responsible; she told him no one yet knew answers to any of those questions. He said that his plane seemed to be headed back toward the World Trade Center, but then changed his analysis of the situation: "No, wait, . . . we're going south. . . . [W]e're over a rural area."[57] He abruptly told her, "I gotta go," and ended the call. At 9:44, he made his third call, this one of just under a minute in duration. His wife reports having just seen the reports of the plane crash at the Pentagon seconds before his call and therefore fearing that the plane in the rubble in Washington, D.C., might have been the one on which her husband was traveling. She quickly told him of the latest strike, and he repeated the news to those around him. He asked her if she had learned anything more since the last call regarding the responsible parties or the overall terrorist plot and the planes involved. She told him: "They think five airplanes have been hijacked. One is still on the ground." He told her that he doubted the veracity of the bomb claim, then asserted, "They're talking about crashing this plane into the ground. We have to do something. I'm putting a plan together [with s]everal people. There's a group of us. Don't worry, I'll call you back."[58] Although there is no independent confirmation of this, Deena Burnett reports that he later called her a fourth time, at 6:54 a.m. Pacific time, less than ten minutes before the plane crashed. He asked her whether there were any new developments regarding knowledge about the attack and inquired about their three children, but deferred speaking to them. He then told his wife they were waiting until the plane was over a rural area, at which point they would attempt to take back the plane. Her reaction was strong: "No! Sit down. Be still. Be quiet. Don't draw attention to yourself." He reiterated that they had to act if the hijackers intended to use the plane as another flying bomb and that it was of no use to wait for authorities to intervene: "I don't know what they could do anyway. It's up to us. I think we can do it." He then told his wife to pray and asserted, "Don't worry. I'll be home for dinner. I may be late, but I'll be home." She recalls this final conversation lasting less than two minutes.[59]

The objective dearth of empirical grist for the mill is fairly obvious here. Despite the media's portrayal of a frenzy of calls emanating from the plane, the number of actually substantive conversations that tell us anything concrete about what was going on inside the plane is quite small, and the amount of communicative material in those calls is strikingly paltry. The cumulative verbatim transcripts, for example, of all four calls Tom Burnett made to his wife, which are reconstructed from her memory on the web site of the Thomas Burnett Jr. Foundation, give something on the order of a mere 700 words. That is precious little in the way of concrete information on which to hang a narrative.

At approximately 9:57, a passenger assault on the cockpit began, and most of the calls were concluded by this time. The flight data recorder indicates that at just about the same time, the plane began a turn to the east. Two minutes later, at 9:59, at an altitude of about 5,000 feet, "2 minutes of rapid, full left and right control wheel inputs resulted in multiple 30 degree rolls to the left and right."[60] Then, from 10:00 to 10:02, "there were four distinct control column inputs that caused the airplane to pitch nose-up (climb) and nose-down (dive) aggressively."[61] The plane briefly ascended to 10,000 feet while rolling right, and then dove into the earth at 10:03:11 going approximately 563 mph. According to the 9/11 report, "the hijackers remained at the controls but must have judged that the passengers were only seconds from overcoming them."[62]

Narratives about events such as the crash of United Flight 93 can seem simple. Indeed, the Flight 93 story, as it has been created, cultivated, and consumed in much of the American public sphere, can be reduced to a single brief sentence: villains try to attack national capital with hijacked plane, but heroes foil the effort. However simple this appears, though, it is instantly clear that we need more than mere facts to come up with such a narrative, and we need much in the way of undergirding cultural material—values, beliefs, myths—to invest that simple narrative with the emotional, visceral power it is intended to have and has for many if not most who hear it in the United States.

Two concepts I take seriously in thinking about cultural narrative are the anthropologist Clifford Geertz's ideas of thick description and faction. Geertz believed that cultures consist of stories that can be narrated more or less like a novel. Indeed, they are so narrated in natural settings and by social actors going about the business of their everyday lives inside the culture. For illustration of this idea, we can turn to a brief examination of one of the chief cultural narratives in American society. This is a story, or set of stories, about the possibility (in some versions, "possibility" is replaced by "inevitability") of anyone low in the social pecking order making his way up the status ladder with the right amount of hard work, the right values, and a few breaks. "Rags to riches" stories in the vein of novelist Horatio Alger are but one incarnation of that cultural narrative. One can encounter many more simply by spending a few hours watching American television programs and films. The 2006 box-office smash *Pursuit of Happyness*, starring Will Smith, is a recent cinematic example. Here, a doubly disenfranchised man, poor and African American, has a dream of material prosperity and puts everything on the line to pursue it. He has tenacity and intelligence, gets a break or two, and ends the film wildly successful in material terms. The film is loosely based on the true story of the entrepreneur Chris Gardner, but the turning of a complicated biographical trajectory into a cultural myth requires frantic purification and stylization. The cinematic version of the narrative does not include any discussion of the social help Gardner got in his effort to pull himself out of the street. Gardner has been vocal in his praise especially of Glide Memorial United Methodist Church in the San Francisco area, which provided him with temporary housing and other material resources when he was homeless. The film also fails to give us a sociological context for considering Gardner against the backdrop of the many thousands of others who were more or less in his same situation in America during the Reagan administration, occupying the same structural place and possessing the same skills and tenacity, who did not become millionaires, and who in many instances met dismal ends in lifelong poverty or prison. It does not consider the moral question of how praiseworthy the Gardner/Smith character is to quit his job with no immediate prospects for another in order to pursue an exceedingly risky dream when he is the sole caretaker of a small child. Still more tellingly, it does not offer even the beginnings of a critical perspective on the moral framework that undergirds the narrative: the idea that material prosperity is and should be the central goal of a human life. The Smith character does not even sugarcoat this piece of the narrative. He decides on his dream career path impetuously after asking a man he sees exiting an expensive sports car what his occupation is and receiving the reply: "I'm a stockbroker!" The Gardner/Smith character thus learns he wants to be a stockbroker solely because stockbrokers drive expensive sports cars. It is of great significance that even the highly intelligent viewers who are my students almost never notice any of these aspects of the film's plot as constructions of a cultural mythology when I use the film for teaching purposes. Geertz's work suggests that this has much to do with how seamlessly the desired narrative of the film fits into the existing set of culturally dominant stories and myths in American society. One is easily absorbed into the thrust of such a story precisely because one already deeply knows and enjoys its narrative elements.

The rags-to-riches narrative is of course elsewhere too. It is invoked by our advertisers constantly, to sell us things. It is invoked by our politicians as well, in this case to sell us political policy decisions. What it is ultimately invoked to sell, however, is something more fundamental than products and political platforms: it is a sense of what America is and what it means to be American.

Geertz's work informs us that studying the presence of the rags-to-riches narrative in American society requires careful attention to detail and a novelist's eye for the nuance of dramatic development. Culture exists as a dramatic narrative that is both in the heads of culture members and externally present in texts and ritual practice produced by them in their daily lives. The analyst of culture has the task of reconstructing those stories, which requires an observational style Geertz called thick description, a careful and exhaustive eye for the dramatic detail of a narrative, and a writing style he called faction, a mixture of objective fact-driven information and attention to dramatic development that is most common in fictional writing but that Geertz argues should also be the model for those who would describe culture. In my classes, there are always some students who, in commenting in their term papers on a work we have read in the course, say, Durkheim's *The Elementary Forms* or Max Weber's *The Protestant Ethic*, will refer to these books as "novels." I always correct this error, but Geertz's point puts their mistake in a new light. Just how are our works of empirical, sociological description different than novels? Perhaps at least partly in ways that do not speak well to the ability of sociological texts to effectively describe the dramatic thing that is culture.

How narratives affect us has something important to do with what we turn into collective memory of important events. Over the past decade, the 9/11 Memory Consortium has undertaken a national study of memory about 9/11 in which respondents were interviewed at intervals of one week, one year, three years, and ten years on their recollection of various aspects of the day's events. When compared with their memories of factual elements of the day and even of their own feelings with respect to those events as expressed in the first survey only a week after the attack, subsequent surveys show increasing unreliability and inaccuracy. As more time passes, people forget more and more of the detail that they knew in the early going, and they even forget about the content of their own emotional reactions. A good deal of this has to do with the natural brain processes of remembering and forgetting. But inaccuracy is not accompanied here by an increasing sense of the fallibility and feebleness of memory. Due to the charged nature of the events of 9/11, people are emotionally invested in knowing about it, and they remain quite convinced of the visceral accuracy of their memories even when the evidence is against them. This is consistent with what we know about earlier national tragedies, e.g., the Kennedy assassination. The cliché is that everyone of the right age remembers precisely where she was when she got the news, and large percentages of people echo this adage. In reality, however, many people misremember those details, despite their continued fervency of belief in the accuracy of the memories. Some of what is going on here is that subsequent cultural framings of the events in question may alter and divert original memories in directions more consistent with collectively held and widely echoed narratives. The preexisting cultural narratives and myths will inevitably shape what come to be our memories of past events when those events brush up against core narratives of our people. People also tend to interpret memories of past events in light of current circumstances and contexts, so their recollection of their emotions, for example, may have more to do with an effort to make those emotions comfortably fit a perception of their personality and politics than with how they actually felt. We develop a canonical version of our memory of 9/11 that may contain significant errors and is at least as much an artifact of the post-event process of constructing life narratives as it is a factually accurate recollection of the actual event.[63]

In a venerable work that remains one of the most insightful books on the social nature of memory, Maurice Halbwachs illuminates why there can be no such thing as pure historical memory. We are always in the presence of social groups of reference that determine what we remember, because it is those groups that winnow from the immense volume of past experience the specific items which are deemed of significant relevance to the life of the group to merit remembrance and commemoration.[64] Nations are only perhaps, in our world, the most prominent of these groups; other groups, such as families, have their own established collective body of history.[65] And it is not so simple as those groups accurately capturing what happened in the past and enshrining it in established history, for the very importance of the memory leads to embellishment and augmentation with other material from other times, especially from the present moment.[66] In this sense, memory of Flight 93 is always at least in part about what the groups currently invested in remembering it are going through in the present. Collective memory is not only ideas, but also practices. Halbwachs offers religious examples such as the Catholic Mass, as he is explicitly following his mentor and colleague Émile Durkheim's distinction of the core elements of religion as beliefs and rites, but it is a simple enough matter to see that secular collective memory works in the same manner.[67] Forgetting too has a profoundly social element: "to the extent that the dead retreat into the past, this is not because the material measure of time that separates them from us lengthens; it is because nothing remains of the group in which they passed their lives, and which needed to name them, that their names slowly become obliterated."[68] It is in sum incorrect to speak of the past as "preserved." We should think of it instead as "reconstructed on the basis of the present."[69] More recently, another writer puts the matter in a similar fashion: "Pure memory does not exist; it is a redefinition of the past as a function of a present reality."[70]

Part of the problem of ever getting to the "true" story of any historical event is the lack of completeness. Any story of 9/11 that aspired to completeness would have to include elements that are never presented in most mainstream narratives of the event, such as the experiences of people who were not at all touched by the event despite living very close to the various sites at which the dreadful action unfolded. Interviews of

New York residents in the aftermath of the attacks revealed abundant evidence of individuals who sunbathed while the towers were collapsing, or casually had friends take souvenir photos of them posing smiling atop their apartment buildings with the flaming World Trade Center towers as a backdrop.[71] A few minutes of video from the CameraPlanet archive on 9/11 apparently shot by a group of young men watching the first tower collapse from their apartment is further bracing evidence of just how startlingly blasé people (and perhaps especially those living in a major metropolis such as Manhattan) can be in reaction to even the seemingly most astounding, unprecedented things. One of the men in the video can be heard saying in a flippant, unimpressed voice, "Dude, wasn't that news guy we just saw on TV in that tower? He's dead [laughs]! He's done. . . . Classes aren't canceled yet? That should cancel 'em! [laughs] This one's [the other tower] gonna fall! [laughs] It's done."[72] In this light, collective memory is necessarily but a representation, and so too are all the memorialization efforts that it generates, and the work of the representation is not simply to become "a mirror of the now absent thing . . . [but to] transform the real."[73]

Thinking America with Flight 93

The collective memory and meaning of Flight 93 cannot be approached without a consideration of the broader cultural landscape in America in which death, and particularly catastrophic mass death, is understood. In every society, death is the most looming existential difficulty, the liminal situation *par excellence* that every society has to successfully handle with its cultural materials if it is to prove capable of convincing its members to get on with life and not descend into depressed entropy at the realization that all are indeed doomed. In modernity, catastrophes that bring sudden, violent, horrific death to large numbers of people present a unique set of cultural challenges. These are the apparently meaningless, chaotic, nihilistic experiences and events that most challenge our symbolic systems of meaning, and for this reason cultures must work particularly hard to narrate and structure them into coherent and understandable entities, even to turn them into sources of comfort and strength for members of the social group. In the next chapter, I look at the cultural question of death and the peculiar American response to this aspect of human existence as a necessary first step in understanding Flight 93's meaning.

In the remainder of the book I turn to an examination of the various sites in which the narratives, collective memory, and meaning of Flight 93 have been produced and are constantly being reproduced. Some of these are actual physical places at or near the crash site. Over the past several years, I have done a good deal of investigation at the two central such locations: the temporary memorial that existed at the crash site from only days after the crash until the fall of 2011 when it was cleared to make room for the construction of the permanent Flight 93 National Memorial, and the Flight 93 Memorial Chapel just a few miles away from the crash site. An individual chapter (chapters three and four, respectively) is dedicated to each of these. In both of those chapters, photographs of the sites and the materials present there are provided to aid the reader in the journey through the narrative work going on there. In chapter five, I discuss the design for the permanent Flight 93 National Memorial and the cultural context of its emergence. The memorial object in that chapter is both a text, that is, a memorial design, and also the initial stages of the transformation of that text into a physical structure, which had just gotten underway in the fall of 2011 when I was writing this book. A movement from physical sites of memory (which are still inevitably partially mediated) to fully mediated sites begins in chapter five, and in chapters six and seven we enter fully into mediated locations of narrative, memory, and meaning. These latter two chapters analyze popular media sources that narrate the events that took place on the plane and describe the characters involved in the drama. I first take on the collection of biographical books written on a number of the Flight 93 passengers, then turn to the several films that have been made about the flight. Chapter eight considers the interview data I amassed at the temporary memorial site. The final chapter is a culminating reflection on what the memorialization of Flight 93 tells us about American culture and society in the objective moment of crisis it is currently experiencing.

All societies make some things, places, beliefs, symbols, practices, and people sacred, separating them from the mundane and the everyday and assigning them a higher position, one that inspires awe and reverence tinged with terror. It takes only a few moments of observation at the Flight 93 National Memorial and the Flight 93 Memorial Chapel to see sacralization at work. The questions the cultural sociologist asks are: Why *these* particular narratives of sacredness? Why this particular trajectory into the realm of the sacred? This is what the book is intended to investigate.

In Richard Snodgrass's recent book *An Uncommon Field*, he juxtaposes exquisite photographs of the temporary memorial site in Shanksville with brief texts of his own production. The insights are viscerally powerful, as Snodgrass is giving us the account of a pilgrim, of someone in a position vis-à-vis the event much like that of the volunteer at the site Snodgrass quotes saying "[t]his place has entered my heart."[74] Much can be seen from there. Yet the approach is too close, the investment evidently too intense to allow the kind of perspective required to inform readers of the broader structures and contexts that are always there influencing, when they are not wholly determining, what we can experience in places and with symbols like these. In one poignant passage, which is juxtaposed to a photo of the distant flag representing the crash site that perfectly captures the visual experience of the temporary memorial in the simultaneous sense of profound proximity and distance it emanated, Snodgrass describes the plane's impact and the consequent making sacred of the land into which it buried itself: "[T]he fragments [of the fuselage] were absorbed into the earth. Became inextricably part of it, like the sand and clay and silt. Except that now the earth was part human. Sacred earth."[75] Moving, to be sure. But, at the most basic level, inaccurate. For we know that the 44 bodies[76] that were plowed into that tract of earth on that day were not the first ones to be laid there. In *The Wild Ass's Skin*, Honoré de Balzac poetically invokes the treatises of Georges Cuvier, the great French naturalist of the early 19th century, and reminds his reader of "the millions of people which the feeble memory of man and an indestructible divine tradition have forgotten and whose ashes heaped on the surface of our globe, form the two feet of earth which furnish us with bread and flowers."[77] That field in Shanksville, like virtually every other such field on the planet, almost certainly holds the dispersed mortal remnants of human beings stretching back centuries, indeed millennia, and thus it cannot be the simple fact of bodies interred there that gives the site the stunning meaning it clearly has for Snodgrass and many others. This book is an attempt to explore the symbols and narratives that have been used over the decade since the crash of Flight 93 to distinguish the most recent group of human bodies to be laid to rest there from all their predecessors and to make the site a shrine in their honor.

Invoking the anthropologist Claude Lévi-Strauss, Michael Schudson asks a question about his book's great event that gets right to the heart of the matter in the evaluation of the intellectual contribution of the study. Does an investigation of the complex cultural object known as "Watergate," of how we remember and forget the event, the characters involved, and the stories surrounding it, yield useful insights into the much larger object, American culture, that produced it? Yes, his book emphatically declares, Watergate is "good to think with."[78]

Flight 93 is also, in this sense, good to think with.

2

Death, Horror, and Culture

Making Sense of the Senseless in Memorials

Death in Human Culture

Death is, considered in its most basic elements, a simple phenomenon. An organism comes into being, it consumes and grows, and then, after a time, its growth is halted by its consumption by some other organism, or by the inevitable return of its living matter to the inert according to the second law of thermodynamics. Life could not be what it is without death (and vice versa) and the two make up the basic conceptual pair in the consideration of sentient matter. The overwhelming majority of the universe is made up of lifeless matter, and death is the destination of every living thing.

This seems straightforward enough. But death in the human world is, for us, rather more difficult to understand, charged as it is with powerful emotional valence. At the most literal level, there are few things more ubiquitous in human life than human death. In the year in which I wrote the first draft of this chapter, more than 50 million people among the seven or so billion who were then alive perished, whether from hunger or thirst, disease, accident, purposeful action by other human beings in the forms of war and murder, self-annihilation, or the debilitating effects of aging. This amounts to about one death per year for every 140 or so people on the planet, a figure that begins to sound more intimate than the gross total does. One might on this ground be inclined, absent other information, to think death should be something close and readily available to the consciousness of the average human being, something reflected on with regularity given its frequency. After all, human beings are perhaps the only living entities on this planet who are aware that they themselves must die. This tremendously complicates the affair for us. We hate and fear death almost as an automatic consequence of this realization. The anthropologist Ernest Becker postulated that the very origins of the hero are fundamentally tied to the fact of death. Without this primordial, most primitive of human terrors against which to measure human bravery and mastery, much of what we understand as the great achievements of humankind is incomprehensible. Only the terror of death produces the possibility of the overcoming of that terror through heroism and outstanding human accomplishment.[1]

But even if we follow Becker in seeing the trembling before death as a human universal, we must acknowledge that death is not present in the same way to all peoples, for different cultures and civilizations have taken radically different positions on the matter as a social reality. The Aztecs seem to have considered death fairly constantly and even saw it as one of the central facts about a life. Those who died well were celebrated and believed to go on to a glorious afterlife in paradise. Men who perished in combat or women who died in childbirth were believed to have the most regal post-death existence.[2] In the centuries since the Spanish conquest, Mexican culture, imprinted with a Spanish Catholicism itself centrally concerned with the meaning of death, has retained a focus on death that is absent in much of Europe and the West. In Octavio Paz's poetic terms, "for the inhabitant of New York, Paris, or London, death is a word that is never pronounced because it burns the lips [while t]he Mexican, on the contrary, frequents death, makes fun of it, caresses it, sleeps with it, celebrates it, it is one of his favorite playthings and his most permanent love."[3] More recent and systematic analysts of Mexican culture have reported essentially the same finding.[4]

Some other kinds of societies have worked hard to efface death from popular consciousness. Philippe Ariès's history of European death traces the emergence of *la mort apprivoisée*, or "tamed death," in the Middle Ages, where death came to be seen as something that could be sensed in advance and prepared for by those with the proper vision. A model is provided by the knight Lancelot, who, wasting away after the death of Guinevere, distinctly feels his death coming, lays down his arms, then stretches out on the ground, his arms crossed, and begins to pray.[5] In this incarnation in the emerging West, death is outrageous only in its sudden form (*mors repentina*), and the proper, tamed death requires an entourage to serve as spectators.[6] In modernity, by contrast, death becomes something that no longer alerts us of its coming, and because

we cannot be sure as to the final moments, we become fearfully dominated by death throughout our lives and in all moments.[7] The cultural
consequence of this tremendous fear is sequestration. Whereas the man
of the Middle Ages "paid attention to death, as death was a serious thing
that should not be treated lightly, one of life's strong moments, grave and
fearsome," death was not for him "so fearsome as to reject or flee from
it, to pretend as though it did not exist, or to falsify its appearances."[8] It
is in the modern West that death becomes so terrifying that it must be
hidden away and a "pitiless constraint" must be placed on public grieving, which comes to be seen as something "morbid" and impermissible.[9]

In this kind of society, death is never to be spoken of publicly and
one is to work as hard as possible to avoid it in any of its forms, even
those that the Aztecs would have seen as valorous. According to the
philosopher Jean Baudrillard, life comes to be evaluated here in more or
less purely quantitative terms, and the only acceptable death is one that
arrives after many, many years of life, accompanied by no pain or suffering. Most death in the modern West, it turns out, is of this rather prosaic
and unspectacular kind. A very large number of us will die in a hospital
or hospice, buried deep within an organizational context for sequestration of the dying that makes them essentially invisible to everyone else.
The work done by those on a terminal ward in a hospital to avoid taking too seriously the humanity of the patients under their care sheds
a penetrating light on death in its mundane appearance in our world.
Once persons are socially ascribed as dying persons, they enter a special
status, and a specific kind of cultural work is required to place persons
into this category. This might seem counterintuitive; do we not know
objectively when someone is or is not suffering from some illness or
other malady serious enough to categorize him as "dying"? The matter
is not quite so clear as all that, since existentially and objectively, we are
all of us dying from the moment we are born, or at least from the time
at which our bodies achieve adulthood and begin the biological decline
toward death.[10] But in our usage the term refers to those who have been
in some way differentiated from the rest of us, who are placed into some
predictive state wherein we believe their deaths are significantly more
imminent than our own. Once this classificatory work takes place, the
dying person in American society is, whenever possible, placed into
institutional contexts that are carefully constructed to make possible the

routinization of dying in ways that, in addition to frequently contributing to a tremendous sense of separation on the part of those defined
as imminently dying, serve to effectively immunize the rest of us from
the thought of our own deaths. A representative interchange between
two staff members in such an institution as one shift replaces another is
indicative of this kind of cultural work:

A: You look tired.
B: I am. Lucky you, it's all yours.
A: I hope it's a quiet night. I'm not too enthusiastic.
B: They all died during the day today, lucky us, so you'll probably have
   it nice and easy.
A: So I saw. Looks like three, four, and five are empty.
B: Can you believe it, we had five deaths in the last twelve hours.
A: How lovely.
B: Well, see you tomorrow night. Have fun.[11]

The extramundane fact *par excellence*, the disappearance from the world
of an entity that had previously existed in a conscious state, is by this
kind of process made banal and unremarkable. And yet David Sudnow,
the ethnographer who captured this conversation, shows in this study
that even here, in the routine world of hospital death organization,
some deaths remain exceptional and retain the power to break these
frames. The death of a child can make even experienced nurses break
down in tears.[12] Something about this particular event in human life, at
least when it takes place in contexts that do not conform well to organizational grooves, potentially eludes the emotional deadening that the
weight and habit of institutionalization brings about with so much else
in human life.

In our everyday lives, as we go about the business of living, we generally bracket death, in a manner one might explain by necessity. How,
after all, could we dwell on it at length constantly, or even every time
we encountered it in some manner during the day, for example, when
reading the paper or watching the news, and still get anything done?
How could we allow ourselves to settle in to the full depth of the fact
that vibrant, warm individuals we knew in some capacity had stopped
breathing and been consigned forever to the cold earth if we hoped to

be able to go on with our own lives? In the language of the Romantics, the ability to rationally and peaceably come to terms with one's own death or the death of the loved one was a de facto indication that one did not actually love life or the lover, and madness in the face of these facts was the evidence of a profound soul. Whatever we make in moral terms of the prosaic refusal to entertain death in everyday life, the evidence of this nonchalant brushing over of the fact in most of the occasions on which it is encountered is omnipresent. It is a rule followed almost always: treat death as any other fact not directly germane to the topic at hand, to be related and passed over quickly. But what cultural work is necessary to provide us with this rule?

Understanding death as a cultural fact, as something that is not fully reducible to (though it is also inseparable from) a discussion of the science of biological organisms or an exercise in reasoning and logic, is so difficult that even some who have thought very hard indeed about it nonetheless fail to get fully to grips with it. The philosopher Shelly Kagan dismisses the commonly held belief that "we all die alone" as an objective falsehood deriving from logical misunderstanding and confusion.[13] From his perspective, it is acknowledged that death may be ritualized differently in different cultures, but this fact is seen as an aside to the more fundamental investigation of the meaning of death in human life, which involves the work of logically cleansing the way we talk about it. The statement "we all die alone" is proven untrue, Kagan argues, by recognizing that, if we mean simply that we are all physically alone at the moment of death, it is evident that some people at least certainly do die in the company of others. If we mean that our own death is something that only *we* can experience, then there is nothing unique about death here as compared to other experiences, since no one else can experience taking a shower, or shooting a jump shot, or walking out the front door for us either. But Kagan's approach falters precisely in his trivialization of the role of culture in the experience and meaning-making of death. Logical purification work of the type proposed by the analytic philosophers is itself an eminently cultural game, as anthropologists have been demonstrating for more than a century now, and this demonstration has been further sharpened by the sophisticated work of the present generation of sociologists of scientific knowledge. Only certain kinds of cultural animals even recognize the variety of thinking we call "logic," and at least some of those who recognize it nonetheless refuse to enthrone it in the way characteristic of analytic philosophers. Getting outside of the game of culture is considerably more difficult than Kagan acknowledges. If we seek to investigate the meaning of death for human beings, we are led unfailingly to investigate culture. Death, it can reasonably be said, reveals culture and "[e]ven more than that, culture matters only because man is mortal."[14]

The meaning of the statement "we all die alone" in the modern West depends centrally on a basic fact of the cultural framing of death in societies like ours. In cultures that sequester death and demonstrate what can legitimately be called an obsession with youth and vitality, and that insist on denying the reality of mortality even (indeed, especially) in the company of the objectively dying, and that endeavor nearly always to put the dying away in institutional spaces distinctly separated from the quotidian worlds inhabited by those not suffering under an imminent but only a more abstracted and distant death sentence, a profound and nearly universal accompaniment of dying is a sense of isolation more total than that suffered by any outcast group with the possible exception of the most serious criminal offenders. The statement is thus true in the cultural sense insofar as the dying are thoroughly and carefully removed from the presence and the consciousness of the living to the extent possible in contemporary America and other similar societies. Kagan's rejection of all historical and cultural context as secondary at best to the issue betrays a fundamental misunderstanding of the deeply situated nature of human life and meaning-making. His approach also fails to come to terms with the purely emotional power of story and narrative in human life. Death, like all other meaningful components of a human life, is something that requires narration in order for humans to understand it. Logic would purport to strip away narrative in order to get to the "truth," but logic is itself a kind of story, albeit frequently a comparatively boring, one-dimensional, and emotionally handicapped one that does not move many of us nearly as much as some other narratives do.

It is not a difficult matter to find examples that demonstrate the nearly unbearable solitude of the dying in some cultural settings. In Akira Kurosawa's classic film *Ikiru*, an elderly bureaucrat is told by his doctors, in a carefully coded language that he nonetheless comprehends fully well, that he has terminal stomach cancer and will perhaps live six more months. Kurosawa brilliantly captures the emotional solitude of the man, as he sits despairing at a table on the other side of which are arrayed the doctors and nurses who accompany him physically but can never be with him in any meaningful way at this devastating moment in his life. After he leaves the hospital, the doctors talk among themselves. One asks another, then a nurse, as he nonchalantly puffs a cigar and undoubtedly looks forward to the next case, what they would do if they were given the news they had just delivered to the bureaucrat, but all are clearly unable to even begin to get their minds around the question. They look concerned, as they must, and as they have been trained to do, and they do recognize the seriousness of the fact, and yet, entirely because it is not them but him, there is no possibility of their entering into that isolated space he now inhabits and will dwell within until the end mercifully comes.

Another evocation of dying as fundamentally unmitigated solitude can be found in the heart-breaking description given by the husband of the British journalist Ruth Picardie of a scene that took place the night before she succumbed to metastasized cancer at the age of 33. The two of them are putting their infant twins to bed, having just read them stories, and the children begin singing a lullaby, which their father joins. Picardie, already physically destroyed by the disease that would claim her life in under 24 hours, tries to participate as well, with one of the children sitting on her lap, but her voice is so frail and weak, and the energy she can contribute to their profoundly cultural game so slight, that the child on her lap intuitively recognizes her increasing distance from the world he inhabits and from life itself. He quietly moves to the bed to join the father and the other child, leaving Picardie in a chair in a darkened corner, visible only as a silhouetted shade, her fading voice barely carrying across the room. Her husband recalls this as a moment in which the primal reality of the loneliness of the dying struck him with unrelenting, obliterating force.[15] It takes a certain distance from human experience to claim that this moving realization, saturated in cultural wine of ancient vintage, is no more than a logical error on the part of Picardie's husband, driven by insufficient clear-headedness.

The cultural is the unavoidable ground of the human thinking and experiencing of death. Martin Heidegger, perhaps the 20th-century philosopher most focused on the question of the experience of death, presented a more nuanced framework for understanding death than that of analytic philosophy, and part of the nuance had to do with his recognition of the place of culture in the human approach to finitude. Heidegger argued that, although we can represent, or stand in for, Others in many everyday situations, the death of Others cannot be experienced as such. This is a result of the fact of human separateness. When the Other dies and thereby makes the transition from *Dasein* to "Being-just-present-at-hand-and-no-more," i.e., no longer a conscious, living entity, and also not a mere inanimate material object that was never alive, but rather "something unalive, which has lost its life," we can, in our deeply social nature, in a sense accompany him: "In tarrying alongside him in their mourning and commemoration, those who have remained behind *are with him*, in a mode of respectful solicitude."[16] Yet, he is clear that this is not the same thing as actually experiencing his death: "The dying of Others is not something which we experience in a genuine sense; at most we are always just 'there alongside.'"[17]

It is difficult to say precisely what we do know about the death of the Other, although it is certainly not the experience of death itself. To die is something one can undergo but once, and we cannot use the experience as a basis for comparison to the experience of Others in the same way that we can, for example, know something of what other people are "going through" when they suffer pain and illness, having 'gone through' them ourselves. Indeed, even though each *Dasein* is called to "take upon itself"[18] its own dying, there is a sense in which we can reasonably say that *Dasein* does not truly experience even its own death: "When *Dasein* reaches its wholeness in death, it simultaneously loses the Being of its 'there.' By its transition to no-longer-*Dasein*, it gets lifted right out of the possibility of experiencing this transition and of understanding it as something experienced."[19] It is, Heidegger ironically notes, precisely the fact that we are unable to reflect upon and understand our own deaths in this experiential sense that makes the death of Others, which we cannot experience but which we can witness and continue to puzzle and marvel at after the event, all the "more impressive": "In this way a termination of [another] *Dasein* becomes 'Objectively' accessible . . . [and] *Dasein* can thus gain an experience of death, all the more so because *Dasein* is essentially Being with Others."[20]

Now, in the modern West, the typical approach to death involves seeing it as "a mishap which is constantly occurring," and always to someone else.[21] Of course, we know that death is a certainty for every mortal, but Heidegger argues that the general reaction of someone learning of the death of another is to reassure himself by thinking, "Death certainly comes, but not right away." This might appear a reasonable, well-adjusted response, but the "not right away" constitutes a dissimulation in that it hides "what is peculiar in death's certainty—that it is possible at any moment."[22] The Catholic thinker John Henry Newman presented a similar set of categories with the concepts of notional assent and real assent. Notional assent to death is recognition of the logical proposition that humans as a category have mortality as one of their core characteristics, while real assent is the coming to acceptance of the inevitability of one's own death, not in merely logical terms, but as an emotional matter as well. For Heidegger, not only do the mass of men willfully delude themselves with an avoidance of the reality of death, but they even castigate any who reflect upon death with what they see as an inappropriate intensity. They do "not permit us the courage for anxiety in the face of death."[23] Heidegger endeavored to present death as something to be faced authentically, that is, as a reality that ought always to be faced squarely as such, in its immediate, visceral sense, and not as a deferred future conclusion to a path we currently travel and as a fact only insofar as it is something we see happening to Others around us.

So the problem of death was a cultural one for Heidegger, insofar as he posits a cultural response to it. It is the lack of care of the modern mass man that has created his dilemma. He is wholly wrapped up in his trivial commercial pursuits, gossiping and chattering in the indiscriminate gatherings that are the sad substitute for collective public life in modern capitalism. What is needed is a return to a structure of meaning, whether the philosopher's sophisticated system or the simpler method of the religious peasant for whom Heidegger always maintained a profound respect. In the latter case, in which the authenticity of the philosopher is not possible, the structure of meaning is a collective exercise in mimicry designed to reassure us about our deaths. So long as we can accept the meanings and follow the actions of our fellows in their traditions and rituals, we are reassured. When we begin to question the stories and doubt the efficacy of the actions, or when objective shifts in the culture and social order enfeeble the old meanings, we enter anxiety. We can achieve immortality, of a sort, through personal investment in the symbols of our collectivity, for, although we die, the family, the tribe, the country lives on.

Death and the Idea of America

It is certainly true that rituals, beliefs, and meanings surrounding death are particularly important in defining any society. In a book on the social meaning of death, Edgar Morin wrote that the ways in which we ritualize death are the most primitive aspects of contemporary societies and they therefore show us what is most deeply human about us.[24] If we doubt the lingering, phantom presence of the primitive even in our contemporary practices and ideas surrounding death, he argues, we have only to look to something as mundane as the still common practice of naming newborns after deceased elders of the family as a living remnant in contemporary culture of the most primitive notions of souls migrating inside a family and reincarnating after the death of one member in another.[25] Claudio Lomnitz's *Death and the Idea of Mexico* takes Morin's claim seriously and makes just such an approach to understanding Mexican history and culture. One might well charge that the task is quite more compelling in a case like this one, where death is and nearly always has been such a prominent part of national identity. But does such a vision make sense in a country, i.e., the United States, where death, while obviously present as a cultural sign of significance, is in many ways occluded, willfully cast into the shadows, and, if not forgotten (as this is an impossibility), at least studiously and actively avoided most of the time? To be sure, Lomnitz does not directly answer these questions, as his main concern is Mexico, but he certainly does suggest that affirmation is defensible. All nations have "tutelary signs," or "national totems," and "the management of death, and indeed the ability to kill" are foundational elements of any state's claim to rule.[26] It has been said that all nations are founded on an act of fratricidal violence and death, and, though it may be an overgeneralization to name death as a universal national tutelary sign, it may well turn out that at least some of any given nation's totems must have to do with the particular manifestation of death as a sign in the dominant culture of the nation.

Let us try then, briefly, to look for death's place in America's totems. A historical vision informs us that death was not always in America what it is today. In America at the time of the Puritans, as in the England from which they had come, "the nights were blacker, the days more silent, and the winters more terrifying and cold" than we can today imagine, with horrifying death by starvation and disease an everyday companion for the mass of society.[27] The religious precepts of the American Puritan, based in the ferocious doctrinal combination of *sola fides* (and so the irrelevance of any earthly deeds to salvation) and the predestination of eternal damnation and salvation of souls (which meant that even faith could not save you if God had already marked you before birth for Hell), death and anxieties concerning post mortem fate were the inescapable companions of all. Children's school primers taught the alphabet and death simultaneously: "G—As runs the *Glass* / Mans life doth pass . . . / T—*Time* cuts down all / Both great and small."[28] Puritan ministers such as Cotton Mather and Jonathan Edwards spoke the brutal truth to even the smallest of their flock: "Yea, you may be at Play one Hour; Dead, Dead the next."[29] Here, remarkably, we find an early American culture much closer in the central role it assigns to death in its broadest narratives to the Mexico described by Lomnitz than to its contemporary incarnation.

By the mid-1700s, however, a less exacting religious sensibility had become dominant, and its more sentimental and ultimately Romantic vision of death replaced Puritanical dread and asceticism. This was evident in discourses on death, but more visibly in gravestone art, which saw a shift from the predominance of the grim Puritan death's head to a proliferation of cherubs, angels, and other pleasant heavenly representations of the afterlife.[30] Romantic America remained, like its Puritan predecessor, focused on death, but now, instead of the terrifying harbinger of suffering and isolation, death was seen as deliverance from physical suffering and reunion with lost loved ones.[31] Until at least the mid-1800s, this Romantic vision of death as the beautiful transition into the community beyond the grave, which was yearned for all the more as earthly community grew more fragmented with the rapid growth of commerce and cities, was dominant.[32] But however much this new death culture shared with its Puritan predecessor the placing of death front and center in life's concerns, it also set the stage for the rise, in the late 19th century, of what we might call the modern American culture of death.

Commercial, technological, and scientific progress combined with the optimism of the Romantic view of death as spiritual release to produce a third American culture of death in which it began to be understood as something to be hidden away. Children begin to die much less frequently in modern America, thanks to the advance of medical science and practice, and the cultural pedagogy on death consequently moved to eliminate nearly all teaching of it to the young.[33] The idea that simply talking too honestly about death to young children can psychologically traumatize them, still a widespread ideology today, was born in this period. Death became something that is not to be thought of until old age, and even then it can be put off with the aid of medical science. A certain hyperyouthful effervescence was enshrined as the goal of all people, even those who are objectively not at all far from the grave, in large part as a logical consequence of our desire to sequester death. Increasingly, death is something the good middle-class American may never see unless and until it strikes him or a loved one, and even in the latter case, most will not have the experience of watching the loved one expire in the home to be commemorated there by family and friends.

There are some seemingly confounding facts in this narrative that have been pointed to by others who believe contemporary America does not sequester death. James Green, for example, rejects the applicability of Ariès's thesis to post-1950s America and cites the influence of Elisabeth Kübler-Ross's well-known stages of death acceptance, which he believes to have been digested and then superseded in today's American culture by a new genre of *ars moriendi*. Green provides a few examples, which he would like to see as representative, of the "good death" in modern America. One of these he even labels the "Everyman" of American death; this is Morrie Schwartz, the former professor who became famous in his dying days because of Mitch Albom's best-selling book *Tuesdays with Morrie* and several appearances with Ted Koppel on *Nightline*. In examples such as the case of Schwartz, Green alleges, we see an American approach to death that is not fearful or retreating, but more and more accepting and embracing. There is evidence of something we might call a home burial movement, vividly portrayed in the documentary film *A Family Undertaking*, in which citizens reclaim the right to care for their dying at home and dispose of their bodies in ritual ways of their own choosing instead of relying on the sequestering institutions of the hospital, the hospice, and the funeral industry, and thereby reinsert death in the heart of everyday life. Much too has been written and said recently about the omnipresence of death in our mass media, which would seem to indicate, among other things, an escape of death, at least in its mediated and mostly fictionalized forms, from sequestration.

However, the broad notion of death as something we work strenuously to hide from ourselves in American culture remains hard to fully refute. Norbert Elias was referring to the West generally, and Europe more specifically, when he described an attitude toward death centrally informed by a rejection of mutual human dependence, an embrace of isolated individualism, and a "collective wish-fantasy of eternal life in another place,"[34] but this characterization is particularly applicable to American society, which is undeniably less morally collectivist, more radically individualist, and more explicitly religious and oriented to the supernatural than virtually any other Western society. More evidence that American death is something deliberately shrouded by the mist of social disapproval and fear can be found in the seemingly mundane fact of the country's astronomical health care expenditure, a huge fraction of which is spent by (or on behalf of) patients near the end of life on the latest experimental medical procedures in largely unsuccessful bids to extend their lives. American health care policy is subject to many influences, including the operations of for-profit pharmaceutical and medical technology industries driven fundamentally by their interest in selling their products to as many customers as possible and regardless of any evidence that many of those customers might derive little or no benefit from the purchased drugs or procedures. But the foundational force driving the profound desire of many American patients and their family members to seek every existing possible medical response within their financial means to the encroachment of death is cultural. The very organizational logic of the hospital, which is the site of major illness and death for most Americans, is founded on the rejection of death. The hospital as institution tends to position death as a foe to be confronted and bested, and, despite the understanding that this particular foe wins all wars in the end, this can contribute to sequestration and depersonalizing alienation of the dying, who are a threat to the commitment of the hospital to the healing process. Bureaucratic modes of efficiency and depersonalization are put into play to make dying sensible in a way that both saves the institution's sense of its own mission (by hiding the dying in a death ward separated from the rest of the hospital) and, simultaneously, contributes to what has been called the "stripping process" by which the dying are robbed of their personhood through renaming and reclassification.[35] That this institutional process accompanies, for the terminally ill, the concomitant phenomenon of the gradual loss of body control and function makes it all the more difficult to bear.[36]

Constant advances in medical technology, which are particularly evident in the United States, outflank any existing definitions of death as a natural phenomenon. When a person with a heart or lungs that are not functioning, facts that announce imminent death absent immediate intervention, can be technologically prevented from expiring, the entire edifice on which the question of the "proper time to accept death" stands is seriously shaken. The American reality is that our fear of death is so great that we tend to embrace, at least as legally responsible family members looking on at our grievously ill kin, any possible medical delay of the terminal moment, and in a society as advanced in medical research as ours, there are many such means to apply to that end. The anthropologist Sharon Kaufman has shown that hospital culture, its own institutional beast to a degree but also deeply influenced by broader American cultural values such as radical individualism, is marked by at least four major characteristics that indicate and contribute to the American sequestration of death: patients and their families are given significant autonomy to make decisions about care, usually in the absence of profound medical knowledge of their likely utility, which frequently leads to decisions to continue treatment long after the point at which such treatment is likely to be efficacious; palliative care constitutes a kind of offense against the hospital's raison d'être, and so it is generally rejected so long as there are any curative measures to be tried; hospital personnel are trained to avoid even invoking the possibility of death until shortly before it becomes wholly inevitable, which contributes to the difficulty of realistic decision making by patients and their families; and, finally, although most Americans will die in a hospital, for various reasons (including the political decision to attempt to bring Medicare costs under control in part by reducing or eliminating payments for many kinds of palliative and end-of-life care) those institutions tend to look to discharge patients recognized as beyond curative treatment.[37] It is patently obvious that the pathologies of the American medical institutional framework with respect to death are symbiotic with our overall dread and refusal of death. American death remains, for most of us at least, "messy, painful, full of contradictions, and fearful."[38] We might suggest that, if the smiling, cavorting skeleton of the Día de los Muertos celebration is Mexico's central death-related tutelary sign, it is the suffering, dying patient hidden away from the eyes of the living in the bowels of the hospital terminal ward that occupies this central symbolic place in the United States.

And yet, this may still be too uncomplicated. For alongside this proposed national sign of death in America, there is another, darker mode in which death is powerfully present in American culture. This is violent and spectacular death as an aspect of contemporary American media culture where we find a transgressive desire to escape the bureaucratic imperative of the "good death" that arrives at the end of a long, productive life and instead meet the challenge of death with an embrace of spectacular, sudden death of self or of observed others. Jean Baudrillard argued that members of mass-mediated, advanced capitalist societies come to understand the explosive deaths in which the daily news is always saturated as a symbolic exchange that constitutes resistance to the logic of the dominant form of death provided to citizens in those societies.[39] In violent, sudden death, and especially in the dark binary pair of suicide and terrorism, Baudrillard sees an act that puts death back in play in our social exchange network. In primitive societies, death and the dead could be, indeed had to be, bartered with and considered as active participants in the human world, but modernity attempts to defeat death and thereby remove it from the cycle of exchange with the weapons of medical technologies. Americans, in this vision, come to experience violent, spectacular death as a terrifying, bracing reassertion of death into the cultural landscape, fearsome and awe inspiring, clearly, but perhaps the only way to elude the fetters of the dispirited, slavish form of death present in the terminal wards of the hospitals. Baudrillard saved the most controversial element of a troubling theoretical position for an essay on 9/11. There, he alluded to what for many Americans is a nearly unutterable possibility: "The fact that we have dreamt of this event—that everyone without exception has dreamt of it, because no one can avoid dreaming of the destruction of any power that has become hegemonic to this degree—is unacceptable to the Western moral conscience. Yet it is a fact, and one which can indeed be measured by the emotive violence of all that has been said and written in the effort to dispel it."[40] In the same experience of horror at the thought that what is unthinkable can happen, there is also the realization of a scarcely recognized desire to escape the prison of the thinkable. When we are forced by an event to contemplate the possibility that everything we take for granted can be undone, terror at the loss of the given is accompanied by a kind of ecstasy at the miraculous emergence of possibility where none had previously existed. The stunning power of Baudrillard's insight is easily lost to the automatic moral judgment we are all encouraged to immediately level by cultural taboos that would endeavor to prevent even the thinking of such thoughts. It may be that some of the undeniable thrill one experiences in watching, for example, the otherworldly footage of people walking in Manhattan streets that ten seconds previously were sun-drenched and now are the very stuff of nightmare visions of blackened and hostile alien worlds has to do with the basic survival instinct. It is the raw euphoria of the life force expressing the dizzying realization of the privilege of witnessing the deathly dreamscape of tortured sleep while fully awake but without actually suffering or even facing the death it brings. The inability to fully explain or account for this feeling does not suffice as a denial of its existence.

It might be argued, following Baudrillard, that catastrophic death events such as the terrorist attacks of 9/11, especially given their spectacular mass-mediated tenor, present a possible acid to the solid crust over human consciousness constituted by Newman's notional assent and Heidegger's "death as that which does not come right away." The purely quantitative magnitude is an important element in this. The deaths of so many in four rapid strokes separated by just more than an hour is a fact harder to relegate to the same irrelevant status we assign to any single death of a stranger. But numbers are not the whole of the story. The nature of catastrophe itself must be understood as essential

to the terrible meaning such events take on and the deep mythological cultural work that is necessary to rob them of their monstrous,
malevolent power.

Catastrophic Death: Risk and Rupture

Events of collective, catastrophic death such as those that took place in
the United States on September 11, 2001, dramatically indicate the risks
inherent in contemporary social life. The men and women who boarded
the four planes and those who perished in the World Trade Center and
Pentagon likely had no inkling that what would happen to them that
day was even a remote possibility, and yet all of us recognize, when we
take a moment to explicitly reflect on the matter, that death could intervene and end our lives in myriad ways every day as we go about our
business, and it is a disconcerting fact that we have almost no control
over most of these risks. What could a passenger on Flight 93 have done
to cheat death that day? Taken another plane, perhaps? This exercise
in alternative history is entertained in many of the recountings of the
story of Flight 93. Waleska Martinez, according to the account of family
members, contemplated changing her flight the night before because of
a nightmare, but ultimately did not do so. The image of Mark Bingham
rushing at the last minute to reach the plane that would kill him is a
poignant one in the established narrative. What if traffic had held him
up only ten minutes more? But of course such thinking is after the fact,
and does not in any way alter the actual risks and dangers entailed by life
in modern society. One cannot know in advance that the hypothetical
second plane is not also targeted for hijack, or in fact that it is not the
one doomed to hijack and crash, while the first plane, which one fore-
goes boarding as a result of trepidation about risk, lands safely. Even if
neither plane is destined for hijacking, either might fall from the sky as a
result of mechanical failure or an accident with a flock of birds blocking
a motor, and there is no way to predict whether this or another plane is
the one that will turn out to be the statistical anomaly. The realization
that we live in such a world of uncertainty and lack of control flies in the
face of our basic understandings of progress, of the idea that our world is
subject to more expertise, more technical precision, more organization
and rational planning than any human world that has heretofore existed.

Risk in human society is not an unchanging constant. The sociologist Anthony Giddens has expertly framed the central differences between the major risks faced by human populations in premodern societies and those we face today. In the former, the main mortal risks had to do with the natural environment, which killed frequently in the form of natural disasters, epidemics and plagues, and unpredictable weather, and violence from bands of roaming marauders and criminals. In our world, the sources of the most important risks to our lives have fundamentally shifted. Many of the risks of purely natural origins have been eliminated or greatly mitigated. Infectious diseases have, in some cases, been altogether eradicated, and, in others, greatly reduced by medical science, and, although earthquakes, floods, and the like still happen, science and technology can often warn us of them with advance time for escape or protect us with varying degrees of effectiveness by means of stronger living structures and barriers. Human violence is still a risk, and indeed now on a regional and global rather than purely local scale. Though legal structures and police provide protection from the kinds of small bands of attackers faced in premodernity, we now have industrialized and nuclear war and terrorism to fear. These risks of violence are heightened in unknown, terrifying ways by the manner in which the very environment of modernity can, in the hands of the malevolent or in the mere event of accident, instantly transform into new and ghoulish forms of death. So, on September 11, 2001, the marvelous constructions of the engine of American capitalist production and organization, those massive towers, were turned into crashing mountains of tons of debris that rained down on and instantly exterminated many, and the horror of the fact was only amplified by the sense so many had just seconds before that it was impossible for even a direct hit from a 747 to bring down these impenetrable pillars of America's strength and know-how. An important new source of risk in the contemporary world has to do with the abstract systems and structures of modernity. The same food and energy systems that nourish our bodies and power our devices can also poison us and expose us to fatal amounts of radiation. Transportation systems that enable us to move around our countries and internationally with considerable ease also kill more than a million of us around the globe every year, and they contribute massive amounts of pollution to the environment that is the primary cause in many deaths.[41]

So disasters and catastrophes occur frequently, and we can accurately say even systematically (that is, as an inevitable, predictable consequence of the kind of social system we inhabit), in societies like ours. A professional sociology of disasters and catastrophes has now existed for a few decades, but it tends to focus on institutional responses to dire collective events and the differential suffering from disasters experienced by groups defined along gender, race, and socioeconomic class lines, at the expense of a full-blown effort to understand catastrophic death in cultural sociological terms. This seems especially so in its American incarnation, and we might well pose the question as to whether mainstream American sociology is in fact just as heavily invested in the sequestration of death as is the larger national culture. It might well be seen as a telling point that when death escapes sequestration in American society, it is nearly always in the form of the "good death," that is, as the death of someone who has already lived what is generally considered a reasonably full and long life and who faces the news of a terminal illness or condition that will eventually, but not overnight, prove the agent of his end. When we turn to death as a consequence of risk society, and when the dead wear the masks not of the elderly but of the young and vibrant, and when the death to be faced comes not after months of decline and preparation, but in an instant that destroys the body of the deceased and thereby reveals in the most horrific way our mortal vulnerability, and when that instant brings not just one death but many, then we find American culture and American academia remarkably silent.

Social reaction to catastrophe is not as easy to describe and understand as it might seem at first glance. It has been argued that, in the early modern period, disaster in America was romanticized and seen as a welcome element of color and excitement in otherwise drab existences. In this earlier period, according to Kevin Rozario, catastrophe "forced the abandonment of suffocating conventionalities . . . [and offered] the opportunity to forge a genuine community," whereas in contemporary America disaster is something only to be dreaded, an unavoidable portion of risk that, if realized, brings only mortal suffering, and indeed brings it in psychic form even if unrealized.[42] It has been a stock claim of much of the sociology of catastrophe that different kinds of disasters have predictably different effects on the human groups they touch. Natural disasters, it is claimed, unite and morally bring communities together, while human-produced disasters fragment them and produce conflict in the process of assigning blame for the disaster.[43] These distinctions, however, become somewhat harder to maintain once one begins to operate in the context of contemporary risk society as discussed by Giddens. Many if not all seemingly natural disasters can be shown to have distinctly human causes that operate alongside natural elements to produce the full extent of the catastrophe. Hurricane Katrina was a natural event, but it was able to do the great damage it did in New Orleans because of particular human inputs, most importantly, the human decision to build a large, heavily populated city on land sitting well below sea level and defended from water by improperly constructed, poorly maintained levees and barriers. Powerful earthquakes can produce massive or very limited tolls on human life depending on the standards in building construction enforced in an affected area and the ability to quickly and effectively communicate scientific information about warning tremors to the public. As such factors are increasingly well known to publics, the matter of blame and responsibility has become a central aspect even of so-called natural catastrophes in contemporary societies. Arguably, in risk society, there is more similarity in so-called natural and human-produced catastrophes than difference. Both are generally strongly affected in likelihood and severity by specific human interventions (or the lack thereof) into the minimization of given modern risks. The hermeneutic of risk is what is paramount in all such catastrophes.[44]

In the old natural/human-produced dichotomy, terrorism would seem to be purely of the latter type, yet the production of moral unity among victim populations seems a regular feature of many if not most terrorist attacks. In cases of terrorism where the attacker is not a member of the attacked community, and perhaps even in cases where he is (e.g., the Oklahoma City bombing of 1995), blame can be clearly assigned outside the group, even if there are complications, as in the case of 9/11 and the criticism of the federal government's ineffectual response to advance intelligence data indicating that al-Qaeda had a great interest in attacks of just the sort that it carried out on September 11, 2001. Indeed, it is the easiest of matters to mobilize simple narratives of insider and outsider in such situations, and especially so when insiders and outsiders differ in fundamental identity characteristics such as religion and race. Psychological research in terror management theory has shown that people who are reminded about their own mortality (and we might suspect this is heightened in societies where death is generally sequestered) tend to more harshly judge and morally separate themselves from people seen as outside the basic cultural symbols of their society and show greater respect for religious symbols understood as traditional to their society. In representative studies, municipal court judges whose mortality was made salient to them tended to set higher bonds for hypothetical women accused of prostitution, and subjects reminded of their mortality were less likely than others to use culturally resonant religious symbols such as crucifixes in ways understood as sacrilegious, even if the religious object was the best one available for an assigned practical task such as hammering a nail.[45] We should expect catastrophic death connected to acts of terrorism believed to be carried out by cultural outsiders to tend to produce significant moral unity within the community and significant aggression toward those seen as outside it.

One short-term response to catastrophe at the collective and individual level, then, might well be characterized as rage. In the immediate aftermath of the 9/11 attacks, there was a brief spike, albeit one rather less impressive than many academics had warned, in verbal and physical attacks on those who, due to their physical appearance, took on the role of stand-in for the hijackers, who had themselves been effectively removed from possible judgment and punishment by their own annihilation in the completion of their acts. Many who did not insult or strike at perceived Arabs or Muslims nonetheless entered the vengeful rage state that made the American movement to war in Afghanistan, and then Iraq, child's play for the politicians who headed it. While one might posit a certain substratum of human experience of death that, if not susceptible to definition as rage simply put, nonetheless has rage as one of its natural expressions, the ultimate framing of angry reactions to catastrophic death is still wholly cultural. In an anthropological reflection on death, Renato Rosaldo described his inability to understand the traditional Ilongot practice of headhunting by grieving family members after the death of a loved one. Rosaldo had difficulty effectively framing their frustration at the Philippine government's outlawing of the practice, until his own wife fell to her death during a research trip in Luzon, and then he too found himself lusting for vengeance against indiscriminate, innocent parties. The question is clearly cultural, both at the Ilongot end and at our own, for certainly there are members of Rosaldo's own tribe who would have no trouble whatsoever comprehending the fact that the Ilongot long to take the heads of tribal enemies when their loved ones perish and who refrain from such a response to the emotional intensity of loss of a loved one not because of any more advanced state of humanity, but largely because of their understanding that the response of the legal system to such rage would be crushing and permanent. It may well be too that those individuals recognize that rage can be expressed collectively as well as individually, and while headhunting cannot be countenanced in the modern West, in response to at least some cases of death, the collectively exercised extermination of parties adjudged guilty, through trial or war, can still be accomplished. In this sense, it may not be off the mark to argue that the American response to the 9/11 attacks was a kind of national collective version of Ilongot headhunting.

The sociologist Gaëlle Clavandier offers a compelling framework for understanding the cultural work that goes on around collective, catastrophic death. A primary cultural act surrounding such events is the tremendously important one of naming. The first step toward understanding something, whether terrible or wonderful, desired or feared, is to give it a name; this is the primordial human act of asserting order and control.[46] The ease with which Americans began to say "nine-eleven" to refer to the attacks of that date, and the fact that virtually every American knows instantly what is being referred to with that economically elegant term, may not seem a remarkable fact, but it is. The serendipitous correspondence of the date with the three-digit emergency phone number, and therefore its easy memorization, perhaps helped ensure the universal acceptance of the term, and a short, nondescriptive name for the event is already indicative of some of the initial cultural work required to obfuscate its most awful elements.

Clavandier describes the universal tendency in catastrophic death to speak in terms of a reified, personified, and malevolent entity as the causal agent of the event. In a disaster involving a collapsed dam, the wave generated by the escaping wall of water is spoken of in awed terms as a kind of living, evil being; when a nightclub bursts into flames and young dancers are suffocated because their escape is prevented by a turnstile, this object becomes a fearsome creature with intentions of a sort; a train that derails and is hit by another, killing dozens, is described as "crazy."[47] With respect to 9/11, we see this same process at work; the most powerful example is perhaps that of the malignant second plane, intelligent and animated with evil intentions, that proved at least for a moment capable of something many believed impossible, i.e., shaking Americans out of their complacent sense of superiority and invulnerability. We might well understand what is going on in this feature of the catastrophe as a refusal of the structural framing of catastrophic death that is an inevitable consequence of the framework provided by the notion of risk society. Risk is a statistical probability, a fact of certain institutional arrangements that has nothing to do with the intentions of individuals and everything to do with the accidents of structure that escape and frustrate those intentions. In assigning malevolent agency to the planes that were simply being manipulated as tools by human individuals, we symbolically reassert a vision of a universe in which agency matters, even if not only and always for the good. This desire for a world in which structural facts, such as the real exposure to risk in given situations and the reality that some percentage of those who run such risks will inevitably succumb to them, can always be translated into the language of actors and agency is perhaps behind the most common way of making sense of the horrific phenomenon of those on the World Trade Center towers who plummeted from the windows to death on the streets below in the minutes after the planes struck. Although the official statistics of mortality recorded those deaths as homicides due to their clear causal connection to the criminal act of the hijackers, the jumpers were commonly considered by everyday observers to have deliberately taken their fates into their own hands and chosen the means of their own ends by leaping rather than suffering the indignity of an imposed death by smoke inhalation.

Catastrophic death is also generally framed as an initiator of liminal experience, that is, of an experience that constitutes a violent rupture with the ordinary and reveals some previously unknown and horrible facts or situations.[48] The memorial of the catastrophe is intended to help us forget the event itself and to remember instead the myth to which it has been attached and the core elements of the commemorative story, i.e., the names of the victims and the moral unity produced by their tragic demise. The catastrophe, and specifically the death that it brings, is "that which cannot be tolerated by man and by society."[49] The memorial itself must not recall the horrific elements of the catastrophe, in the case of 9/11, the towers collapsing, the bodies crushed and mutilated, the jumpers, or for Flight 93 specifically, the plane impacting the earth and the bodies being instantly turned into steaming gore. It must also refrain from recalling the unbearable emotions of the victims crying for help, buried in the rubble of the towers, or the families screaming inconsolably.[50] An event of catastrophic death also makes sacred the places where it occurs, although it is not clear, however much memorialization seeks to hide the horrific aspects of the event, if that sacralization is fundamentally in the direction of purification (the innocent victims and their heroic efforts to save their own lives and the lives of others), making "accursed" (the evil perpetrated on the victims), or some complex combination of the two.[51] In particularly immense and violent physical catastrophes such as in the case of the destruction of the World Trade Center towers, the space is deformed on a grandiose scale that cannot be missed by any onlooker, but even when deformation of the site is much more symbolic than physical, as in most of the cases Clavandier examines, the power of the meaning of this deformation remains immense. We speak of the deformation of the land in terms of injury and impurity: the wound in Manhattan where the absent towers once stood, the hole in the Pentagon, the despoiled earth in Shanksville. The site is fearful and cursed, but also blessed, a sanctuary, a cemetery, or a chapel where the visitor finds both trepidation and balm. This is a crucial theoretical point to which I will return in forthcoming chapters. Finally, catastrophic death must be encompassed in a narrative that forces death to give way to "the necessary victory of life" and to an affirmation that "the situation will not be reproduced [and] that lasting changes have been brought about" to "return to normal."[52] This element of the memorialization of catastrophic death looms very large indeed in the narrative most centrally embraced in the mythology of Flight 93, as we will see later in the book.

The memorial dissolution of catastrophic death is aided by the general cultural fear of death we have been discussing and by the sheer capacity, in bustling societies like ours in which the tragedy of one day instantly melts into oblivion in the wake of hundreds of new bits of trivia masquerading as news the next, to forget and to forget quickly. Whatever the evidence that, in the moment, the attacks shook many Americans to their existential core, snapping them out of the everyday and into a brief realization of the monstrous violence and fear felt much more commonly by other segments of the human population, the available data seem to indicate that 9/11 has affected Americans only very abstractly and weakly in the long term. In general, we have not much changed our behaviors post-9/11 out of fear of terrorism. A 2008 study by the National Consortium for the Study of Terrorism and Responses to Terrorism found only relatively slight alterations in American attitudes and knowledge of terrorism as a result of the 9/11 attacks. For example, while large majorities claimed they have become "more vigilant" since 9/11, and significant percentages claim to know others who are doing specific things in response to terrorism (e.g., avoiding air travel or travel to areas likely to be terrorist targets), when subjects are asked about specific things they themselves have done in response, the percentages responding affirmatively are quite low.[53] One T-shirt I saw at the dedication ceremony for the permanent memorial for Flight 93 in September 2011 summed up this sentiment—which was also communicated, albeit in generally somewhat less vernacular language, by President Bush and other national political and business advocates of a consumerist response to the attacks—in a Sharpie-scrawled message: "No terrorist is gonna mess with my vacation." Respondents in the NCSTRT study self-report only very moderate levels of knowledge of the color codes of the Homeland Security Advisory System, what the government has done to prepare for terrorism, and where to get information if a warning is issued because of a terrorist event.[54] And now, more than ten years down the road, a significant shift in the thinking about 9/11 is already well underway in the public sphere. When the film *2012* was premiering in theaters, trailers showed a plane flying between two towers, which collapsed just after the plane passed through. Mark Harris, writing in *Entertainment Weekly*, suggested that "you can mark the sight of those falling buildings as the moment when Hollywood's attitude toward 9/11 devolved from *We should be careful* to *Oh, lighten up.*"[55]

Death, Terror, and the Destroyed Body

When the simple, already liminal fact of death is augmented by accident or malice or both, i.e., when deaths take place among those seemingly very far from "natural death" because of some chance malfunction of a large and deadly machine, a freak natural phenomenon such as an earthquake or a bolt of lightning, or the action of a human antagonist or animal predator, then it becomes still more endowed with the eerie glow of fear and repulsion. To truly experience the horror of this kind of catastrophe, mass media news reporting, which is itself an already sanitized object beholden to cultural regulations and taboos concerning what journalism can show viewers, will not do. In the present age, catastrophes frequently are reported not only by professional journalists, but also by everyday citizens with handheld video cameras and smart phones, and the Internet provides a site for much of the information they produce to be communicated to publics. In this unedited, raw footage, the sheer vastness and raw intensity of catastrophic events is more sensuously evident than in the carefully polished video and accompanying reportage of the professionals, and terror comes precisely from the magnitude of the chaos. It is this sense of being small and inconsequential, in the midst of some massive and malevolent event, that is so viscerally communicated by the shaky amateur camera technique that has become de rigueur in many movies that seek to unsettle viewers.[56] A virtual stroll through YouTube reveals a sampling of the chilling on-site footage of the strikes on the World Trade Center towers and their collapse. In one such video, we watch the burning towers from what appears to be only a few blocks away while voices discuss the designs of a helicopter hovering nearby: "This guy's trying to land. . . . [L]ooks like there's people on the roof," intones one, and just as his colleague responds "There gotta be!" there is a terrible rumbling and the South Tower begins to collapse. Immediately, screams erupt from the vicinity and the cameraman, or someone else nearby, expels a litany of blood-curdling intonations of the same repeated phrase: "OH MY GOD! OH MY GOD! OH MY GOD!" He goes on for what seems an eternity, his cries expressing a sense of unbelief, literally calling on a supernatural force to intervene and stop the impossibility, his voice quivering near the end of the litany perhaps with the realization that there will be no such intervention and that the closest thing he has yet experienced to total ruin is now at hand.[57] In another video of the South Tower's collapse, from near Trinity Church just south of the WTC complex, the cameraman stands seemingly mesmerized as the demolition cloud, a massive phantasm of disintegrated concrete and pulverized human flesh,[58] descends on him at impossible speed, from every angle, only seconds before he enters the shelter of a building, his lens spattered with the dust that contains the remnants of just extinguished human life.[59]

Catastrophic death of this kind produces absolute destruction in human bodies, reducing them to fragments, ash, or less still. Sometimes its material evidence is somewhat more substantial and for that reason still more horrible. One first responder at the World Trade Center recounts a chilling encounter with a woman whose body from the waist down was destroyed at the impact, her lower half "unrecognizable," yet who was somehow still conscious and talking to him as he did triage at the scene, ghoulishly reminding him, "I am not dead," while he was putting a black tag around her neck to indicate to others that she was in fact well beyond help.[60] Gruesome images of victims at the Pentagon were entered into evidence in the Moussaoui trial and they demonstrated the horrific nature of the injury inflicted on bodies by the raging fires produced by exploding airplanes and ignited jet fuel. One can also still find video of people jumping from the towers after the two impacts; this is some of the most disturbing footage from a harrowing day's events.[61] In one bit of video included in the History Channel's *102 Minutes That Changed America*, which is a remarkable minute-by-minute account of the time span from the first crash at the North Tower to that same tower's collapse, two women watch objects fall from the stricken North Tower from their apartment window with a growing sense of dread, and one asks a question whose answer she already knows: "What are those big, heavy things falling at a rate that a piece of paper would not fall? Oh my God!" As they try with a patent lack of success to convince themselves they are seeing chairs or other office debris falling, their conversation is interrupted by the second plane barreling into the South Tower. They erupt in cries of fear. As one shouts, "It's terrorists!" the other asks helplessly, "What do we do?" They both then fall into shocked sobs before they rush to leave the building.[62] In addition to the horrible photographs just discussed, the jury at the Moussaoui trial also heard phone calls from two people who were trapped in the North Tower and died when it collapsed. The voices of Melissa Doi and Kevin Cosgrove are the very substance of terror as they describe the distressing situation in which they inexplicably find themselves to their respective emergency operators. Doi's voice is just above a whisper, struggling against the smoke in the air, as she half-incredulously begins to realize the truth, which is that no one can possibly reach her in time: "I'm gonna die, aren't I? I know it, I'm gonna die. I'm gonna die. I'm gonna die, I know it [sob]. Please, God. . . . [I]t's so hot, I'm burning up!" The operator responds energetically to Doi's question: "No, no, no, no! Say your prayers, ma'am, we're gonna think positive 'cause you gotta help each other get off the floor!" Doi's answer to this is shattering in its resignation: "Can you stay on the line with me, please? I think I'm dying." She goes silent and succumbs to the smoke while still on the line. Cosgrove impresses the listener with his energy and outrage; he is demonstrably frustrated and angry with the inability of the operator to provide any immediate assistance and adamant in his demands that they do more. After she tells him to calm down and conserve oxygen, he sarcastically responds, "Tell God to blow the wind from the west!" In the last seconds of the call, he repeats his last name for her: "Cosgrove, must have told you a dozen times already, . . . we're overlooking the [World] Financial Center, . . . three of us, two broken windows." Abruptly, there is a low rumbling sound and Cosgrove screams, "Oh God!" The call terminates as the building collapses around him.[63] The knowledge of what happened to these two people we hear in the awful final minutes of their mortal existence is almost too much to bear.

The crash of Flight 93 at the massive speed it had attained at impact produced near-total annihilation of the bodies of the victims. The total weight of the passengers on board was in the vicinity of 7,500 pounds, but less than a tenth of that weight in human remains was recovered at the crash site. This consisted entirely of small pieces of skin and tissue, teeth and bone fragments, and a few hands and feet. Most of the remains were unidentifiable, and most of the passengers were identified through DNA evidence. The cause of death was given as "fragmentation due to blunt-force trauma" and recovery workers noted the striking absence of blood or any other palpable material evidence of the 44 people known to have been on the plane.[64] For all intents and purposes, the passengers simply ceased to exist in the physical sense at the moment the plane hit the ground. The catastrophic damage done to their bodies by the velocity of the plane is so radical as to be difficult even to imagine, and, unlike in New York City and Washington, D.C., there were no visual cues even to provide clues here. There was no image comparable to that of the World Trade Center's "Falling Man," no visual horror to subsequently be hidden from the outraged view of those who had seen it, which is precisely what happened with the anonymous Falling Man, who appeared briefly in the pages of a few newspapers and then, after an outcry from some readers, was never seen again except in the pages of scholarly tomes and little-read histories.

Such complete trauma, the very disintegration of human bodies into next to nothingness, makes human cultural universals in response to death difficult to fulfill. Even identifying victims positively is a chore. In many cases, no delivery of remains to next of kin can even take place, as the physical traces used to identify the victim may be so small as to be imbedded in or sprayed on some other object, e.g., a piece of cloth or seat cushion, and not easily detachable. Jeremy Glick's wife, Lyz, describes receiving some of her husband's teeth from the investigation of the site and morbidly speculates that the powdery substance coating his recovered datebook may well be the exact equivalent of "dust from . . . African mummies" she recalls from her days as an anthropology student.[65] The human need for funeral ritual involving the body, at a minimal level some basic rite to dispatch the deceased's material remains through burial in the earth or dispersal via some practice guided by cultural beliefs, goes back deep into human prehistory. There is some evidence in contemporary America that older, more traditional practices of disposal of the dead through enclosure of the body in a casket and subsequent burial in a cemetery are in the process of giving way to a practice that was once seen as a fundamentally un-American manner of treating the dead, i.e., cremation. But this has not been a simple transition and arguably a good deal of the explanation for the difficulty has to do with the movement away from rites geared toward an integral human corpse and toward practices directed toward a literally incinerated, destroyed body. Proponents of cremation initially attempted to equate burial with impurity and disease, and touted cremation as pure by comparison, but this effort was unsuccessful precisely because of the deep-rooted cultural belief in American society that the dead body should not be significantly altered by any human intervention prior to interment. In many cases, this had to do specifically with Christian doctrine that, in many evangelical and other incarnations, preached a literal resurrection of the actual body at the coming of Christ's reign, and therefore saw the destruction of that body prior to burial as an insurmountable obstacle to this resurrection. Since the 1960s, cremation has been recast as more aesthetically beautiful, simple, and environmentally friendly and responsible than burial, and it has made significant gains in American funeral practice and belief. It may be too that criticisms of the profiteering of the funeral industry, popularized initially in the 1960s in Jessica Mitford's *The American Way of Death*, have made some contribution to the growing acceptance of cremation.[66] In this sense, American funeral practices would seem to be moving in a direction of greater rationality and modernization, and even secularization if we take that term to mean not the disappearance of religion but rather its growing confinement to the private sphere.

Yet even if in the carefully controlled case of cremation, Americans are increasingly able to contemplate the incinerated human body without extraordinary horror, it remains true that Americans approach catastrophic death that incinerates, or rends, or otherwise destroys bodies as atypically monstrous and terrifying. We must refine matters still a bit more in order to understand why 9/11 deaths evoked what they did. It seems clear that some of what is happening in the way Americans approach the catastrophic death associated with 9/11 can be understood by the radical distinction we tend to make between the dead and ravaged bodies of those regarded as cultural Others, which are seen as unfortunate and unpleasant but can be tolerated in newspaper photographs or television footage, and the destroyed bodies of our own countrymen, which are horror incarnate and must be banned from the public sphere entirely. Indeed, pulverized corpses of certain foreigners perform a narrative task important to the reproduction of a set of deeply held American cultural beliefs of our exceptional place in the world, as described by John Taylor: "Death is rarely seen in ragged human remains unless they are foreign. . . . [These foreign corpses] imply that outside [our country] chaos is the norm, and life is cheap."[67] The extreme horror at 9/11 deaths may also be related to an unconscious realization of precisely who the

victims were. The rhetorical response to the question of who, demo-
graphically speaking, died in the attacks has stayed within the bounds of
morally comforting messages: people of all races, classes, genders, ages,
nationalities, and religions, this moral framework assures us, were the
victims of this attack, and this is why all should be equally outraged by it.
But statistically speaking there are demonstrable patterns in the demographic makeup of the victims. Males and whites were greatly over-
represented among the dead. Of the 2,723 victims, more than 75% were
white, and roughly the same percentage were men.[68] On Flight 93, the
gender balance (omitting the hijackers) was exactly equal, with 20 men
and 20 women, but the racial imbalance toward whites was even more
exaggerated than in the overall 9/11 victim total. Of the 40 people on the
plane, only three were black, and none of those three were passengers;
they were all members of the flight crew. One passenger was Asian, and
one was Hispanic. Nearly 90% (fully 35 of 40) of the crew members and
passengers were white. With these numbers in hand, interpretations of
the meaning of the act can be mobilized that are harder to mount in
the face of the rhetorical move to see it as an attack on "all of us." One
can from this perspective perhaps conceive of the horror of the typical white, middle-class American onlooker, and especially those in this
group who are male, in the face of the devastation of 9/11 having to do
not only with the generic aversion to catastrophic, unpredictable death
that rends bodies and makes it impossible to properly ritualize their exit
from life, but also with the realization that, here, for once, those bodies
belonged not to raced and cultured Others, but disproportionately to
other white, middle-class American men.

As a consequence of these cultural facts, American public memorials
to catastrophic death are as a rule quite bloodless, literally and figura-
tively. At the Oklahoma City bombing memorial, the issue of whether
or not to bury unidentified human remains from the explosion at the
memorial site proved divisive. Many of the survivors and family members adamantly opposed "transforming the site into a cemetery."[69] In
the end, the "common tissue" of those killed in the blast was not buried at the site, but in a memorial grove of trees at the state capitol.[70]
Death and destruction are generally dissimulated at such memorials in
a deliberate forgetting and occluding of the ontological fact of death.
The effort is to attend to other things: remembrances of the lives of

those lost, demonstrations of the will to ensure that such things will not happen again (or at least that their recurrence will be struggled against mightily), and evidence of how the communities involved were able to overcome the tragedy.[71] As we will see in the chapters that follow, the memorial efforts regarding the crash of Flight 93 have followed these unwritten but culturally strict prescriptions with meticulous care. One might well note that this careful memorial omission of the actual grisly events of the catastrophe is in keeping with the broad effort in funereal architecture to replace the disintegration of the body with the permanence of stone or metal. The desire of the human species to deny the fact of the fragility of our own bodies and lives is venerable and widespread. Yet here again we are thoroughly in the realm of the culturally relative. In Vietnam, there is a state memorial of the Indochina Wars that displays the corpses of stillborn infants and human embryos horribly deformed by the widespread use of Agent Orange. There are even living victims of the monstrous effects of this chemical defoliant who can be seen at the memorial. Compare this to the abstract, antiseptic bloodlessness of the American Vietnam War Memorial in Washington, D.C., and you start to appreciate not only the different points of view of the two societies on the conflict but also the cultural distinctions in their ways of representing the fact of the destruction of human bodies.

In recent years, the study of what has come to be known as "dark tourism" has emerged as an important subfield in the broader area of tourist studies. This new branch of study is a clear growth stock in the scholarly world, with journals, websites, and university positions emerging with some regularity to engage the emergent field. As the name indicates, the optic here has to do with tourist sites and experiences that focus on the macabre and morbid. War memorials, historic sites of heinous crimes and deeds, and places of catastrophic death and suffering are the kinds of objects dark tourist studies explore, and the attitudes of those who seek such sites and are drawn by such aspects of the human world are an important element of this work. While the field is a profoundly interesting one, with potentially much to tell us about catastrophic death in the human experience, it is clear that what is going on at the Flight 93 memorial sites I will describe in the coming chapters cannot be adequately described as dark tourism. Inevitably, as we will see, and despite the intentions of many of the producers of Flight 93 memorials and memory, narratives about the mysterious terror of mass death, and especially of the chaos wrought on the bodies of the victims/heroes, work themselves in complex ways into the memorialization of the plane and its passengers. But they do so in ways that do not lend themselves to either the narrow morbidness of much dark tourism or the unapologetic superficiality of much tourism in general. Instead, these narratives of the horror of death and bodily destruction are ensconced in reverential national cultural myths of God and country, that is, of the American civil religion, and they are symbolically inscribed and decoded with a seriousness and a reverence that distinguishes Flight 93 memorialization and visitors to the memorial sites from tourism of the killing fields of Cambodia, or Bran Castle in Romania, which is marketed to tourists as "Castle Dracula."

One might argue that it is in sites of dark tourism that one finds the most likely challenge to the lie about death that Heidegger describes as the rule in modern human culture. Reverent cultural memorials that are deeply soaked in American civil religion and foundational myths about American identity and heroism such as the work commemorating Flight 93, in contrast, present very little challenge to that lie. Insofar as death disappears in the Flight 93 memorial work to be replaced by the redemptive cultural work of the heroes and the call to mission of American values in the face of evil, we can accurately say that the central narrative thrust of Flight 93 commemoration is toward further occultation of death and horror. The work done by the American civil religion, and also by the dominant religious perspectives present in Flight 93 memorial work, is not the same work Heidegger suggests is done by the simple but stone-hard death-focused peasant religion he admires. Whereas the latter is focused on the ongoing spiritual requirement of preparation for one's own death, the American civil religion and the dominant American versions of Christianity that inform Flight 93 memorialization offer stories of the marvelous deaths of heroes that serve ultimately, as we will see in the rest of the book, to distance us from those heroes. These stories do so by raising the heroes so far above us that we cannot hope to attain their status, and they encourage us to focus on their heroic triumph and pass quickly over their deaths. In this sense, this kind of memorial work is almost inevitably profoundly culturally conservative.

3

The Sacralization of Shanksville

The Emergence of the Temporary Memorial Site

Shanksville is situated in Somerset County, Pennsylvania, near the Allegheny Mountains in the southwestern part of the state. It is approximately an hour's drive from Pittsburgh, two miles north of the Pennsylvania Turnpike/Interstate 76/70, and just under 20 miles north of the Maryland border. Somewhere in the vicinity of about 250 people live in this tiny community of a few streets, a post office, and a general store. In the language of Pennsylvania state governmental administration, it is a borough, the rough equivalent as a form of municipality to what many other American states call towns, too small to be classed as a city. All Shanksville's streets placed end to end would add up to under a mile in length.[1] "Quiet" is an understatement to describe these streets. In all the many trips I have made into and through town, on my way to the two memorial sites I studied or to pick up food and supplies at the town grocery, I do not recall ever seeing anyone actually walking the streets of Shanksville.

The top industry in Somerset County is recreation, and state parks, resorts, and outdoor-life opportunities abound. Agriculture is the number two industry, and coal production has been of significant importance historically here.[2] But these days job opportunities in Shanksville are scarce, and the population is overwhelmingly older, as younger natives steadily migrate out for work. This is Red State America. Evangelical churches are everywhere along the various roads leading to Shanksville, bearing aggressively and unapologetically conservative Christian messages, e.g., "Jesus is Lord!" and "Go forth and sin no more!" One of the first indications to otherwise uninformed travelers headed east along Route 30 that this is the part of the country where Flight 93 went down is a billboard outside Stoystown at a fork in the road. It features a plane, coming directly at the viewer, on a field of stars

FIGURE 3.1. Flight 93 billboard near Stoystown. Photo: ATR.

and stripes, with Jesus standing below. The first several times I saw the billboard, he too donned the colors of the American flag, though he now sports entirely yellow garb. The message on the billboard ties the moral meaning of Flight 93 to that of abortion: "Flight 93 Born Hero's [sic] Gave their Lives to Save Lives Life is a Precious Gift Save God's Unborn Hero's [sic] America Must End the Terror of Abortion" (figure 3.1). It is readily apparent here that one is well outside of Manhattan and Washington, D.C., both physically and ideologically. And while one might chalk it up to an idiosyncratic editorial decision, it is also reflective of something important when the first interviewee cited in *Quiet Courage*, a book about the response of Shanksville to the crash written by a local physician who was involved in the recovery and rescue effort, describes what she was doing when the crash occurred: "I was reading the Bible that morning" (12). It is not difficult to imagine numerous residents of the area emulating this morning activity on that and subsequent days.

The first time I visited Shanksville, one object struck me immediately by its omnipresence. American flags were draped seemingly everywhere, on front doors, hanging on fences, and providing the color of ornate patriotic decorations dangling from porches and planted in front yards. The country store, Ida's, where over the several years of my research I have bought innumerable sandwiches and soft drinks, boasts a large flag on the front door. Mailboxes frequently bear the name of the local newspaper, the *Daily American*, although the word "Daily" is so small as to be invisible from a distance and what one sees while driving down a Shanksville street is a line of mounted mailboxes proudly announcing "American." When I learned of the name of the local paper, it seemed to me an almost inevitable fact. It is idyllic small-town Americana patriotism in ideal typical form. During the time I was doing my research there, roadside signs bearing an image of a flag stretched across a red, white, and blue countryside pointed visitors in the direction of the crash site. Frequently, other flags were visible as background to these signs. The overall effect was hypnotic; even when there was no flag in my line of vision, I had a tendency to imagine it there nonetheless. Flags are the center of much of the symbolic and mythological work around Flight 93, as we will see in this and the several chapters to follow.

On our initial trip to Shanksville, as my wife and I passed Hauger's Auto Shop and Sales on Lambertsville Road heading out of town, we encountered a hand-drawn sign with a crude image of an airplane bearing the number "93" that informed us that we were now very close, less than two miles away. The first time through town, in late 2004, we were almost entirely reliant on the signs, and thus I had a good, practical reason to pay careful attention to these details. But these signs are also an important textual trace of the event of September 11, 2001, that in the vision of some commentators turned this sleepy Pennsylvania borough (or, more correctly, the airspace above it) into the first battlefield in the War on Terror.

On that first visit, it was raining and foggy as we arrived, in the dusk of early evening. We had left Lewisburg, 180 miles away, later than anticipated, and we had gotten lost along the way. There was a chill in the air as we stepped out of the car in the parking lot of the temporary memorial. In the shrouded twilight, we walked up to the Park Service staffer on duty and asked where the plane had hit ground. He led us to a spot just in front of a collection of mounted red, white, and blue angel figures and pointed into the distance to what he said was a large flag a few hundred yards off in the mist-cloaked field. I learned later that the flag could be easily seen in the light of day, but we could not make it out at all that evening. We stood there in front of these angels, which I did not yet know would be the inspiration for the title of this book, and looked into the gloomy distance for what seemed a very long time, to the place where the plane had flown into the earth at nearly 600 mph, so hard and so fast that a nearby home suffered structural damage akin to that caused by an earthquake, even though no debris struck it. My camera registered the photos I took of that scene with a ghostly fog cloaking all the images as the steady drizzle continued and the dissipating light grudgingly but inevitably gave way to night. I very clearly remember thinking that the scene could scarcely have been more conducive to stimulating thoughts of the spirits of the dead, somewhere off in the field, hidden in darkness and drifting brume, dispassionately and silently watching their human seekers, even had it been prepared by a movie or stage crew to just that end. In his book *Field Notes from Elsewhere*, Mark Taylor writes, in language I can well understand, of his first visit to the World Trade Center site after the 9/11 attack, accompanied by his son, who was in the American Express building just across the street from the towers on that day and who left the area when he saw people leaping to their deaths from the crippled towers:

> We had repeatedly heard that TV and film could not do justice to the scene and that was right. It was not merely that screens are too small and camera angles too limited; rather, the reality confronting us was not only visual but, more important, visceral. The only word to describe my response to what we saw: awe. Contrary to every expectation, a strange religious atmosphere pervaded Ground Zero. There had been much talk about the role of religion in this conflict but very little understanding of what religion really involves. . . . While religion often gives people a sense of meaning and purpose in times of personal and social crisis, its symbols, stories, and rituals also carry people to the edge of life, where unmasterable power always threatens to erupt. Throughout history, religion has been associated as much with terror and anxiety as with love and peace. For a few brief moments on September 11, the veneer of security was torn to reveal a primordial vulnerability that neither defense departments nor advanced technologies can overcome. For me, and, I believe, for Aaron, the encounter with this awesome power was a religious experience that left nothing unchanged.[3]

If such was the atmosphere at Ground Zero, which, though certainly grim, was nonetheless populated within a relatively short time after the attack by the banal, comforting sounds of automobiles and people rushing along on their morning commute, and with the urban comfort (for the cosmopolitan viewer, in any event) of omnipresent concrete and blacktop, buildings still intact and human commerce humming along at its everyday clip, how much more amplified this mystical sense of dread of the primordial enemy, death, in this hillside field, which was empty but for the whispering trees in the distance and what could well have been ominous, phantom visitors out in the gloaming? And yet in recounting our emotions in such times and places, it is difficult to avoid falling into clichéd stylings. Did I feel wonder and awe? Yes. But I cannot say how much of that might have been driven by my sense that this is what I was morally obligated to at least try to feel in such a theatrically perfect spot. For I had already been prepared, prior to my visit, as every other American who had read a newspaper, watched the news, or consulted a webpage that discussed the fate of Flight 93, for a certain kind of experience of the site and of the commemoration of the event. Indeed, as an American, the preparation for how to respond to this hillside where Flight 93 crashed had been going on for the entirety of my life. When the plane crashed and the first efforts to narrate the event got underway in Shanksville and elsewhere, there was no clean slate on to which the story was written, but rather a well-annotated document of already-existing frameworks of meaning into which any narrative of Flight 93 had to fit.

"The End of Serenity": A Frame for the Picture

A photo taken by a woman from nearby Indian Lake (a borough actually slightly closer to the crash site than Shanksville) of the immediate aftermath of the crash has achieved iconic status in the cultural narrative of Flight 93 through its wide distribution in mass media and on the Internet and, in a more limited fashion, via direct sales of copies of the photo by the photographer herself. As Val McClatchey, a local real estate agent, tells the story, she had been watching the *Today* show and learning of the events in New York City when she heard the plane roar overhead, ran out to her front porch, and snapped one shot.[4] She quickly copyrighted the photo and gave it a title: "The End of Serenity." The image evokes a picturesque country scene from a mythical American rural past, a red barn and a smaller red building (perhaps a tool shed) on a gently sloping green hillside, woods visible in the background, below a clear blue sky. The only contrast in this idyllic scene of pastoral harmony and calm is the menacing black cloud that dominates the center of the photo, the aftermath of the crash of Flight 93.[5] The photo looks like a country postcard gone horribly awry, the bulk of the visual elements conveying peace, tranquility, hearth, stability, and rural tradition, and the one blemish effectively throwing all of that peaceful order into radical doubt and chaos.

In endeavoring to understand the symbolic material that makes "The End of Serenity" work, we are operating at the level of what the mythologist Gilbert Durand called anthropological archetypology, which consists of cultural work at a stratum even below that of myth, one wherein the objects that will become the elements in myths and rituals are formed. Durand writes that anthropological archetypology has the task of "identify[ing], in all human manifestations of the imagination, these groupings or constellations where images converge around an organizing nucleus."[6] A central narrative structure from the American social imaginary, the opposition rural/industrial, is paramount in making sense of the photo. The machine-in-the-garden trope in the American cultural memory[7] is what enables the image to be instantly placed into a broad mythic structure of the American collective consciousness in which a pastoral aesthetic and ethic are challenged by the machinery of industrial America. The threat in this narrative is not radical Islamic terrorism; it is contemporary technology and industry in the danger it poses to an imagined traditional, rural order of American society. Seen in this register, the narrative of Flight 93 takes on a rather different hue than that of some other 9/11 narratives, generated as they are overwhelmingly by the attack on the World Trade Center. The chief images of the latter, which are aesthetically centered on the explosion of United Flight 175 as it crashed into the South Tower, evoke a purely modern, technological holocaust. Here, we have the machine menace of the plane-turned-bomb plowing into the gigantic symbol of American technological and financial accomplishment, that is, a modern technological apparatus in opposition to another modern apparatus bearing testimony to engineering and technical prowess. But a more complex narrative of America's past and her present is evoked by "The End of

Serenity." It calls on a profound set of basic mythical oppositions in the American imaginary: rural heartland/alienated city; natural/technological; simple/complex; farm work/big business. Any culturally competent American viewers of the photo are able to implicitly and instantly place it within those oppositional structures.

The narrative power of "The End of Serenity" is such that it nullifies any effort to present the events of 9/11 as, in an adaptation of the claims of the terrorists that is sometimes invoked by indigenous critics of American international politics on both left and right, originating in a critique of American technological, business, and military power. If the attacks are directed solely against American icons of technological (the World Trade Center) and military (the Pentagon) power, then the terrorists can potentially be understood as defenders of some more primal, pastoral, "natural" way of life that is threatened by that alienating, technocratic, militarist power. "The End of Serenity" has the symbolic effect of making the events of 9/11 into an attack on far more enduring, deep-rooted American cultural traditions: the farm homestead, the pastoral countryside, the pure and independent American life of the frontier. It matters little that the myth of pastoral purity that is tapped here is fictional, an imaginary plenitude unrealizable in reality, a "myth of the rural middle landscape,"[8] or that the attack on that pastoral purity was unintended by the terrorists (who were aiming for a decidedly nonbucolic target, the Capitol Building or the White House). The narrative power of the image draws on forces stronger than those of logic.

Alternative narratives concerning Flight 93 have also taken up "The End of Serenity" in their own efforts at meaning-making. A number of bloggers and authors of conspiracy-laden books about 9/11 have suggested that the photo is evidence that the official narrative about the flight cannot be true. The form of the cloud of smoke, they argue, is inconsistent with a plane crash; the mushroom shape of the plume is closer to that of an ordnance blast. Some[9] have endeavored to demonstrate that the photo reveals in its details that it could not have been taken from the location claimed.

These attempts at alternative narrative construction rely on elements of the American social imaginary rooted in populist distrust of official and state power. Similar conspiratorial beliefs hover around other significant events in American history, e.g., the Kennedy assassination and the moon landing. Such beliefs have arisen concerning other elements of 9/11 and their purported visual evidence as well. There exists, for example, a narrative about the attack on the Pentagon that interprets the visual evidence as indicative of a missile strike rather than the crashing of American Flight 77. These conspiratorial narrative structures are in basic ways not wholly unlike the "rumor of Orléans" analyzed by Edgar Morin in the book of the same title. He showed how a widespread urban legend in Orléans, France, that circulated virulently for a brief time in 1969–70 concerning the alleged kidnapping of young women while they were in clothing stores trying on new fashions and the subsequent selling of the women into prostitution in exotic locales was actually a hidden discourse related to fears of liberated female sexuality and anti-Semitic sentiments (all the involved stores were Jewish owned).[10] 9/11 conspiracies also frequently emerge from an unstated set of cultural debates that exist somewhere underneath the actual events at issue. We might, for instance, note the ways in which the conspiratorial narratives surrounding the events of 9/11 frequently intersect with critical narratives about Jews and Israel. Some of the narratives explicitly present the attacks as the work of an Israeli force, e.g., the Mossad, working to provoke the U.S. into a war with Islamic foes or as the product of a radical pro-Israel group inside the United States.[11] These narratives tap into deep elements of the social imaginary having to do with fears of shadowy outsiders (government officials, Jewish or Israeli agents) working in American society to destroy it from within. They do not need to directly invoke all the elements of those narratives in order to bring them into play in the meaning-making of readers. More, even in the face of considerable counterevidence, they are often attractive narratives for significant numbers of people. A Zogby poll of August 2004 showed that fully half of New York City residents surveyed believed that at least some American political leaders "knew in advance that attacks were planned on or around September 11, 2001, and that they consciously failed to act."

I will return to conspiracy theories in more detail in the discussion of the Flight 93 permanent memorial design in chapter five. But, before we can talk of the planned permanent memorial, we should first turn our attention to the commemoration process that took place at the crash site for nearly ten years prior to the start of its construction.

The Temporary Memorial: Gifts, Flags, and Angel Patriots

Almost immediately after the fate of the plane became widely known, local memorialization work began. Some Shanksville residents used their own homes and front lawns as sites for small, spontaneous memorials in the immediate aftermath of the crash. One of these is still on display, although not at its original site but at the Flight 93 Chapel a few miles away (figure 3.2). It consists of a poster board perhaps 12 square feet in size containing a simple message of thanks to the passengers of Flight 93 and signatures and salutations from dozens of individuals who attempted to approach the crash site in the first hours and days after the plane's impact. It was erected, along with numerous other similar poster boards, a large flag, and a cross, in the yard of a local family who lived in a Shanksville home located near the police barrier that was set up in the immediate aftermath of the crash to block traffic to the site. In addition to signing their names to the boards, visitors who were thwarted in their efforts to get to the crash site left flowers and other items in the yard. This is perfectly in keeping with what we know about how spontaneous memorials have come about in other such situations. In a book on the Oklahoma City Memorial commemorating the bombing of the Federal Building there in 1995, Ed Linenthal describes the same practice: "Immediately after the bombing, people gathered at the safety perimeter several blocks away, at Sixth and Hudson, and made offerings of 'poems, cards, flowers, stuffed animals.'"[12] Similar memorial objects appeared in other Shanksville yards or along streets traveled by workers at the crash site. One local woman used bed sheets as giant thank-you notes to rescue workers and volunteers.[13] As Joy Sather-Wagstaff has argued, these spontaneous memorials or "commemorative folk assemblages" can be understood as "intentionally arranged formations and displays of material culture . . . that emerge at sites of death or other public sites of mourning [and constitute] a means for publicly paying respects to the dead while producing numerous social effects . . . including participation in imagined communities of mourning, belonging, closure, and spiritual or emotional healing."[14] The origins of this practice are difficult to trace, but academic interest in it dates back only about a quarter of a century, and the emergence of the phenomenon as a widespread, global practice in the face of traumatic death is certainly

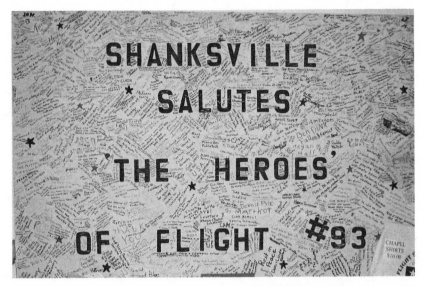

FIGURE 3.2. "Shanksville salutes the heroes" poster board. Photo: ATR.

a recent phenomenon.[15] It seems clear that the radical individualization of many contemporary societies has something to do with the rise of spontaneous, grassroots memorialization, along with the criticisms of traditional institutional forms of ritualization of death, both religious and secular, in much of the Western world that have accompanied this individualization.[16] In Shanksville, as I will show in the remainder of this chapter, we see evidence of an ongoing process of incorporation of spontaneous, individualized memorialization, which often represents a way of speaking back to formal state and church memorial efforts, into more traditional state-driven memorial processes, and in a later chapter we will see how the plan for a formal, permanent memorial, driven in large part by institutions of the American state, has nevertheless endeavored to directly incorporate elements of the ground-level, spontaneous memorialization that was evident in the temporary memorial to Flight 93. We also see, although this vision requires some theoretical decoding of the practices that produced the temporary memorial, that what appears hyperindividualized in some respects is nonetheless deeply tied to collective cultural and symbolic needs of a primordial variety.

By the day after the crash, something of a small city of a few hundred people sprang into existence on the hillside overlooking the crater. This city was populated by a revolving team of search and recovery workers, police, agents of various government agencies, and media. Two citizens of this new city, Rick Lohr, the director of the Somerset County Emergency Management Agency, and Bill Baker, the 911 addressing specialist for that same agency, assembled what became known as the "straw memorial" at the command center of the rescue mission.[17] In their account, this began with something like a dozen bales of straw as a base to support flowers, flags, stuffed animals, candles, poster boards, and other items left by inhabitants of the temporary city on the hilltop. As the memorial items grew, so too did the number of bales of straw on which the former were stacked. Within a few days of the crash, families of the passengers began to arrive in buses escorted by state troopers, and they brought personal items that were left at the straw memorial as well. A large flag was mounted at the site, and later a local pastor, James Vandervort of the Christian Missionary Alliance Church, and a few of his congregants took a wooden cross they had constructed and decorated with a white cloth up to the site to post. In Vandervort's account of the event, there was a brief conflict as to whether it would be permitted. State police supported the erection of the cross, while FBI agents at the site initially balked on the grounds of religious diversity, telling Vandervort this Christian symbol might be read as exclusionary by visiting passenger family members who were not Christian. One FBI agent invited him to contact the Somerset rabbi to attempt to broaden the religious symbolism at the site. Vandervort told him there was no rabbi in Somerset. In short order, American religious sensibility, in its dominant Christian guise, won the day over any commitment to by-the-book secular public policy: the FBI agents relented and permitted the cross to be erected.[18]

Once the search-and-recovery mission was completed and the area (with the exception of the actual crash site) was made accessible to the public again, the memorial was moved several hundred yards up the hill to Skyline Drive. As the land is privately owned, property owners were asked permission to place the memorial. Flight 93 National Memorial Curator Barbara Black, who has been closely involved with the Shanksville memorial from the very early days, told me that the environmental resource management group who were consultants to the excavation of the plane and helped in the recovery effort selected the original site of the temporary memorial because it had a direct sightline down the hill to the point where the plane hit. They negotiated with landowners to designate the space for the memorial and then turned responsibility for the site's management over to the county. The site initially sat on the side of the road nearest the crash, but some years later, in September 2008, the entire memorial was moved to the other side of Skyline Drive when the original landowner, a coal company that had established an agreement with the National Park Service for yearly renewable leases, decided for unknown reasons to end the agreement. The Families of Flight 93 then came to an accord with a second coal company that owned much of the land on the hillside and purchased enough property on the other side of the road to house the temporary memorial.[19] During the time I studied it, prior to its removal in the late summer of 2011 as construction for the permanent memorial got underway, the temporary memorial was situated in a dirt and gravel lot of several hundred square feet, bounded by a wooden fence a few feet in height. Among the first objects visible after turning off Skyline Drive into the parking lot were two poles, perhaps 20 feet tall, bearing the U.S. flag and the Pennsylvania state flag, and the same wooden cross that was initially placed by the Christian Missionary Alliance Church, some ten feet in height and draped with the white cloth that in many Christian denominations signifies the risen Christ.

An opening in the fence adjacent to the parking lot permitted entry by visitors. Situated just a few yards to the left of this entryway was a small wooden shelter in which the Park Service representatives and local law enforcement on duty could retreat from inclement weather. The building, which featured a deck area from which Park Service staff frequently delivered the short lectures on the history of the crash that they provided as part of their service, also held a guestbook, a large book of photographs related to the crash, a notebook containing the official transcript of the voice recording of the last minutes of the flight, and information regarding the permanent memorial project, including some graphic designs provided by the architect.

Around the perimeter of the memorial site were arranged a collection of large monuments and plaques created and donated by various organizations and individuals. Many of these were at the site from the first year or two after the crash, although newer ones could be seen there too. The United States Federal Air Marshal Service, an educators' delegation to a university in Maryland from South Africa, various car clubs, at least one Boy Scout Troop, a local elementary school, and the United States Judo Association were among the many groups represented in these memorial objects. The messages they bore were of thanks and warning. A stone sternly cautioned: "The heroes of Flight 93: never forget them lest we be attacked again"; a plaque mounted on the large cross and bearing several Marine Corps badges read, "Civilians cannot and will not understand us because they are not one of us. The Corps: we love it, live it and shall die for it. If you have never been in it, you shall never understand it"; a sign left by a local Johnstown Catholic school announced that schools in the Johnstown diocese have offered over 8,500 rosaries for the victims of 9/11.

At the other end of the memorial site area sat a row of benches, which, viewed from the rear, did not seem at all extraordinary and might have been imagined as merely practical in purpose. When large groups visited the site, Park Service staff sometimes presented their informational lectures from the front of these benches while the group listened comfortably seated. When one moved around to view the benches from the front, their central memorial feature stood out: the names of each passenger and crew member of Flight 93 were carved into the wood of the back supports. The benches were made and donated by students from a cooperative religious community in Farmington, Pennsylvania, the Spring Valley Bruderhof; according to the Park Service volunteer Ambassador coordinator, Donna Glessner, "They adopted the site early on as a place where people could use comfort."[20]

Moving back toward the staff building, on the side of the building opposite the entryway to the memorial, one found what was perhaps the central element of the temporary memorial, if not physically then certainly in terms of its effect on visitors to the site.[21] This was a steel fence 40 feet[22] in length, perhaps ten feet high, on which were draped myriad objects associated with the flight and with the symbols of the national imaginary (figure 3.3). Barbara Black told me that the original purpose of the fence was eminently practical, to "attach things to so they wouldn't blow away, as it's always windy up there," but over the years it became an essential part of the temporary memorial. Hanging from the fence, mounted in all manner of ways, were thousands of objects and

FIGURE 3.3. The fence at the temporary memorial. Photo: ATR.

images. There were religious medals and icons, firefighters' and emergency workers' uniforms, other items of clothing bearing messages of sympathy and identity with the passengers and crew, as well as many, many American flags, some sporting the traditional red, white, and blue stars and stripes, some with augmented symbolic banners and messages related to Flight 93, the Twin Towers, the Pentagon, and other 9/11 symbols. The range of material was startling, and the basic aesthetic effect a wash of widely varied colors, textures, and sizes. All of these items were donated by visitors to the site or others who had them delivered there precisely that they might be made part of this participatory public aspect of the temporary memorial.

Gifts to the Heroes

In addition to the fence, objects were frequently left at other sites at the temporary memorial. The ground at the foot of the large cross and the collection of flag angels mentioned earlier in this chapter was often covered with objects left by visitors, and several large plaques and monuments with flat surfaces were covered with small trinkets (figure 3.4). The objects left by visitors that were present at the memorial at any one time represented only a small percentage of the entirety of such objects that were left at or sent to the site over the years since the crash. There is a storage room in the Somerset office of the Park Service that overflows with such material, and a larger Park Service storage space nearby houses still more. Park Service employees swept over the site with some regularity to remove objects that would be damaged easily by weather or that might be carried off by the wind, and they were deposited in the Somerset office. The sheer volume and diversity of these objects is breathtaking. According to Barbara Black, the Park Service placed very few restrictions on what people could leave: "Nothing permanent or long-lasting, so no huge monuments, [and] they couldn't plant things because we didn't own the land,"[23] but beyond these minimal rules, gift-giving visitors were given wide latitude. In the storage facility can be found entire boxes of toys: dolls, figurines, rubber balls, plastic army men, and many toy jets. Other boxes contain sports items: balls, helmets, caps, and jerseys, and one set of red, white, and blue boxing gloves bearing the inscription "America Fights Back!" Still others bear collections of CDs filled with music related to Flight 93 and 9/11, e.g., Bruce Springsteen's "The Rising," and many homemade and self-titled discs with titles such as "The Day the World Stood Still." There are boxes of religious medals and pendants, religious icons (angels, crosses, and saints of all sizes and shapes, rosaries, bottles of holy water), and Bibles and other religious books (often with handwritten notes of dedication to the passengers of Flight 93); boxes of military objects, license plates, framed objects, handkerchiefs, bandannas, and glassware; boxes of ribbons (mostly red, white, and blue), patches (frequently bearing the name of some local fire or police department), coins and commemoratives, hats and caps (often with messages and identities scrawled on them), stuffed animals and tote bags, signs and banners, and plenty of T-shirts and personal items of clothing, one of the most common fetish items in our culture.

Many of these objects bear text, and a good number of the objects collected at the Somerset archive are in fact written messages of one variety or another. The archive contains reams of written material from visitors

FIGURE 3.4. Trinkets left at the temporary memorial. Photo: ATR.

and others from around the world. Note cards were provided at the site for those who wished to leave a personal note, and these were routinely collected. Visitors frequently left, without explicit prompting,[24] handwritten notes or more elaborate texts they prepared in advance of their visit to the site. Most of these are brief and highly formulaic, expressing one or more of a very common set of three themes: (1) giving thanks to the emergency services workers or to the deceased passengers themselves; (2) a religious blessing given to same, to their families, and/or to the U.S. as a whole; and (3) a promise never to forget the event. The passengers are sometimes thanked in very personally invested terms, as though but for their action the note writer him- or herself would have perished: "We are alive today because of you";[25] "Thank you for saving everybody!"[26] Some writers even look forward to the day when they will be able to thank the passengers face-to-face: "I hope to meet you in heaven";[27] "Looking over the site where you heroes lie, I just want to reach out to that spot and give you all a big hug and tell you thanks for everything you all did that day. Jesus is doing it for me. I will die someday and then I will be able to hug you. Thank you, Thank you for everything."[28] A sample from one randomly selected day, November 13, 2006, gives a sense of the great degree of conformity of the notes to these few central themes and tropes: "May we never forget the lives that were lost"; "May you all be happy being with our Lord"; "Dear God, We thank you for our brothers and sisters of Flight 93 . . . who's [sic] gracious gifts and ultimate sacrifice will never be forgotten." The phrases "Never forget!" "We will never forget!" and similar formulations (e.g., a particularly emphatic "I WILL NEVER FORGET ANY OF YOU!!!!" with several underlines, on a note dating from early 2002) are omnipresent, almost as though the writers understand how difficult a thing collective memory actually is to preserve and are crying out against that looming and inevitable darkness of oblivion.

The uniformity of the vast majority of the texts makes those that differ even slightly from these norms stand out jarringly, even though they also adhere to various narrative blueprints. One writer made explicit what was certainly understood by many others who left messages at the site, i.e., that their notes would themselves become part of the memorial: "I feel very special and honored that I will be a part of this honorable memorial."[29] Direct political commentary is rare, although an implicit nationalist politics in support of the war efforts in Afghanistan and, later, Iraq is frequently encountered. Of those messages expressing views on the politics of war more explicitly, almost all are on the prowar right, and, although I could not read every card in the archive, I could not find even one that outwardly questioned the two wars that have emerged from 9/11. One of the very few messages I found that expressed *any* criticism of the Bush administration's response discussed the Patriot Act, as well as the cultural politics involved in the selective media attention given various passengers on Flight 93:

> When word first came of the passengers who fought back, we heard of Mark Bingham. He played rugby, he was a big guy. His mom spoke proudly of him. As the days went by, we heard less and less. Todd Beamer's wife was all over the news. But what of Mark's partner? I am glad Melissa Etheridge wrote "Tuesday Morning" on her *Lucky* CD to preserve his memory. Now our country wants to pass an admendment [sic] to deny our rights. So much harm has been done in the name of

freedom these past years. May our country turn back and preserve our freedom, save us from the Patriot Act.[30]

Most of the stronger prowar sentiments I found in the archival collection were by writers who pointedly identified themselves as military veterans or currently in military service. One representative such writer, who identifies himself as a retired lieutenant colonel in the U.S. Air Force, put his thoughts thus: "You thwarted the evil effort to destroy our government, institutions, and way of life."[31] Another wrote: "George [Bush] has gone after the wrong country—He should have gone after Saudi Arabia until it is a glass bowl—no nation building!!!"[32] There are also many notes that allude to the military service of a family member: "Our son joined the Army and fought in Iraq to defend our country as did all in Flight 93—God Bless you and keep you";[33] "My husband went away for 2 years to help the freedom cause";[34] "My husband is serving in Iraq in 2008 for Operation Freedom."[35] Especially in the first year or so after the crash, but later as well, writers who lend their support to military efforts in the Middle East use symbolically charged terminology such as variations on the phrase "Let's roll!" e.g., "Thank you, Flight 93, and let's keep rolling."[36]

Some of the notes endeavor to make a still closer personal connection to passengers on the plane. One soldier claims to have fought in Iraq with a close friend of passenger Jeremy Glick: "They were the first to fight in this new war, they will not be the last, En Avant!"[37] Another asserts a relationship with Andrew Garcia: "A tribute to Andy from a friend. . . . I knew Andy during the 1960s–1970s and had not seen him since. He was someone who you would always remember. I salute his part in taking down Flt 93."[38]

There is little in the way of explicitly anti-Islamic sentiment in the messages visitors left, and indeed, somewhat to my surprise, I found anger only rarely expressed, as in a note that read: "To hell to those higackers [sic]."[39] Some writers do delve into the more radical religious cultural narratives of the Christian right to describe the events of 9/11. In several such cases, religious pamphlets or other published writings with a warning that the 9/11 attacks were something of a signal from God that America has strayed from the proper path were commented on by the visitor in the margins, then left at the site. One visitor left a copy of an essay, published in a local newspaper, by Robert Lind entitled "Where was your God on Sept. 11?" The piece responds to those who doubt the goodness of a God who could permit such atrocities to take place by claiming God's presence that day in preventing some people from boarding the planes, keeping some others away from the towers, and holding the buildings up long enough after the plane strikes for some people to escape. The essay ends with this passage: "[God] cried that 19 of his children could have so much hate in their hearts that they didn't choose him, but another god that doesn't exist. Now they are lost forever." Another visitor left a copy of a pamphlet "The Twin Towers" from a series titled "Moments with the Book" (apparently published in Bedford, Pennsylvania): "I believe God has been saying for a long time 'WAKE UP, AMERICA! You are pushing Me aside and forgetting who I am. You are representing Me as a permissive God who is tolerant of evil. You "call evil good, and good evil" (Isaiah 5:20).' If this terrible tragedy causes us to stop and hear His voice, then at least some good can come from it."[40] Many notes express belief in the miraculous presence of the Christian God at the crash site: "When I heard that a bible was not destroyed, when Flight 93 went down hear [sic], I quickly thought the bible had a shield pertect [sic] by God."[41]

There are many boxes of art and messages left by children, most of whom apparently visited the sites with their school classes. Most of these innumerable hand-drawn American flags are essentially identical.[42] Some come with messages: "I love that flag"; "God bless America"; "Keep going, we're right behind you, you're doing great"; "No one scares USA." Like the adult notes and messages, many of the children's messages are explicit words of thanks for emergency responders and the passengers. Some starker child art depicts such images as planes on the verge of crashing into the towers. Fictional culture heroes such as Captain America (accompanied by a text reading "Hero's [sic] of Flight 93, rest in peace") appear as well. Perhaps the most compelling aspect of this collection of children's memorial art and letters is its moral and aesthetic uniformity. Doubtless some of this has to do with the fact that most of these are individuals who were producing their work under conditions that could reasonably be described as coercive: i.e., teachers or parents bringing children to the site whether they would chose to come independently or not and assigning them a more or less formal task to complete as part of their visit. But it undoubtedly owes a good deal also to the deep well of cultural mythos that even young Americans dip from when they fill their expressive jugs. As we have already seen, similar conformity to unwritten symbolic and narrative rules is present in the materials adults left at the site as well. There are for example many poems written by visitors that read as variations of the same meta-text. The basic framework consists of a brief description of the passengers uniting in the fateful final moments and acting as one, tragically failing to save their own lives, but succeeding in their true goal of saving national symbols and the lives of others and living on in a heavenly existence and in the eternal honor and memory they are awarded by those still living. One representative poem reads:

> Dear Heroes, Everyone is born with a purpose, No matter how large or small, When your purpose was presented, You united in the face of fear, You took the hands of strangers, and fought the fight of your lives, for the goodness of man, the love of life, and the right to freedom, You each laid down your own life, for the lives of so many others, Although we can't tell you now, please know we are grateful, Even though I didn't know you, Your actions make me proud, You'll be forever in my prayers, and you will always be my example . . . of true American Heroes.[43]

Gift Exchange and Heroic Sacrifice

Why would visitors to the site leave objects there? What sorts of motivations could they have, and what meanings are they attributing to their action? Some possible explanations are psychological in nature and perhaps rather less than flattering to those who engage in this practice. Ed Linenthal cites the account of a local official who recalled how, in the aftermath of the Oklahoma City bombing, the city council was bombarded with calls by people "who would call and read a poem. It was very, very important to some people that we listen to their poem. It was not enough for them to send it. They wanted us to hear it."[44] It is hard not to detect a kind of narcissism in such reactions; such callers seem convinced that their contribution to the mourning of the tragedy offers something so uniquely important that it cannot be permitted the pedestrian treatment given to the contributions of others. It seems likely that some of what drove gift leaving at the temporary memorial and the Flight 93 Chapel has to do with a desire visitors felt to tie themselves to the sites in some way. Alphonse Mascherino, the late founder of the Flight 93 Memorial Chapel, told me he thought some people left objects and then took photos of them at the temporary memorial site as testimony to their presence and therefore to their very personal connection to the place: as he put it, they were thinking, "Look, it's *my* little Army man, or *my* hat at the Flight 93 memorial!"[45] This style of commemoration may have simply become the "thing to do" by sheer weight of history. Much like folk epigraphy, or the popular practice of scrawling messages directly on public memorials in a kind of commemorative graffiti, this begins somewhere, in the wake of some such traumatic event. The practice is then reported in the press and by word of mouth, and it is visually obvious at the site as well. It gets a response from archives and historians and then trickles into the public consciousness as the accepted process for interacting with the memorial.

The giving of thanks and gifts to the heroes at the temporary memorial and the Flight 93 Chapel can be best understood as deeply implicated in the cultural need for ritual. Though the death of the Flight 93 passengers is obviously not an act of sacrifice in the purely religious historical sense (i.e., with a victim offered according to specific rules to achieve religious goods), we might well call it an act of "auto-sacrifice." The passengers are here placed carefully into a framework of meaning wherein they become willing martyrs for a set of values which, in death, they come to symbolically represent in material form at the memorial. They move from their initial status as profane, unremarkable, quotidian individuals to become sacred entities through their own violent destruction. In so doing, they symbolically evoke one of the central sacrificial myths in American society, which originates in American Christianity but which has spread outside the confines of that religious community, and indeed outside of religion proper and into the American civil religion. The passengers willingly give themselves as necessary sacrificial victims[46] in an act mirroring, if still structurally inferior to, the founding act of Christianity, i.e., the sacrifice of Jesus Christ. Although they are heroes and not gods, and therefore cannot be physically resurrected, they nonetheless symbolically rise again in the memorial and thereby remain in relations with the rest of us. We see the power of this

Judeo-Christian narrative of heroic self-sacrifice in the symbolism of a number of patriotic narratives of American political history, e.g., the fall of the defenders of the Alamo, or the martyrdom of the Civil War dead.

The leaving of gifts for the heroes is an important element of the ritual interaction with them, and still other ritualistic elements of the relations between the martyred heroes and the members of their grateful cult are apparent at the Flight 93 Chapel, which I examine in the next chapter. The gift giving cannot be seen as part of a literal sacrifice, wherein the victim bestows a boon on the surviving celebrants of the sacrifice in his destruction and they are therefore called to treat the victim with certain ritualistic respect before his immolation and pay homage to him afterward, but it certainly is an action that adheres to all the central definitional elements of ritual: it is formulaic, repeated, and collective, and it is connected to a set of symbols and narratives that can reasonably be classified as the ritual's governing myth. The act is spurred by the action of the auto-sacrificed passengers, who are, according to the terms of the myth, understood to have given the rest of us a great gift in bringing the plane down short of its goal, and it constitutes a fulfillment of an obligation to return the good deed and pay homage to it in whatever limited way possible.

The relations between the heroes and their cult are defined then in large part by the mandatory giving and returning of gifts.[47] As the heroes have given the ultimate sacrificial gift, visitors to the memorial are called on to reciprocate with simple thanks or with more elaborate offerings. Structurally, the social imaginary is here calling on the same primitive human needs as were answered to by the Aztecs' sacrificial gifts in return for the life giving of the sun. As we are given, so we must reciprocate, if we would avoid shame or worse. The role of the hero in the social order sheds some additional light here. The hero is, according to the historian Henri Hubert, "like the living symbol or emblem of a definite society":

When a society gains consciousness of itself through its heroes, it feels that it takes its origin, its blood, its name from the prestige of their authority, their strength and their worth. . . . Divine symbols of societies, ideal actors of their histories, models of merit, examples of virtue, moral types and characters, heroes have passed by degrees from religion to heroes of literature, in the evolution of drama and epic that originates in the feasts. All heroes, in whatever degree, as symbols and types, help individuals and groups become conscious of themselves.[48]

In chapter six, I will have much more to say about the construction and functioning of the Flight 93 passengers and crew as cultural heroes; here, Hubert's definition is perhaps sufficient to show us what the hero is for the society in which he emerges, and why the establishing of formal relations with him is therefore so important. The process of hero creation is part of the production and reproduction of cultural myths of the tribe, or the nation. The Flight 93 passengers who rose up and attempted to take back the plane once the intentions of the terrorists became plain are no longer mere individuals. They have become charged with a mythological significance that relates to deep cultural beliefs about being American, and this structurally changes them. They cease being primarily unique individuals with particular sets of traits both positive and negative, and they become the very representative form of fearlessness, practicality, duty, religious faith, selflessness, and patriotism that is present throughout a long tradition of cultural narratives about American identity.

The Flag as American Totem

We have already seen something of the importance of the role of the American flag, in both unedited and revised forms, in the symbolic world of the temporary memorial. The essential role the flag plays in the production of civil religious narrative in the American context has to do with its totem-like capacity. Recent (and ever-recurring) discussions in the realm of national politics about a constitutional amendment to ban the burning of the flag powerfully illustrate this. Is the flag merely a piece of cloth, paper, or other material that cannot be realistically considered in a class apart from other such raw materials, or is it rather something *sacred*, an essential piece of the narrative of the American civil religion that should be rigorously protected from profanation and degradation? Broad cultural concern with destruction or irreverent treatment of flags certainly suggests they might occupy a special place in our symbolic mapping of the world. In the last attempt to pass a flag desecration amendment to the Constitution, in the summer of 2006, the required two-thirds majority was easily secured in the House, and the proposal fell only one vote short in the Senate. Had proponents garnered this one additional Senate vote, the measure would then have been dependent on securing victory in two thirds of the states for passage, an entirely conceivable outcome. It is clear that there is significant feeling in the U.S. that the flag is deserving of special care and protection not generally provided to symbols of our political universe. We might do well to recall here that legally even the president can be insulted, and in the vilest terms, so long as his life is not threatened.

In an unfinished work on the nature of the nation as a collective body, Marcel Mauss directly compared the national flag to the primitive clan totem. As more simply organized societies had symbols that represented both clan members and the animal, plant, or natural phenomenon from which they believed themselves to have sprung, so more complex societies have symbols that serve as markers of national identity and collective historical origins. The former has its animal-god ancestors, while the latter has its cult of fatherland and each requires symbolic material to represent those mythical systems to members.[49] The flag's use in the Flight 93 temporary memorial certainly suggests its sacred status. The memorial flags directly tie the national symbolism of the traditional stars and stripes into the specific events of 9/11. Similarly, the power of the totemic image in the society that worshipped it was formidable, as Émile Durkheim showed in his masterwork on religion, in which he described the process in primitive clan societies whereby the totem was regularly glorified and charged anew with sacred energy. During the intense ritual experience of the ceremonies dedicated to the celebration and regeneration of the totem, the totem animal or plant itself was present, and its emblem was everywhere. It was marked on the body with ink or some other substance, drawn on banners and on the costumes of celebrants, and even literally on the faces of clan members, who literally believed themselves to be materially of the same substance as the totem. In this symbolic form the totem was effectively an "emblem, a true coat of arms," parallel in essence to the coats of arms that graced the castles, shields and swords, and other key possessions of feudal European nobles.[50] Members of totemic clans not only wore the image of the totem on their bodies in the form of drawings, tattoos, and scarrings. They also sought to resemble it themselves, and hence bodily modifications of a specific variety with that goal were often obligatory. When the totem was a bird, for example, the men might wear its feathers; in the tortoise clan, the men might shave their heads and leave six curls at appropriate angles to mimic the legs, head, and tail of the animal.[51]

Durkheim provided several compelling examples of the sacred power of the totem image, largely drawn from the pioneering ethnographic work of Spencer and Gillen in central Australia. Clan religious life there frequently involved an object called a *churinga*; Durkheim noted that similar objects existed in northern and southern Australia—the *nurtunja* and *waninga*, respectively—and the latter closely resembled a flag.[52] The *churinga* were pieces of wood or polished stone, usually oval or oblong in shape. In some cases they produced noise when whirled through the air. The totemic group generally had a collection of these objects. They were kept in a special location, the *ertnatulunga*, generally a cave in some remote location unknown to those considered profane, i.e., boys who had not yet been initiated into manhood, and women, neither of whom were permitted to touch or even see them.[53] The *ertnatulunga* itself was made sacred by the contagious touch of the *churinga*, so a man in danger of any sort who sought shelter there was safe from harm. The *nurtunja* was kissed by initiates during their immensely exacting initiation ceremonies, and they thereby entered into relations with the totemic principle in it. This enabled them to endure the frightful ordeal of penile subincision without anesthesia.[54] The *churinga* healed wounds and sickness by the merest touch, yet the only thing distinguishing it from other objects of wood and stone was the totemic mark it bore.[55]

The relationship between the totem and the clan member was complex and demanding in specific rules of contact and avoidance. One could not ingest or kill the totem animal or plant of the clan.[56] There were some exceptions and mitigations to this harsh rule. For example, in cases of extreme hunger, or imminent danger from the totem animal, the rule might be broken, but a subsequent propitiation for the offense was required to be made. In clans of the water totem, obvious difficulties were presented. Clan members would die without water, yet they nonetheless could not drink it unassisted but only from the hands of someone in another phratry.[57]

This prohibition on contact with the totem might seem contra-
dicted by the obligation of the clan member to wear the totem image.
Still more complexity is seen in the fact that clans considered human
beings by nature to be profane, and yet clan members were believed to
be the sacred totem (totem myths frequently depicted original humans
born surgically, by axe blows, etc., from animal ancestors).[58] The seeming contradiction had its resolution in the fact that in totemic systems
humans, though in general profane, were nonetheless understood to
have sacred energy (the totemic principle) concentrated in certain parts
of their bodies, especially the hair and the blood.[59] During ceremonies,
the *nurtunja* was anointed in human blood, and some clans drew the
totem during religious rites on soil soaked in the blood of clan members.

In a key chapter in his book, Durkheim addressed the totemic principle, that is, the source of its sacredness and its power. It is important
to understand precisely what was being claimed when, for example, a
member of the crow clan claimed to be the totem. He did not mean
he was literally a bird, but rather that both he and the crow were animated by the same fundamental source of power.[60] Totemic societies
saw the whole universe as powered by forces that with a few exceptions took the forms of animals and plants. This force that resided in
the totem was a moral force, arousing both fear and respect. Durkheim
summarized an account he cited from a member of a North American
totemic group, the Dakota, regarding the nature of this "diffuse power,"
which the Dakota called *wakan*, as follows: "*wakan* . . . goes and comes
through the world, and the sacred things are the places where it has
alighted."[61] As a general term, Durkheim adopted a Melanesian word
for such power: *mana*.

The totem is thus essentially a representation or a symbol of something beyond it. What is the thing standing behind the totem? It is this
power of *mana*, the totem being or god in its abstracted form, but it is
also something else, Durkheim contended. The clan, that is, the social
group, is also what is symbolized in the totem, which means the social
group and the totemic principle are essentially one.[62] We come now to
perhaps the most famous of the key terms in Durkheim's analysis: collective effervescence. When human groups are assembled together and
driven by common aims, they become filled up with a certain kind of
energy. This kind of phenomenon can be transitory, for example, a man

exhorting a crowd, or it can be more sustained, such as during "some great collective shock," e.g., the Crusades, or the French Revolution.[63] Durkheim described a number of compelling scenes from aboriginal Australia in which clan members gathered together and engaged in various moving and physically exciting rites, some sacrificial, some mimetic or imitative, and some commemorative, all of them involving mythic narratives of their descent from the totem ancestor and the requirement to regenerate its principle within themselves and in the world if the clan were to have the power to sustain itself. In the midst of this overwhelming barrage of physical stimulation and symbolic information, the clan members were made literally ecstatic (from the Greek *ek-stasis*, meaning "to move outside oneself").

Yet how does the idea of the emotional, collective power that is generated at collective ritual ceremonies get transferred to the totem symbol itself? The answer is not self-evident, since, as is made clear in Durkheim's description, this energy is actually generated by the simple phenomenon of the collectivity in proximity, ritually focused on rhythmic and intense activity, i.e., by what might seem a purely material, physical set of facts. But for the member of the clan, the feeling of effervescence and the totem symbol are united by the omnipresence of the totem image at the moment of the experience of effervescence. The actual phenomenon that generates the force, that is, society itself and the experience of the intoxication of vigorous collective exertion, is a complex, difficult thing to comprehend.[64] The symbol of the totem simplifies and crystallizes this complex reality, and in fact comes to replace it. Durkheim returned here to the idea he had earlier presented of the totem as an emblem. When a soldier at war is killed, he is often said to have "died for his flag," by which we mean that he died for his country. We might think ourselves perfectly capable of sorting the two out and recognizing their distinction. After all, we know the flag is not the country, but only a scrap of cloth. And yet many a soldier in many a contemporary society has perished in combat while attempting to reclaim an actual flag abandoned in territory lost to the enemy, despite the fact that it is perfectly clear that the country will not perish if that one flag is lost, and the war will not be won simply because it is reclaimed. Just as the clan member with his totem, the soldier "forgets that the flag is only a symbol that has no value in itself but only brings to mind the reality it represents [and] treat[s it] as if it was that reality."[65]

The totem is a symbol of the whole society that can be thought of in the same frame of reference as a modern flag, and it is embodied by the members, indeed often literally inscribed on their bodies in the form of tattoos and scarifications in addition to its presence in their physical being as the totemic principle in the form of their hair and blood. Its power is generated through collective assemblies in which mythical stories of the relation of those present to the totem are told and reenacted, during which the symbol of the totem comes to be charged up with the residue of the emotional energy of the assembly. All this provides a penetrating lens for examining the workings of religious and national symbols, rituals, and collective identity and memory in modern societies like our own, distant as we are from these totemic groups in many ways. At the Shanksville temporary memorial, the sheer number of flags made it effectively impossible to avoid encountering the symbol at the site—it was literally everywhere one turned. Though explicit ritual effervescence of the type Durkheim described was generally not present at the temporary memorial site,[66] i.e., visitors to the site were not engaged in the kind of strenuous physical action and collective mimicry and entrainment that produces what Randall Collins calls emotional energy,[67] it was nonetheless visibly evident that visitors were frequently intensely marked by the symbolic energy produced by the omnipresent totem flag and other emotionally charged symbols. Text was directly added to the surface of the flag in order to make explicit the meaning of the events in national symbolic terms, and the mutation of the flag into a very specific symbolic statement of the events allowed for a funneling of the flag's symbolic capital into new directions.

Augmented or alternative flag designs abounded at the memorial site. For some time, a plaque was posted to the fence with the design of a "9/11 flag" and an elaborate description of its symbolism. According to the text, this flag boasted a field of blue representing the sky, the medium of the attacks; three red stripes that represented the sites where the planes came to ground and spilled blood; two white stripes standing in for the two towers of the World Trade Center; and a large star, composed of 50 smaller ones, with a white center representing the Pentagon

FIGURE 3.5. "93" flag. Photo: ATR.

and a smaller red core representing Pennsylvania, the site where "the Brave Heroes" struck back. A number of these augmented, transformed flags also flew high above the fence at the memorial. These included an American flag with the field of stars transformed from rows in a sea of blue to a protective circle of 50 stars surrounding a huge "93" and the text "Our Nation will eternally honor the heroes of Flight 93" emblazoned directly on three lines of white stripes in the main body of the flag. This flag was both hanging on the fence and represented in a marble commemorative plaque near the entry way of the memorial (figure 3.5). Two other flags that were not alterations of the American flag but original creations to symbolize and sacralize the events of September 11, 2001, could be seen atop the fence: a red flag with text reading "Never Forget" and an image representing the two towers inside a pentagon, itself inside a larger circle, and four stars representing the various crash sites (one in each tower, one in the Pentagon, one at a point in the circle); and a blue and black tri-bar flag with four large stars representing the four planes (see figure 3.3).

Other American flags with text (e.g., "God Bless America") written directly on the bars could be found at the site. Some of the flags stretched the traditional civil religious narrative all the way into frank Christian American patriotism. Two such flags are collected at the Park Service office in Somerset. They aggressively proclaim the meaning of 9/11 as the response of an angry Christian God to a nation insufficiently fearful of him and as an opportunity for the nation to "come out in Jesus' name." Here, 40 crosses (one for each passenger) fill the blue field on the flag and the text on one of the two flags reads: "In this world we live in, many fail to claim, Our Father who art in Heaven, they use his holy name in vain. They fear no evil, in what they say and do, they take the precious gift of life for granted too." Still other flag imagery directly engaged other culture-war conflict and tension. One monument at the site juxtaposed the American flag with the flag of the Southern Confederacy, and seemed to directly equate the Flight 93 passengers to the rebellious soldiers of the South. These last few examples make an important point regarding the tenor of cultural symbolism at the memorial. As in any such site, completely monolithic meaning is impossible. Even though the bulk of the symbolic material at the site pointed to a common narrative of civil religious piety, some symbolic material there complicated that meaning structure, adding specifically denominational religious or political content that many who would readily pledge fealty to the civil religious narrative would perhaps reject.

Perhaps the most intriguing bit of flag symbolism at the memorial site was that found at the end of the site abutting Skyline Road. Just in front of the benches and next to the large wooden cross were a row of slate angels, created by a local business and mounted on small poles that raised them two to three feet off the ground. Each angel was emblazoned with the name of a passenger and they each featured the red, white, and blue design of the American flag on their breasts (figure 3.6). The Angel Patriots, as I have come to call them, which were a long-lived feature of the temporary memorial,[68] offered a near perfect summary of the civil religious narrative. They bore the totem flag symbols,

FIGURE 3.6. The Angel Patriots. Photo: ATR.

colors, and patterns. They displayed the names of the heroic martyrs.
They took on the shape of entities that, in the religious traditions of
many faiths, including the Christian, are located somewhere between
the realm of the gods and the world of humans, structurally the same
location occupied by culture heroes, who are neither divine nor human
but a mystical combination of the two arising from the powerful magic
of their deeds. Those entities are winged, and thus ascend into the heavens; the miming of the movement of dead souls into the heavenly sphere
of the plane the heroes rode on their final journey is here encapsulated
with neat precision. There is one other powerful bit of meaning present in the Angel Patriots, a meaning that evokes dread but is nonetheless essential in that very horror to the civil religious myth, which I
will explore in the next chapter. Here it is enough to put a name to the
cultural process I will theoretically elaborate later: the Angel Patriots
were funeral markers, but not of the human individuals whose names
they bore. They were the totem body itself, flag hero corpses, slain in

combat, in the interpretive understanding of members of the Flight 93 hero cult, and they were therefore symbols of the dreadful power of the American nation over life and death.

During their time of display at the memorial, the Angel Patriots were constantly adorned with various gifts left by visitors, which included everything from flags to flowers to personal trinkets. The ground below Honor Wainio's angel was covered with seashells. Often the gifts showed some knowledge of the life of the passenger in question or of the media coverage of the crash. For example, someone placed an Ohio State University cap on the ground below Todd Beamer's angel (figure 3.7), as one of the photos of Beamer that was featured in much media coverage of his death shows him in such a cap. Visitors who left such gift objects were both affirming their own personal presence at the memorial and enhancing the civil religious hero myth.

FIGURE 3.7. Gifts left to the Angel Patriots. Photo: ATR.

The Ambassadors

In addition to the material culture just described, another unforgettable aspect of the temporary memorial was the group of friendly individuals wearing bright red shirts that indicated their position as Ambassadors from the Park Service. During the existence of the temporary memorial, they were an essential part of the institutional face of the Flight 93 memorialization effort, but, like most other parts of this institution, they emerged essentially spontaneously and took on their ultimate shape only over time.

In the fall of 2008, I spoke with Donna Glessner, the volunteer coordinator of the Ambassadors, who was involved with the memorial since its inception, about their origins. A long-time resident of Shanksville, she recounted how, in the early months after the crash in the fall and winter of 2001, she began to realize the importance the site was going to take on. She recalled seeing someone in a car with an Indiana license plate taking photographs of a local fire truck in October and thinking, "I'd seen the first tourist":

> A number of us came to this conclusion that there needed to be someone at the memorial, . . . a caring sympathetic ear. . . . [I saw] how frightened and anxious everyone felt, how lost. . . . [P]eople really just wanted to tell you about their experience. . . . [I]nitially there were no signs, no flag down in the distance, and people would stand in that bare field and not have any idea what they were looking at.[69]

Some early visitors would ask if the plane had gone down in a nearby pond or take pictures of the scrap yard at the top of the hill, believing that was the crash site. Troubled by the fact that there was no source of information and assistance to these uninformed but curious and emotionally invested visitors, Glessner contacted her friend Barbara Black, the Flight 93 National Memorial curator who was already in late 2001 beginning the labor of collecting and archiving material culture and oral histories related to the crash, and asked her if she thought there was a need for volunteers at the site. In a manner that tells much about cultural life in small town America, although, as Glessner makes clear, "not because we felt it was a religious mission or anything, but just because in a small town a church is a way to meet people," Glessner and a few friends announced in their church, Shanksville United Methodist, one Sunday that they were seeking volunteers to help out at the crash site and that a training session would be held in the days to come. A total of 17 volunteers were at that first training session on January 26, 2002, and among those present to instruct them on how to do the work they were setting out to do were Black and Terry Schaefer, the Shanksville fire chief. The individuals who would only later come to be called the Ambassadors learned logistical facts about the crash (where the plane went down, where and how wreckage was discovered) and were briefed on the kind of directions likely to be useful to tourists (where to find a local gas station and restaurant, how to get back to Route 30 or Interstate 76). They were also given a phone number for journalists to contact for press information. Initially, the crash site was staffed by these volunteers only on Saturdays and Sundays, when free time was easiest to find, and individual Ambassadors worked two-hour shifts. Many, though not all, of the Ambassadors were retired seniors with considerable volunteer time. From that first winter of 2002 through the following one, there was no shelter on the grounds for Ambassadors to use for protection from the severe elements up on the hilltop (bitter winter wind, merciless summer sun, and no trees) while waiting for tourists. One early Ambassador was a local pastor who was able to give the rest of the crew instruction on grievance counseling, a useful skill given the emotionally distraught state of more than a few visitors in the early days. Only much later were the Ambassadors officially approached by the Park Service, who offered them training in visitor rights, CPR, and first aid. Glessner told of rare emergency situations at the site involving tourists (cases of sunstroke, someone who fell and broke a leg) and explained "you feel responsible for these people." The Ambassadors were instructed to make entries into a log book concerning their shifts, and these are now collected in the Somerset archive. Most of the entries are no more than a few lines and give mundane details of the weather and brief accounts of the density of visitors for the day, e.g., "Beautiful day—warm—light breeze, few visitors (44)" from the 2:00–4:00 p.m. shift on August 17, 2004.

In May 2006, in what Glessner describes as a "peaceful coup," the National Park Service officially incorporated the Ambassadors and further institutionalized training. By the summer of 2008, the Ambassador staff numbered some 45, most of whom lived in the Shanksville area, though at least one was making a three-hour commute to the site. Already, a sense of the identity of the group and of its mission was evolving, both through formal institutional mechanisms and more informal avenues.

The Ambassadors quickly recognized that they would have a not insignificant role to play in the maintenance of collective memory about Flight 93. Glessner noted that in the early days after the crash, tourists could be counted on to know basic facts about the plane from media coverage, but within a few years, it became obvious that memory concerning the events on Flight 93 and its place in the larger story of 9/11 was beginning to wane. Ambassadors were increasingly asked questions that revealed ignorance of even basic details of the event: Were there any survivors? What time of year was it when the crash occurred? Ambassadors were shocked to be asked whether they personally had been on board the plane. Some visitors had forgotten the significance of Todd Beamer's "Let's roll" phrase and asked about its ubiquity at the site. Glessner observed that it is perhaps understandable that memory has weakened, especially given that "there's so much out there that's incorrect." Even in recent years, she told me, there was still interest, albeit relatively infrequent, among visitors in one of three main conspiracy theories surrounding Flight 93: (1) that the attack was a false-flag, inside job of the American ruling establishment; (2) that the plane was actually shot down by American jets; and (3) that the permanent memorial design is actually a mosque.[70] Some critics were confident enough about their suspicions as to bring it up in the midst of Ambassador presentations to groups of visitors, which sometimes made for lively interchanges, but it was, Glessner said, much more commonly in one-on-one encounters with visitors, after formal presentations to groups, that these beliefs were articulated in hushed tones.

Glessner cited several of her colleagues among the Ambassadors in describing their own sense of their cultural work at the memorial: one man, retired from his job in the oil distribution business, told a journalist, "I used to be a businessman, but now I'm a storyteller," while another described their work thus: "we've become historians." Both are correct. The narratives communicated by the Ambassadors made up an important contribution to the ongoing construction of a Flight 93 mythology insofar as they were, during the time of the temporary memorial, the sole representatives of any official American institutions that visitors to the site encountered. Glessner soberly described the responsibility for such a role as "kind of scary," and clearly understood the complex nature of this interpretive work. Initially, she described her own narrative stance as "nothing but the facts, just the facts," but

> very quickly, certain Ambassadors began doing interpretation, in the Parks Service sense of the word. They were assigning values to things that happened, in the way of, like, this was the bravest deed ever, or this was like the second Pearl Harbor, those kinds of interpretive [things]. I really rebelled about that. I didn't think that was right. I didn't think it was our place to do that. But over the years, whether we've become more authoritative or what, but now we all sort of, even I tend to use some phrases like that, that go beyond just the facts. . . . [I]t feels okay now to do that. It does.[71]

As an example, she juxtaposed her own mode of noting that the plane was only 15 minutes from Washington, D.C. ("I just let that fact out there and let people think what that would have meant"), to that of other Ambassadors who would elaborate more emotionally ("just imagine the death and the destruction and the loss to our government"). The line between fact and myth is difficult and perhaps impossible to find, and indeed it may be misguided even to seek it: we are perhaps thoroughly inside myth as soon as we begin to communicate about such things at all.

The formal Ambassador addresses to gathered visitor groups were "in the Park Service plan" envisioned as in the range of ten to 12 minutes, but, according to Glessner, most tended to be about twice that in length, which is fairly close to the experiences I had listening to perhaps 15 or 20 different versions of the presentation over the time I spent at the memorial. She described the energy Ambassadors receive from this work in compelling terms: "Many Ambassadors will say, 'I'm tired, I'm overworked, why did I agree to do this?' and then you go out there and you feel so confident that you're doing the right thing because people are so appreciative, and you come out feeling energized, you feel like you have done the greatest thing you could do for your country or your fellow man." Though, according to Glessner, the average span of a volunteer's commitment to a project is brief, perhaps two years, most of the Ambassadors in 2008 had been at the job for at least six, and most of the original group from 2002 were still there when I spoke with her. By 2008, the training process had become considerably more formal. A booklet was culled from the accumulated information packets from the first few years, and training was divided into three steps: potential Ambassadors would first meet with leaders of the project and talk generally about its history and its future trajectory; then in a second session the trainee would learn logistical information about the site and being a volunteer, e.g., where to locate keys, what to do in emergencies, and what literature to hand to interested visitors; and finally, in a third session, they would receive formal training on the presentation to be delivered (or, as Glessner put it, "what is the story all about?"). Trainees were given a large FAQ document and information contained in a binder with photos that was used as a kind of guidebook by some Ambassadors as they walked through their presentation. Glessner described the text in the following terms: "I won't say it's the text, because everyone is explaining things in their own words, but there are talking points. . . . [W]e can't have people out there saying things that aren't right. . . . [So] you're looking at a photo, and behind it there are talking points that go with that photo, and then flipping, talking points for the new photo." The trainees were also given copies of the 9/11 Commission Report and Jere Longman's book on Flight 93, *Among the Heroes*, which, as we will see in chapter seven, is firmly planted in the same civil religious narrative told by the symbols at the memorial site.

Two September 11 Mornings at the Flight 93 Temporary Memorial: 2008 and 2011

Most days at the temporary memorial were, as the Ambassadors' log entries attest, uneventful: in winter, very few visitors, and in other seasons, occasional spurts of tourist busloads framed by longer periods of a small trickle in which seldom were more than 20 people on the site at the same time. Around the anniversary date of the crash, the level of energy rose at the site. Politicians, recognizing the important role 9/11 and Flight 93 play in the cultural imaginary and in the narrative of American identity and mission, scheduled appearances to deliver addresses charged up with the symbolic material they hoped would demonstrate to those they serve how fully invested they are in the American civil religion. Much can be learned about the resonance of the Flight 93 narrative in American political discourse from what was said by these exceptional visitors to the memorial during the commemoration of the day the plane crashed.

On September 11, 2008, I arrived early at the site, drawn by the scheduled appearance of Arizona senator and then Republican presidential nominee John McCain, at the time engaged in a furious, bitter struggle with his Democratic opponent, then Senator Barack Obama of Illinois, in which many of McCain's supporters and fellow Republicans were launching controversial discursive attacks on Obama that accused him of sympathy with Islamic terrorists such as those who hijacked Flight 93. The national political discourse at the time was fairly crackling with intensity. I did not have to wait for Senator McCain's turn at the podium for a speaker to present a reading of the symbolic meaning of the act of the passengers that went directly for the cultural jugular. The first speaker of the morning, Ken Wainstein, then director of the U.S. Office of Homeland Security under the Bush administration, in brief remarks of just a few minutes, bypassed the civil religious discourse and explicitly connected the act of the passengers of Flight 93 to that of "the Son of God 2,000 years ago." The then governor of Pennsylvania, Ed Rendell, followed and marked the difference in Republican and Democratic political discourse of the season by steadfastly avoiding any mention of God in his remarks. However, the site's civil religious energy still dictated that Rendell find a way to connect his message to its symbols and meanings. He passionately described Senator McCain's time as a prisoner of war in North Vietnam and thereby brushed up against the American civil religion very deliberately. Here was a man who had nearly given his life, and had given his health and years of his life in captivity, for his country; how could his presence at this site of nationalist sacrifice and mythical nation-saving heroism be questioned as a mere campaign ploy? (It certainly had not escaped the notice of at least some visitors that the presidential election was at this point less than two months away.) Despite Rendell's refusal to entertain the explicitly religious national language of the first speaker, which found symbolic sustenance at this memorial in that large cross standing next to the

American flag at the entrance to the site, his remarks were yet drenched in the cultural narrative of the American nation with a mission that, if not from God, certainly exceeds merely secular explanation and bursts from the temporary memorial like a beacon.

Finally, after much anticipation, Senator McCain spoke. He wasted no time in aiming straight for the cultural binaries of peaceful, democratic heroes and militant, authoritarian antiheroes. He attacked "our depraved and hateful enemies" in no uncertain terms. McCain placed the Flight 93 passengers, personified by Mark Bingham, whom McCain mentioned by name,[72] in a position of clear moral and patriotic superiority to that of the average citizen: "Few of us could say we love our country as well as he." Toward the end of a fleeting but symbolically pregnant address, McCain turned to the same Christian sources invoked by Wainstein: "In the Gospel of John it is written: 'Greater love hath no man than this, that a man lay down his life for his friends.'" He then concluded with this remark about the Flight 93 passengers: "Such was their love, love so sublime that only God's love surpasses it. I'm in awe of it as much as I'm in debt to it. May God bless their souls." Sustained applause followed. McCain had managed to invoke the core elements of the civil religious narrative, patriot heroes whose death mirrored the axioms of Judeo-Christian religious principle, while also pointing to the explicitly Christian trappings that religious conservative Republicans favored. He did not mention Jesus directly, as Wainstein had, but only indirectly and yet in a manner that no Christian, or anyone else for that matter, could miss: by citing from one of the Gospels. One might note that McCain, who previously was recognized as a denizen of the more secular end of the Republican Party and rather sparing in his religious remarks, had already pragmatically moved more to the religious right during the presidential campaign in an attempt to shore up dissatisfaction with his candidacy on the right, and attempt to explain these remarks in that light. The cultural sociologist, however, might well conclude that the symbolic universe into which the good Senator had entered that September morning, ripe with such imagery and narratives, was of greater importance in the generation of this tone than any merely practical political considerations.

Three years later, on September 11, 2011, some things, significant and mostly physical, had changed, but the symbolic work being done at the site had remained largely the same. Construction of the permanent memorial, which is described in chapter five, had by this time been underway for some time and, although much work remained, the outline of the part of the memorial park centered on the crash site was becoming evident. The temporary memorial was gone now, the artifacts that had been there whisked away to storage in Somerset or elsewhere, and the ceremonies for the first time took place down the hill, much closer to the crash site, although now the black framing wall of the permanent memorial served as a distinct visible cue as to the line dividing the most highly sacred space from the rest of the memorial. On one side of the wall rested the stage and the seats that would hold family members and distinguished guests, while beyond the wall lay a golden field of bright flowers, glowing in the late summer sun, and a boulder decorated with gifts that represented the exact spot of the plane's impact. Just the day before, the memorial had been dedicated in a ceremony featuring two former presidents and the current vice president. President Clinton had compared Flight 93 to the Alamo and the Spartan stand at Thermopylae, emphasizing the "deliberate" self-sacrifice of the Flight 93 passengers, who, he said almost certainly incorrectly, "*knew* they were going to die." He expressed his hope that the narrative of Flight 93 would be remembered as long as the Greek stand against the Persians. He concluded with a pledge to push a concerted effort to raise the remaining money needed to finish the memorial. President Bush's remarks centered on a note-for-note recapitulation of the simplest version of the mythology of Flight 93. He described calm heroes learning stoically of their planned fate, deliberating in a considered fashion as to strategy, setting up a vote, and then unflinchingly acting. As he had done in the wake of Flight 93's crash, Mr. Bush leaned heavily on Todd Beamer's "Let's roll!" line, turning it into a trope not merely for the actions of the passengers on that plane, but for the broader American response in the wake of the crash. The binary cultural world of crisis was still powerfully operative in Bush's mind, and undoubtedly, in the minds of many, many Americans, a decade later: "One of the lessons of 9/11 is that evil is real, and so is courage." Vice President Biden followed them, and in a telling moment of his talk, he presented his summary of the two messages contained in the two presidents' remarks. He recalled that President Clinton had noted that the Flight 93 passengers knew that our common humanity is what most unites us, and touted the former president's work in that same regard. He then addressed President Bush as the man who "made it clear that America could not be brought to her knees [and] helped us stand tall and strike back." The remarks about Clinton aroused a bare smattering of a few seconds of restrained, polite applause, scarcely even discernible from where I was seated some 100 yards away from the podium. The statement about Bush, on the other hand, was met with sustained and much louder applause, punctuated with whistles and cheers, showing in no uncertain terms what the lessons of Flight 93 and 9/11 had been for America at least in this place, at this time, for these Americans: the recognition of common humanity takes the back seat to striking back against evil enemies. Biden went on, in the martial spirit that is unquestionably present in a good deal of the material culture and narrative work at the temporary memorial site: "They didn't board that plane to fight a war, but they knew it was the opening shot in a new war. They stood up and they stood their ground. That heroism is who they are. [The terrorists] cannot—they cannot—defeat the American spirit."

On the following day, the 11th, which fell on a Sunday in 2011, the political star power was significantly lessened. The keynote speaker was not a president, or a vice president, but John Hendricks, the CEO of Discovery Communications. He was chosen, apparently, because Honor Wainio, one of the Flight 93 passengers, was a district manager for his company at her death. His largely innocuous remarks were directed toward a vague promise to the families of passengers to complete the memorial. Republican Congressman Bill Shuster, like President Clinton, compared the deed of the passengers to that of the defenders of the Alamo, and also to "Lexington and Concord": in all three situations, he claimed, "Americans banded together and said, 'No, this will not stand.'" The grave historical difficulties in the comparisons are self-evident, as is the infelicity of the equation of the sovereign states of Mexico and Great Britain to an underground network of suicide bombers. It was neither the time nor the place, however, in which one could expect challenge to Shuster's statement.

Governor Tom Corbett, also a Republican, made the most symbolically pointed remarks of the day, and it was his speech that most clearly embraced the more powerful elements of the binary symbolic system at work in the mythology of Flight 93. Unlike his predecessors, who were eager to tie the events of Flight 93 to historically and symbolically similar examples in earlier American times, Corbett flatly refused to make any comparisons. For him,

> the truth is that this place is like no other because the deeds aboard Flight 93 were like no other. . . . [I]t has no companion in history, in my mind. . . . [T]heir uprising marks the moment in history when Americans showed what makes us different. We refuse to be victims. We refuse to settle for the term "survival." Captivity will not suit us. We know that there are things more important than our own lives and chief among them is freedom. That truth rose like the smoke over this field ten years ago. Today our Capitol stands, the city of Washington is intact, the honor of our Republic is yet stronger, because of the strength of will and the sense of purpose of 40 American citizens who chose to be warriors, who chose to sacrifice themselves to protect their fellow Americans. They engaged in that battle armed only with the knowledge that they were right.

They did what they did, in Corbett's interpretation, "to stay the hand of tyranny." He then alluded to a vision of the world historical importance of the action on the plane almost identical to the neoconservative global vision articulated by President Bush in the wake of the attacks. The political end pointed to by the passengers of Flight 93 is, in this vision, nothing less than the transformation of the entire planet to conformity with a conservative American vision of democracy: "The breezes on this hillside whispers [sic] of an unfinished agenda, one of freedom at home and abroad. Of faraway peoples free from the yoke of dictators and bigots. It is filled with lives we must now complete on behalf of those who sacrificed their lives. . . . It is up to us to finish their journey."

The possibility, which is strong given the testimony of phone conversations from the plane and the biographical materials available on passengers, that the motivation of the passengers in the revolt effort might have centered less on any sense of patriotic duty than on their own more mundane and personal desires to survive and get home to their families is conveniently placed here into the shadow of an overarching cultural political ideology. The trope of "freedom," which, as I write this, is the calling card of the Tea Party and other right-wing critics of the

Obama administration's efforts to address massive social problems created at least in part by the excessive freedom from regulation accorded Wall Street and corporate elites, can hardly pass the vision of any reader attuned to the political news without remark. What exactly do Corbett and the others who invoke the term in such simplified discourse mean by it? Corbett, who was elected in the same 2008 election widely interpreted in the political world as a major set of electoral victories for the Tea Party, almost certainly meant at least some of the same things meant by those people who carry the Gadsden flag, which has become something of a Tea Party banner, and the immediate context of the current American political climate almost certainly played a role in the contours of the symbolic terms and language that appeared at this ten-year anniversary ceremony. But much of this symbolic material goes back much further in American cultural history, and there is much in the existing Flight 93 mythology that relies on that same archaic set of cultural narratives and symbols, so the speeches made during this recent annual marking of September 11 easily find support in some of the cultural work that produced what we know as Flight 93. In the context of American mythology and civil religion, then, Corbett's evocation of "freedom," at this site, and in reference to this event, gathers narrative direction from the same mythical vision of the frontier and the rural heartland that is present in the "End of Serenity" photo.

4

Flag Bodies

Commemoration in the Flight 93 Memorial Chapel

About eight miles from the site at which Flight 93 struck ground, along a stretch of a sparsely populated country road dominated by farmland and woods, sits a small chapel dedicated to the passengers of Flight 93. It is eight miles, that is, if one is following the serpentine local roads, but only about half that as the crow flies. If however you are not possessed of the power of flight, leaving the crash site toward the chapel, you retrace your steps out to Lambertsville Road and head back through Shanksville. At the post office, you turn right on to Stuzmantown Road and follow its winding curves, through postcard-picturesque rural Pennsylvania countryside, for several miles until, at the intersection of Stuzmantown and Coleman Station roads, you find a small, nondescript white building, remarkable from the outside only because of the bell tower at its entrance that is taller than the building itself. To one side of the chapel, separated from it by Coleman Station Road, lies a small, plain country cemetery. The late Alphonse Mascherino, the first pastor at the chapel and the man responsible for its existence, once told me, in his assertive, theatrical voice, that he was occasionally asked by a visitor to the chapel, in hushed, respectful tones, if the passengers of Flight 93 are buried in that cemetery. On the chapel's other side is the guesthouse, a modest one-story, four-room home that serves as the temporary dwelling for family members of Flight 93 passengers when they visit the chapel. During annual commemoration ceremonies, it also serves as a kind of group home for assorted members of the passengers' families, invited speakers, performers, and other participants in the ceremonies at the chapel. Over the past several years, Father Mascherino frequently gave me the keys to the house during research trips to Shanksville. My family has accompanied me on nearly all of those trips, and, for a time, my young daughter was there so frequently that she referred to our own home in Lewisburg as "the Riley house" and to the chapel guesthouse as "the *other* Riley house."

Throughout this book, the tension present in my consciousness between the multiple identities and identifications I described in the opening chapter makes itself known in myriad ways and, frequently, it has made the work much more difficult than I might have wished. As a scholar invested in a more or less clear distinction between purely subjective observation and social scientific analysis that aims beyond that to a more objective accounting, I feel the responsibility to look at the phenomenon under consideration as dispassionately as possible, with a distance that will allow a level-headed, *impersonal* account. As an American citizen with strong moral and political positions on many of the issues that are fought over in the construction of meaning about Flight 93, I feel compelled to take stances, to make judgments, and to defend those ideas with which I am in agreement and to criticize those I oppose. As a human being, with deeply emotionally invested personal relationships and the moral responsibilities those naturally entail, I feel bound by specific loyalties and friendship ties to withhold both political judgment and objective scientific evaluation in the interests of human warmth and fraternity. These various perspectives struggle with one another in many of the other chapters in the book. But it is in this chapter, more than any other, that the struggle is at its most compelling. I have deep, and deeply conflicted, feelings about the Flight 93 Chapel. I called its founder, Alphonse Mascherino, my friend, and he made it clear in many ways, not least of which was his frequent habit of presenting me to the congregation as I attempted to sneak in unobserved, that he considered me a member of the chapel's community, and he always addressed me as "brother." There is much in the symbolic work going on at the chapel that I personally find tremendously emotionally moving. At the same time, some of the meanings being generated there, in the form of possible or likely readings of the symbolism of the chapel in the context of the broader American culture, are more difficult to reconcile with my own political and cultural beliefs. And I also know that some of what is revealed here by the scholar in me would perhaps have failed to fit my friend Father Fonzie's own understanding of what is going on there. I know that these dilemmas have no solution, and I know that writing about them poses risks, which I accept in undertaking this task.

The Origin of the Chapel

In the beginning, of course, there was no chapel. The origin myth of the Flight 93 Chapel is itself a part of the mystical, symbolically and morally charged narrative of its meaning. Mascherino told me the story for the first time as we sat in front of the altar on a sunlit morning and a few visitors milled about; he occasionally paused in his telling to assist the visitors or direct their attention to particular features of the place, or to allow me to fumble clumsily with the digital recording device I was using to record our conversation. In the first moments after Flight 93 crashed, he began, memorial efforts sprang up in Shanksville, which were described in the previous chapter. Mascherino pointed to a poster board that now sits atop a table near the entrance to the chapel.[1] This was one of the very first such works, a sign saluting "the heroes of Flight 93" and bearing dozens of signatures and expressions of thanks. It appeared in the yard of a local resident, whose home was situated at the police line that turned back those attempting to get to the crash site in the early moments of the aftermath. The family set it out and pilgrims on their way to the site signed and wrote messages on it before turning away from their quest to locate the crash site. In these early moments after the catastrophe, Mascherino noted (here echoing a theme widespread in the mass media in the early aftermath), the sentiments were

> universally expressive, "God bless America," "God bless the heroes," "God bless the families," and this was being done at the same time that the churches were being filled throughout the nation after September 11 . . . and that expression of faith in God, faith in the expression of religion was so prevalent. . . . [T]hen the story came out that the heroes of Flight 93 prayed together. . . . I understand they prayed the 23rd Psalm . . . for courage and strength, confronted by these terrorists who were hell bent on killing them. In the midst of that turmoil to turn to God and pray, that's what impressed me.

Inspired by his perception of an atmosphere of heightened religious awareness in the wake of the attacks, Mascherino, who was at the time an unassigned Catholic priest from the Somerset area without a home parish, wrote an essay that he titled "Thunder on the Mountain" in which he describes "our hills" of Shanksville as "hallowed ground" changed forever by "Giants who are . . . honored here" as "Heroes." Mascherino's prose is unabashedly hyperbolic: "In the final moments of their lives, they demonstrated courage, strength, purpose and commitment. Their message is clear: to be free, completely free, let no one, let no thing take control. We are Captains of our Destiny, Masters of our soul. . . . [W]e can make a difference in the destiny of the world." Clearly exceptionally moved by the event, he began making buttons bearing the thanks of the town and distributing them to emergency workers at the crash site. The idea came to him in these early days after the crash to establish a memorial site for the passengers where visitors could pray and intermingle in the same ecumenical spirit he believed could be seen at work in the last moments of Flight 93. The temporary memorial site already existed, but "I knew," Mascherino told me, "the government was not going to build a place to pray or that was about God."[2] It was during one of his numerous trips back and forth from Shanksville to distribute the buttons, in late October 2001, that he saw the "For Sale" sign outside the abandoned chapel on Coleman Station Road. He inquired, but was disappointed to learn that an offer had already been accepted. Undaunted, he looked at two other sites, one in the immediate area, another some 30 miles away in Johnstown, but both were prohibitively expensive. His inspiration seemed to have met an abrupt, early demise. But about two weeks after his inquiry, he got a call from the real estate agency handling the property on Coleman Station Road; he was told that the first buyer had backed out and that the property was again available. It was priced at $18,000 and the required deposit was $800, a significant amount to raise for a lone Catholic priest without any organizational backing and few resources of his own. One of those few resources, however, was a personal collection of antiques and Hallmark ornaments Mascherino had amassed over the years. Among other items, he sold six dozen Christmas Barbies, which he had originally purchased at $12.95 each, for $65 apiece. The sale of this material enabled him to make the deposit and later the settlement on the property. In his description of the twists and turns involving the property's status and the constant struggle to acquire the needed money at various steps in the process of purchase, a discourse of the mystical and miraculous is quite present. He emphasized numerous events along the path to the purchase, reconstruction, and opening of the chapel that he explicitly posited as supernatural in origin, and he was quite unrestrained in his praise of what he referred to as the "great generosity of the Power of the universe, you cry out to the universe your need and the universe responds. Cry out to God and before you even ask Him anything, He already knows what you need. . . . I just went along for the ride."

During the Christmas holiday in 2001, Mascherino visited with his elderly mother and other members of his family. He told them of his plans to purchase the church and turn it into a chapel for Flight 93. His family was decidedly unenthusiastic, stopping short of ridiculing the idea but certainly less than convinced that he would be able to pull it off. His mother, however, who was seriously ill at the time and, as it turned out, in the last few months of her life, listened approvingly to his plans. It was during this Christmas season that two important, and in Mascherino's telling supernaturally driven, developments took place. He was still uncertain as to where the money for the closing would come from, as his antique collection was attracting buyers, but in a trickling stream too slow to generate the amount he needed by the required date. His brother-in-law abruptly announced to him, after previously expressing a distinct lack of confidence in the plan, during his holiday visit that he would purchase the whole of the remainder of the collection of ornaments Mascherino was trying to sell so that he would have the necessary funds in time. He also had a prescient dream during this same period. In the dream, he saw the chapel completed, in detail fundamentally identical to the look of the actual chapel today. The symbolic narrative of the chapel, the cultural signs it would contain and which would come to define it, revealed themselves essentially in their entirety to him in this dream. He had at this point measured the church in detail, so he knew well its architecture and dimensions, but he could not yet envision in his conscious moments what it would look like when completed. In the dream, memories of his childhood fascination with Roman cathedrals and of his work some 15 years earlier to remodel the church to which he was then assigned in a nearby county came together and produced the fruit of a full-blown civil religious monument to the heroes. The design was informed, he told me, by three principles that were always before him as he envisioned the chapel: it had to be noble ("of the highest quality"), infinite ("of the longest duration"), and worthy of the heroes it commemorates.

In August 2002, he was, in his words, "out of everything, out of resources, out of energy, out of inspiration," and the chapel was still but a shell, looking much more like the abandoned grain storehouse it had recently been than a memorial shrine to Flight 93. Then, a local 84 Lumber manager who had become aware of Mascherino's struggles phoned Maggie Hardy, the owner of the company, and told her of the situation. Instantly inspired by the project, she gave Mascherino a grant of $23,000 to finish the work, even furnishing the labor required. His narrative here is remarkable, and always, when he repeats this story for the chapel congregation at events, delivered in high dramatic fashion: "She looked at the plans to finish it and said, 'I think this is significant. . . . [I]f you don't mind, I'll do this for you.'" She took over the work on August 31, 2002, and had her team work around the clock, finishing the chapel just in time for the one-year commemoration ceremony on September 11, 2002. Mascherino went on: "I never dreamed it would be possible that someone would come forward and just say, 'I'll do it for you,' and undertake all that work and all that expense. . . . [S]he was here every day and she'd be saying to the workmen, 'you do everything he tells you, I do not want to hear you say "no" to him.' . . . [S]he was absolutely committed." Hardy taped an interview with a local television station about the chapel and, afterwards, told Mascherino, with a sly grin, to be sure to see it when it aired later. In the interview, she recounted Mascherino telling her, "If God wants it finished, God's going to have to do it," then added "I'm not God, but I think God sent me to help him and I will build that church for him." In the fashion of many folktales about supernatural assistance, Hardy performed her good deed and then instantly disappeared: "It was finished on September 10 and I never saw her again, she never came back to the chapel." He finished the story by relating one of the last things she told him after the chapel was completed: "Your carpentry days are over. Now you have other things to do."

FIGURE 4.1. Thunder Bell tower and chapel entrance. Photo: ATR.

A Tour of the Chapel's Symbolic Universe

Such is the narrative of how the chapel came to be, a story that Mascherino routinely delivered with a remarkable combination of dramatic flair and sincerity to the congregations that gather there every September 11. The narrative he wove is undergirded by the actual material structures at the chapel that are in many cases themselves symbols and narrative elements concerning Flight 93, its passengers, and the meaning of their deed. The first thing one sees from just outside the front entry of the chapel, and the first sign that this is not just a farmhouse, is the impressive bell tower, at the top of which rests what Mascherino dubbed the Thunder Bell (figure 4.1). That title, and the phrase "The Voice of Flight 93," are painted on the bell itself, which was given to the chapel by a local man from Somerset. As Mascherino told visitors to the chapel, the bell provides a "mystical relation between the chapel and the crash site," as its ring can be heard several miles away on the hill where the plane went down. He told congregations that the crash site is visible from the top of the 44-foot steel belfry. Numerous times when I was in attendance, he invited someone from the congregation to ring the bell on exiting the chapel as a way of symbolically expressing unity with the deed of the passengers. In doing so, he told them, they affirmed the will never to forget their heroism and to propagate that message to those who had not yet heard it.

To the right of the bell tower is the Memorial Torch of Liberty, a 12-foot metal sculpture crowned by a torch approximating the one held by the Statue of Liberty in its design, and therefore linked explicitly to the American civil religion's narrative structures. The torch is fully functional and at night gives off a powerful quarter-billion-candlepower beam that can be seen for miles in every direction. It is, like many of the art objects in the chapel, the work of a local resident, a retired master blacksmith from Somerset.

Entering through the front door, one immediately discovers that there is no vestibule; once through the door, one is suddenly thrust into the very heart of the chapel. Mascherino told me this was a conscious architectural move designed to contribute to the participatory, democratic sentiment he envisioned for the chapel. A traditional church vestibule provides an intermediate space between outside and inside the church, an additional boundary to be passed through in Mascherino's account before one can truly be welcomed into the spiritual life of the building. The existing internal structure of the old church included a vestibule, but Mascherino had it removed. Here, instead, visitors move, without the need for transitional ritual to attain purification, immediately from the outside, profane world into the core of the chapel's sacred structure. In Mascherino's words, "I wanted people to open up that front door and see the entire vista." He spoke in distinctly mythical terms of an imagined "humble little church of my youth," a prototypical "little church in the wildwood" where despite its humble external appearance "when you open the door, you are confronted with this glory to the honor of God, and who would expect to see this inside a little country church? The glittering chandeliers, the pillars, these are the kinds of things you see in the cathedrals and the great churches of Rome."

FIGURE 4.2. Chapel altar. Photo: ATR.

From just inside the front door, the altar is clearly visible (figure 4.2). The intimacy of the size and scale is a striking feature of the chapel. Mascherino spoke to me frequently of this, and I often observed empirical examples of the intimate interaction between chaplain and congregation enabled by the fact that, as he put it, one can "stand on the edge of the sanctuary and reach out and the person in the front row could reach out and we could shake hands." More than once, I saw him stop to greet someone entering through the front door in the middle of some event. Indeed, the first time I visited the chapel, I had spoken with him on his cell phone when I was uncertain of the way from Shanksville and, after he gave me directions and I attempted five minutes later to enter inconspicuously, he greeted me from the altar as I came through the door and invited me to come up to introduce myself to the group. To my surprise, he was at the time addressing a busload of perhaps 25 or 30 tourists and had apparently taken my phone call in the middle of the address.

At the immediate right on entering the chapel is the meditation room (figure 4.3). Here, one gets a first powerful glimpse of the symbolism at the heart of the chapel's civil religion. Mounted on the wall at the far end of the room is a mural depicting an American flag and bald eagle. Below it, on all sides of the room save that which holds the doorway, hang individual framed biographies of the 40 passengers with photos. Below the biographies runs a ledge bearing votive candles; a visitor can add his or her own candle to the collection to indicate, as in traditional Catholic practice, that one is praying for the souls of the departed. Civil religious and religious iconography and symbol weave seamlessly together here. There is some symbolic complication, however. Below the martial American eagle and flag motif, to the left of the entrance, are two flags that escape the nationalist dominance of the American symbolism. Alongside the biographies of the two passengers who were foreign nationals, Toshiya Kuge (a 20-year-old Japanese exchange student) and Christian Adams (a 37-year-old German wine exporter), stand their respective national flags. In the absence of wind, they remain unfurled and so are visually less imposing than the iconic American flag imagery

FIGURE 4.3. Meditation room. Photo: ATR.

FIGURE 4.4. Eagle and flag-motif sky above altar. Photo: ATR.

on the wall, but there they are nonetheless to challenge the otherwise monotone language of American national identity. It is perhaps also of some relevance for the meanings they have in such a juxtaposition that these are not just any two flags; they are the flags of the two chief enemies of the American nation in the great international conflict that stands as perhaps the main modern generator of meaning in the American civil religion. So, here, in the very entrance of the chapel, and in the context of an otherwise monolithic narrative of American patriotism, one finds symbolic material that challenges the neatness of the narrative of America confronted by her enemies.

The iconic eagle of the Meditation Room also soars behind and above the altar (figure 4.4). This primal symbol of ascension, profoundly linked to American patriotic narratives from early in American history,[3] flies in a blue heaven swept by clouds that are heavenly white in its upper levels and fiery red below. Dotting that celestial sky are 40 stars, each one representing a passenger on Flight 93. Only 38 are visible, Mascherino once explained to me, as they were painted before the eagle was mounted and the icon of flight now blocks the visitor's view of two of the stars. In red letters on the wall directly behind the altar are the words "One Nation Under God." Below that, more text:

> And his name shall be called
> Wonderful
> Counselor
> Almighty God
> Everlasting Father
> Prince of Peace.

This is from Isaiah 9:6, an Old Testament passage frequently pointed to by Christians as prophecy of the coming of Jesus, yet the titles given the national God here are denominationally unspecific and arguably point not to Jesus but instead to the lawgiver Judeo-Christian God described by Robert Bellah as the deity of the American civil religion.

Altar and political monument here become indistinguishable. One comes to this place to worship both the Judeo-Christian God who protects the American polity and that American polity itself. Mascherino's phrase "Thunder on the Mountain" already places the memorial in a powerfully resonant social imaginary for American Christians and Jews. The mythical narrative that Mascherino chose to connect the memorial to is one of the most essential in Judaism and Christianity: that of the giving of the Ten Commandments. In this episode from the Old Testament, the Israelites, after their emancipation from Egypt, arrive at Mount Sinai, where they are told by their God, "You shall be my special possession, dearer to me than all other people, though all the earth is mine. You shall be to me a kingdom of priests, a holy nation."[4] How will this covenant be ritually formalized? Yahweh informs Moses: "I am coming to you in a dense cloud. . . . Go to the people and have them sanctify themselves today and tomorrow. . . . [O]n the third day the Lord will come down on Mount Sinai before the eyes of all the people."[5] There are strict ritual demands made; no one, save for Moses himself, must go up the mountain during this time, nor even touch it, under penalty of death. The Israelites are to go to the base of the mountain where they will be able to perceive the miraculous appearance of their God:

> On the morning of the third day there were peals of thunder and lightning, and a heavy cloud over the mountain, and a very loud trumpet blast, so that all the people in the camp trembled. But . . . they stationed themselves at the foot of the mountain. Mount Sinai was all wrapped in smoke, for the Lord came down upon it in fire. The smoke rose from it as though from a furnace, and the whole mountain trembled violently. The trumpet blast grew louder and louder, while Moses was speaking and God answering him with thunder. When the Lord came down to the top of Mount Sinai, he summoned Moses to the top of the mountain, and Moses went up to him.[6]

At the mountain's summit, Moses receives the Ten Commandments and then descends to the people with this sign of the covenant and of Israel's special status before God.

It becomes evident on close examination of the chapel's invocation of symbols with religious significance how carefully they were chosen to avoid falling too narrowly into one or another denomination's specific religious narratives. The God invoked is, again, not the Christian God. He is a Judeo-Christian deity stripped of the attributes that would too narrowly identify him with one or another religious community and make it harder to reach the wide community of Americans infused with broad, amorphous Judeo-Christian narratives. There is no prominent Christ on the cross at the chapel, and a stained-glass window above the entryway solidly ties the chapel's religious message into the Old Testament. It bears the Hebrew text for "Zion" along with representations of the Mosaic law tablets and a menorah.

It is not hard to locate the ways in which this narrative functions in the visual aspects of the chapel. Flight 93 becomes the voice of God, the thunder and lightning on the mountain that brings the message of chosen status and holy covenant to the people on the ground below. It is a terrible thing to behold, as is the appearance of Yahweh to the Israelites at Sinai, and severe ritual restrictions are necessary in order even to survive the sighting. But the ultimate meaning is the confirmation of the status of America as holy nation. In this way, the seeming defeat of 9/11, the destruction of the entire crew and passengers, and elsewhere the destruction of many more lives and monuments to American success, is all symbolically converted to spiritual and moral victory. America's God chooses a harrowing mechanism for the delivery, or *re*delivery, of the covenant message, but this is only to assure His people of His majesty and the seriousness of the affair. Has He not after all "raised [them] up on eagle wings"[7] to bring them out of their bondage? The eagles in the chapel and on the flagpole at its entrance serve as a reminder of this deliverance. The schemata of ascension in the flight of the eagle is one of the most basic languages of the imaginary; it represents the path upward, toward the heavens.[8] Valorization and verticalization are firmly attached in much human symbolism. As the mythologist Gilbert Durand has noted, the role of the stair or ladder in primitive and classic myth is a powerful example, and not only is it so that "the exemplary means of ascension is the wing," but also that "for the Semitic-Christian tradition, the multiplication of wings is a symbol of purity; wings are the stripes of the heavenly army in the six-winged seraphim of Isaiah's vision. . . . [A]ll elevation is isotopic with purification because it is essentially angelic."[9] We might say much more about the importance of such ascending motifs to 9/11: towers, ladders, stairs, the various narratives of firemen rising up those stairs to rescue the trapped, despite their own interests in self-preservation, and who, in climbing the stairs, move upward toward the heavens, which they finally reach, in the view of many onlookers, by their act of ascension, even as the crumbling tower forces them physically into descent. Planes are obviously a focal object of the events of 9/11, and the role of flight in our collective imagination and dream life is profound. Along with the cinema, which gave us the magic of seeing the dead move about before us, a second magical machine, the airplane, emerged at the beginning of the 20th century to make real something previously attainable only in the realm of the magical. Before there were planes, only angels had wings.[10]

To the left of the altar stands a large plaque bearing each of the passengers' names. To the right, an identically sized plaque bears the phrase "We shall not falter, we shall not waver, we shall not fail," followed by names of political figures associated with the response to the 9/11 attacks: President Bush, Dick Cheney, Condoleezza Rice, Donald Rumsfeld, Queen Elizabeth II and Tony Blair, the late Pope John Paul II, former New York City mayor Rudy Giuliani, former head of the Department of Homeland Security Tom Ridge, former Pennsylvania representative John Murtha, former Pennsylvania attorney general Mick Fischer, and a collection of local officials including the Somerset County coroner and the mayor, fire chief, and assistant fire chief of Shanksville. Red, white, and blue altar candles are mounted below this plaque, and several American flags frame it. Another item of note on the right of the altar is the gift of a former Marine of an Eagle, Globe and Anchor emblem worn on Marine uniforms. It is mounted on a wood plaque with a carved message: "The brave Americans who boarded Flight 93 did not know they would be called upon to become warriors for good in the ever present battle between good and evil. Even so, they excercised [sic] their God given right to freedom by taking a vote and then took Osama's killers to the ground. Since I do not know of any who earned

FIGURE 4.5. "287 Patriots" painting. Photo: ATR.

the eagle, globe & anchor, I am leaving them all one of mine.—Semper Fi." On the right of the plaque is an image of the Archangel Michael, chief of the forces of light in the war in heaven, crushing Satan's head beneath his foot. Just prior to the September 11, 2011, ceremonies at the chapel, Mascherino received a new piece of material culture that immediately took up a place of honor to the right of the altar during the day's events. It was a donation from United Airlines: a beverage cart, as an accompanying plaque specifies, "the exact model that would have been aboard Flight 93" which was "believed to have been used by the Heroes as a battering ram to gain entrance into the cockpit."

One of the most striking pieces of culture in the chapel can be seen on the wall to the right of the altar. It is a painting by a local artist identified on the painting only as "Doree," depicting four planes soaring into the heavens (not crashing downward, but going up and thereby marking spiritual ascension) into the waiting hands of a nondenominational, civil religious God, while below are visible the smoking remains of the World Trade Center, the damaged Pentagon, and the hole in the Shanksville field made by Flight 93 (figure 4.5). The artist titled the painting

"287 Patriots," and I initially suspected this was intended to represent the passengers and crew who had perished on the four planes, but the actual number of those dead on the planes is 246: 40 on Flight 93, 87 on Flight 11, 59 on Flight 77, and 60 on Flight 175. I asked Mascherino about the title and he too was puzzled by its referent. My efforts to contact the painter to inquire about the title proved fruitless. The puzzle of the title, however, clearly does not prevent visitors from viscerally connecting to the message; virtually every time I have been in the chapel, I have seen people gazing intently and with evident emotion at this canvas.

There is another collection of objects at the chapel that are infused with a yet greater symbolic valence, a discernibly more potent variety of sacredness that separates them from these objects I have just described and marks them with a power viscerally felt with a particular intensity by many who visit. Resting in the crook of one of the chapel windows is a hermetically sealed and folded flag in a triangular glass case bearing an inscription that tells viewers it was flown at and thereby consecrated by its proximity to the World Trade Center site on the sacred date of the Fourth of July, 2004. Just in front of this flag sits a chunk of construction block in the shape of a half circle, labeled "Pentagon Remnant 9/11/2001." In another window rests a solder-covered piece of I-beam from the World Trade Center wreckage. Behind the chapel, alongside the fence marking the border between the it and the guesthouse, there is another remnant of the World Trade Center, this one a massive metallic object weighing, by Mascherino's account, close to a ton that has been welded and cut to name Flight 93 and the three locations where hijacked planes struck ground on September 11 (figure 4.6). These objects taken from the World Trade Center and Pentagon sites are places where visitors frequently leave monetary donations to the chapel, although there is a neatly labeled box at the chapel's entrance, with envelopes on top, designed for this purpose. I have watched visitors spend long moments before these objects, touching and caressing them with great care and expectation. During the ceremonies of September 11, 2011, Mascherino showed me a new gift to the chapel, apparently from a local resident, who had retrieved it from the plane's impact site: a small piece of plastic moulding, framed and labeled "Piece of UAL Flight 93 recovered from Impact Site."

Perhaps counterintuitively, in this site where the effort to attain a

FIGURE 4.6. "Flight 93" sculpture from World Trade Center remnant. Photo: ATR.

spiritual energy is so palpable, there is nonetheless merchandise for sale at the chapel. Much of it is displayed on a few tables near the entrance. Among the objects bearing the chapel flag or other messages related to the chapel are T-shirts, coffee cups, pins, caps, coasters, clocks, and plaques and wall hangings. There are even small framed reproductions of the painting "287 Patriots." The chapel receives no funding from the federal government or any other organizations and relies entirely on donations and sales of merchandise to keep the electricity on and maintain the building. Given the presence of consumer items at the chapel, how should one think about its visitors? Are they *tourists*, fundamentally consumers looking for leisurely diversion and opportunities for the acquisition of various commodities, some material and others ideal, as Marita Sturken would have it?[11] Or are they *pilgrims*, deep seekers of spiritual meaning and sustenance, looking for the salve for troubled and inquiring souls, and purchasing souvenirs of their visit only as a contribution to the continued existence and livelihood of this place of spiritual exploration, as is suggested by Rhoda Schuler in an insightful unpublished paper on the religious aspects of the two sites?[12] There are significant problems with either term. Schuler's take is certainly too neat. Even if most visitors come for profound reasons, certainly not all have deep religious affiliations or identities. In my conversations with visitors to the chapel, it has been an easy matter to make distinctions between those clearly absorbed in the idea of the chapel as a deeply spiritual place and those with a more superficial emotional level of immersion in its symbolic work. But classing all visitors to the site as "tourists" is even more problematic. The cultural conversation regarding consumerism at sacred sites is a charged, difficult one, but, in her book on consumerism and the construction of memory at the site of the 1995 Oklahoma City bombing and New York's Ground Zero, Sturken is unable to transcend simple moral condemnation of the "kitsch" objects she studies. American commemoration of such tragedies, in her view, inevitably circulates around consumer items such as the omnipresent teddy bear (these could be found at the Flight 93 temporary memorial as well) that create a "culture of comfort," and this culture of comfort ineluctably leads to "depoliticization" and inauthenticity.[13] It is far from clear, however, that the mere fact that tourist goods are for sale at such sites forecloses the possibility of a deep emotional experience nor that only in the absence of such goods could a properly historical understanding of the event commemorated be possible. Careful study requires that we acknowledge the immense complexity and even contradiction in the ways meaning can work in such places. I have struggled over the distinction between tourism and the pilgrimage. Some who visit the chapel are indeed pilgrims, in a religious sense, a civil religious sense, or both, while others are obvious tourists. Yet still others, and this is perhaps the majority, are some combination of the two that changes from moment to moment and experience to experience. In the end, we might perhaps do best to put aside the pilgrim/tourist distinction as a lens that, if wielded too readily during the course of the investigation, threatens to influence the conclusions before they can even be produced.

The symbolic work at the chapel is not all being done inside the building. Behind the building stretches a garden containing a number of memorial objects. The large remnant from the structure of one of the World Trade Center towers that was already mentioned is, despite its size, not the centerpiece of the garden's commemorative symbols. That role is reserved for the immense black marble block bearing the names and images of Flight 93's crew and the four benches in matching black marble, arranged on a stone octagon, inscribed with the names of the passengers that frame it and the message "A Grateful Nation Will Forever Honor The Courage And Patriotism Of The Flight 93 Passengers." This impressive structure was provided to the chapel by United Airlines. An iconic plane sits atop the monument, its nose tilted, inevitably in this symbolic universe, upward toward the heavens. The garden is the scene for significant activity during the annual September 11 events. On the anniversary date, several large tent pavilions are erected on either side of the brick walkway and octagon on which the marble monument sits. Food, refreshments, and various site memorabilia are sold from these pavilions, and a number of tables are arranged for the convenience of visitors lunching at the chapel. The walkway and the octagon are on this day framed by the flags of all 50 American states. When crowds are too large to hold scheduled events in the chapel itself, they take place under one of the tent pavilions, which is equipped with a wooden stage. On September 11, 2011, on the ten-year anniversary of the attacks, the crowd was large enough that even the pavilion proved too small to hold them all.

An Ideal Typical 11th of September with the Flight 93 Congregation

The symbolic material at the chapel cannot mean anything unless people interact with it in specific ways, and the ways in which they interact with it change the meanings that emerge from the symbols. So we cannot stop at a description of the chapel in the absence of action; we need a description too of what takes place there when people come in search of these symbols. Cultural narratives do not exist as completely autonomous texts. There must be readers to decode their symbols, and those readers cannot do their interpretive work in isolation but must interact collectively at the sites where the elements of the texts present themselves. In this section, I will describe an ideal typical September 11 ceremony to show how meaning-makers come together there to reproduce and share the narratives about American society that are encoded in the physical structures at the chapel. (It was as I was doing final revisions of this manuscript that I learned of Mascherino's death, and I decided for aesthetic reasons to keep this part of the narrative in the present tense.)

Mascherino begins the day's events[14] by briefly and informally addressing the congregation. He is eminently personable and charismatic, full of energy, wit, enthusiasm, and the sparkle of authenticity and authority, and his personality is an absolutely crucial aspect of the overall atmosphere and cultural life of the chapel. Mascherino's charisma is, as is always the case, in some ways rehearsed and acted. Like a trained dramatic actor, an effective religious leader must be practiced in delivering stock narrative lines with freshness and vigor, in reading audience contexts and adjusting to them, in improvising within the limits imposed by structures. I have heard Mascherino repeat phrases, anecdotes, or entire stories nearly verbatim in various presentations at the chapel, and yet each time his voice resonates with authenticity, and the emotional reaction of the audience is unmistakable. Erving Goffman describes the potential problems created by the cynical social actor, who is aware of the performative elements of a social script and becomes too self-conscious of the fact and thereby loses the quantity of credulity in the play necessary for successful drama.[15] Mascherino is no cynical actor. He talks about September 11, 2001, as "the day that changed the destiny of man forever," as the heroes of Flight 93 "showed us how to live." The basic lesson they provided that day, he intones solemnly, was "never surrender." He closes his brief introductory remark with a vibrant invocation of the civil religious hybrid essence of the chapel's symbolic life: "We thank God for the blessings of freedom and democracy, . . . patriotism and faith, one nation under God, no such thing as separation of church and state, patriotism and faith are joined in our hearts." The congregation listens respectfully, even dutifully.

Then the ceremony proper begins with the Pledge of Allegiance. Everyone stands and joins in the recitation, after which they are told to remain standing to sing "The Star-Spangled Banner." A woman who is sitting at the piano (she is part of a musical group that will soon present their talents to the gathered congregants) tries to accompany them, but does not know the chords and plays meandering, disjointed fragments for most of the song. The "Banner," this piece of music that I would guess most Americans are so familiar with as to be capable of identifying it within a few seconds of the opening melody, thus sounds oddly mysterious, the sure incantation of the lyrics by the congregation mingling with the pianist's largely unsuccessful effort to find the tune. Only as the song is drawing to a close does the pianist seem to solve the puzzle and manage to close in the right key. My sense of the performance, which I do not know to be shared by the congregants, is of clumsy, artless, but deeply heartfelt emotional intensity.

Mascherino then introduces the pianist and the group accompanying her on this day as the Senior Serenaders from the Johnstown Activity

Center in a nearby city. The group's leader, a gray haired man perhaps in his late 60s or early 70s, leads them into Lee Greenwood's "God Bless the USA." This song has, by its peculiar cultural history, become a kind of nationalist, conservative political anthem. It was first released in 1984 and was used in that same year at the Republican National Convention. It has enjoyed three separate periods of residence in the top five songs in the country, each of them neatly coinciding with distinct moments of martial nationalist effervescence in the country: first, during the Gulf War of 1991; next, in the wake of the terrorist attacks of September 2001; and finally, in 2003 at the beginning of the Iraq War. Virtually the entire congregation sings along, especially loudly during the chorus: "I'm proud to be an American, where at least I know I'm free, and I won't forget the men who died, who gave that right to me."

Mascherino invites a woman to the pulpit. She sings a song titled "There She Stands," written by a Christian singer-songwriter named Michael W. Smith. Smith performed the song at the 2004 Republican National Convention, where he spoke of visiting with then president Bush in the aftermath of the 2001 attacks and being asked by the president to write a song about the day. "There She Stands" is even more drenched in traditional patriotic imagery than the Greenwood song that preceded it. The lyrics describe the "clear blue skies" and shed blood of veterans represented in the colors and design of the American flag, which the patriotic faithful will raise at the risk of their own lives. As the woman sings key lines in the song, congregation members enthusiastically respond. After the line "someone will risk his life to raise her," a hearty "That's right!" is heard; a loud "Amen!" follows "there she stands."

Mascherino retakes the pulpit and recounts the story of the establishing of the chapel. Though I have heard him tell this story numerous times, on each occasion his delivery is powerful and flawless. The dramatic skills of this former Catholic priest are formidable, and the effect on those gathered is visceral, detectable in a second visually and aurally. He builds the story in a crisp, taut crescendo, bringing his listeners on a thrilling journey, expertly adding colorful flourishes at just the proper instant. The room crackles with intensity as he concludes:

The owner of 84 Lumber . . . came with a check for $23,000. . . . [S]he looked at the plans, . . . and she said, "You know it would be nice if this was finished by the first anniversary, so if you don't mind, I'll just do it for you instead" [loud applause spontaneously breaks out from the gathering], so they started on August the 31st, 2002, and ten days later the chapel was finished [a chorus of expressions of awe follows—one man exclaims "marvelous!"]. Everything you see was created in ten days.

Mascherino then indicates the "Shanksville salutes the heroes of Flight #93" sign standing on one of the gift tables behind the congregation seating area. He describes his impression of the tenor of the words written on that sign and elsewhere in the wake of the events of 9/11:

> Have you been to the site? Have you seen the kinds of things that are written? What does it say? "God bless America, God bless the USA, God bless the families of Flight 93." And the churches were filled right after September 11, remember? . . . [And critics say,] "But where are they now"? Here we are. Just because we take down the flags after the Fourth of July doesn't mean patriotism is dead, and just because the people aren't going to the churches doesn't mean the faith is dead. They just don't go to church, that's all. . . . [F]rom the very start the response of America was an appeal to God. . . . [T]hat demonstration of faith is what this chapel honors, and the faith of the 40 heroes, after they found out they were part of this plot to destroy the United States, in one half hour, . . . 40 strangers got together and decided they were going to do something about it, and they did, they said the Lord's Prayer and they prayed the 23rd Psalm, and they didn't have time to say to each other "What church do you go to"? or "What religion are you"? but they prayed for courage and strength and wisdom and they rose up against the terrorists, and four minutes later the plane crashed in Shanksville, but in four minutes, 40 strangers changed the history of the world forever. What could 350 million Americans do, and we have the rest of our lives to do it? So the chapel is the sign of faith and it's in honor of God and in memory of the holy heroes of Flight 93.

It is not asked in this gathering, and one would probably not expect it to be, what evidence shows that the passengers collectively prayed these two prayers. Lisa Jefferson, the Verizon operator who spoke at length with passenger Todd Beamer, recounted in her book about their conversation that the two of them had, at Beamer's suggestion, prayed the

Lord's Prayer together, but she makes no indication that others were involved. Some news sources reported that Beamer and Jefferson actually prayed the 23rd Psalm, or both that Psalm and the Lord's Prayer, but Jefferson does not mention the 23rd Psalm in her book. A story in the *Greensboro News & Record* from September 21, 2001, by a writer named Kerry Hall claimed crew member Sandra Bradshaw's husband heard "three men . . . whispering the 23rd Psalm" during an eight-minute conversation with Bradshaw. It is not clear from the story how Bradshaw's husband knew exactly how many passengers were involved. It is perhaps not wholly out of the realm of imagination that there is confusion here with the mention made of the 23rd Psalm by President Bush in his address to the nation on the evening of September 11, 2001. The fact that there is no good evidence to support the claim about the collective prayer, however, matters relatively little in the attempt to understand the considerable mythological power of such a claim in such a site.

At the conclusion of his story, Mascherino notes that one of the altar candles has stopped burning. He asks for a member of the congregation to come forward to light it as he holds it forth reverently. An elderly woman in the front row steps forward at his nod, and with genuine pleasure says, "Thank you, I'm so honored," and does the deed.

The Senior Serenaders take the floor again, and the vibrant pianist Rose leads them in a stirring rendition of the hymn "Leaning on the Everlasting Arms." The congregation settles back in after the boisterous musical interlude. A man referred to by Mascherino as "Reverend Tony" then steps to the podium and, to raucous laughter, says, "I think that's a Baptist song, isn't it?" Mascherino adds: "Southern Baptist!" Reverend Tony then refers to Mascherino's earlier reference to the praying by passengers of Flight 93: "When Brother Al mentioned that they said the Lord's Prayer on Flight 93, it's like the puzzle pieces just fit right together, and God is in it." He then performs a startling, emotionally vivid sung version of the Lord's Prayer to the accompaniment of recorded music.

A performing group made of children, aged perhaps six to 12, from the Pittsburgh area called the North Star Kids then march into the chapel in exquisite precision and undertake a carefully prepared presentation on the passengers of Flight 93. One by one, the North Star Kids, wearing identical all-white outfits and bright blue vests (in some years, the vests are red), take the microphone and recite from memory a biographical fragment on one of the passengers. Just prior to the start of the performance, their adult director says they have individually researched the information in their recitations. The collection of biographical summaries is enclosed in a lengthy version of the hymn "You Are Mine," which is a narrative spoken by God Himself in which He tells the faithful that He has "called you each by name." The Thunder Bell is tolled with each name, then the reciting child provides a brief narrative. The details are uniformly hagiographic, indeed, so carefully directed toward the moral perfection of the passengers as to appear to have been written by a single author writing with only that intention in mind:

> He was a quiet, tender, and loving man. . . . [H]e loved his daughter and two sons. . . . [A]lways happy and had a big smile on his face. . . . [K]ind hearted and truthful. . . . [A]lways put his family before himself. . . . [L]oved his family very much. . . . [H]er two grandsons were her greatest joy in life. . . . [A]lways saw possibilities in everyone and everything. . . . [H]e would do anything to spend time with his daughter. . . . [H]ad a heart the size of Texas. . . . [V]ery devoted to helping other women. . . . [N]onjudgmental, easy-going, and polite. . . . [P]eople were struck by his friendliness and appreciation of nature. . . . [B]efore becoming a flight attendant she was a police officer but resigned because her heart couldn't take the pain of the job. . . . [A] wonderful smile that always lit up the entire room. . . . [S]uccessful, outgoing, and optimistic. . . . [L]oved his two daughters and wife very much. . . . [A]irline worker who gave unused airline meals to homeless people.

While a few of the biographical notes veer into the humorous ("Donald Greene, . . . he could open a bag of potato chips, eat two or three, and then walk away"), the overwhelming bulk of this material reads as an emotionally heavy encomium of the saintly dead. In some years, the delivery by the children of these biographical sketches is almost unbearably laden with sadness. Children weep as they say their lines, and the effect is magnetic, as tears and sniffles erupt in the congregation in response. In 2011, one of the young boys was crying inconsolably throughout virtually the entire presentation, and the crowd seemed particularly moved.

FIGURE 4.7. LeRoy Homer's model plane. Photo: ATR.

Mascherino next brings to the attention of the congregation the presence among them of special guests:

> We're always blessed to have family members in the gathering, and today we have members of the family of LeRoy Homer, the copilot of Flight 93 and last year his dear mother, Ilsa, brought to you a special gift: the plane you see on display in a glass case in the corner of the chapel was brought last September 11 [awed exhalation from crowd] and on that occasion Ilsa said, "I have thought about this for five years, everything I own that belongs to my son is a precious treasure and I will part with none of it, but I bring this plane to you, the people of this chapel, who come here to honor my son and pray for him." It's a way of sharing his legacy with us—you see the planes were still hanging from his bedroom ceiling at home and when Ilsa handled the plane she wore rubber gloves and when she put the plane in the case and took off the gloves and gave them to me, she told me, "Father, if you ever have to handle the plane, please wear rubber gloves, my son's fingerprints and his DNA as well are still on this plane. (see figure 4.7)

FIGURE 4.8. Honor Wainio's Christmas dress.
Photo: ATR.

Homer's mother responds, "You make me cry!" Mascherino gestures
to her: "There's mother, right there!" and there is long and sustained
applause from the congregation. Mascherino says, "We love you!" and
Homer's mother thanks the congregation for their reception. There is
more applause. "The family is a treasure. God bless the family!" concludes Mascherino.

The Homer plane (which, note well, is ascending) is not the only
object in the chapel intimately connected to someone who perished
on the plane. There are several other such gifts by family members of
personal items owned by passengers. Perhaps the most poignant is a
dress made by her mother and worn by Honor Elizabeth Wainio on her
third Christmas. It is enclosed in a case along with a card identifying it
and a photo of Wainio as a child wearing the dress (figure 4.8). More
recently, a rugby ball owned by Mark Bingham was donated to the chapel by Bingham's father; it sits in a sealed case atop the case protecting

Homer's airplane (figure 4.9). These objects are surrounded, in the cultural symbolism and discourse of the chapel, with an eerie energy that I will discuss shortly.

The ceremony moves on to another Christian spiritual, "God on the Mountain," performed by the same woman who had earlier sung "There She Stands." The lyrics depict the ease of faith in good times and the test it faces in hardship. The Senior Serenaders follow with two more spirituals. In "One Day at a Time," the pianist provides some skillful gospel harmonizing with verses and choruses. "How Great Thou Art" follows, the pianist playing unsure chords, the whole chapel singing along, but frequently out of tune and uncertain of lyrics. The energy of the congregation seems to have waned slightly by the conclusion of the song, but Mascherino then makes his last address to the gathering and instantly brings them back to a frenzied emotional pitch. Throughout the day, he has frequently tied the meaning of the passenger's act to a deeply mythological American politics of liberty. Their deed, in his discourse, was fundamentally an act of refusal to be told what to do and to instead assert the fundamental desire to live free or die that is the birthright of every American. "Liberty is not an automatic thing," he tells the congregation, "and Shanksville is the place where heroes died so the

FIGURE 4.9. Mark Bingham's rugby ball. Photo: ATR.

light of liberty would continue to burn." This is already heady stuff, but in his concluding remarks, Mascherino ups the ante still further and endeavors to ensure that his listeners understand that these are not simple and secular patriots they celebrate here, but full-blooded civil religious heroes whose act transcends the merely political and touches on the metaphysical:

> I see the stars, I hear the rolling thunder. "Thunder on the Mountain" is the message of Flight 93. . . . [A]s the plane crashed in the fields of Shanksville, it exploded and could be heard all across the hills, and shook the houses, and people heard it for miles around, and it was felt in Frost-burg Maryland, 35 miles from here it registered on the Richter scale, that's how powerful is the message of Flight 93. Once we've understand it, it will explode upon our hearts. Never surrender. Never surrender. On September 11, 2001, the old world passed away forever and can never be restored the way it was. The old heavens and the old earth passed away and behold, God said, "I create all things anew and this time I give you 40 . . . new . . . stars" [spontaneous awed applause from the congregation]— "40 stars to guide you in the darkness of terror."

"What did you expect to find in this field?" Mascherino goes on, in a phrase that perhaps might be at the origin of the misinterpretation reached by some visitors that the passengers rest in the graveyard adjacent to the chapel, "It's just an empty field. *Except in this field, heroes died.*"

Later, as the ceremony reaches its conclusion, he introduces family members of Flight 93's captain, Jason Dahl, who have come in midway through the proceedings and escaped his notice until that moment, and the congregation greets them with a round of applause. As we have already seen, family members and the objects closely attached to them are treated with a special reverence at the chapel. At one September 11 ceremony I attended, Deborah Borza, the mother of passenger Deora Bodley, was in attendance, and Mascherino introduced her at the conclusion of the proceedings. As the congregants dispersed, at least a dozen of them gathered around Borza, reverently shaking her hand and eagerly delivering their words of praise and love. The emotional intensity pouring out of these congregants was fairly palpable, and Borza seemed equally energized by the interaction. The Senior Serenaders then close the ceremony with a rousing version of "God Bless America," the pianist again uncertain of the chords until about midway through, then hammering them out resoundingly to conclude the day's musical offerings.

Everyone in the building is standing as Mascherino calls their attention to the bell tower in the front of the chapel. "You can see the crash site from the roof," he says, "and with the bell there is a mystical relation between the two sites." In the early days of the chapel, he tells them, visitors would sometimes ask him, "What's that sound?" as the bell tolled. His response: "It's the voice of Flight 93." As congregants prepare to leave the chapel, Mascherino encourages them to give the bell a ring as they exit to symbolize their own contribution to the moral project of the heroes of Flight 93.

Making Heroes in the Chapel: The Flag and Other Totems and the Hero's Body

It is perhaps true that no description can be fully analytically innocent, but in the previous section I made a significant effort to avoid the deliberate application of interpretive tools to the extent that is possible. Now, let us try to ground the description in a broader theoretical framework.

Though, again, there are no dead bodies at the chapel, there is a powerful cultural narrative at work there that requires dead bodies, and dead bodies of a particular kind, as its symbolic fuel. Dead bodies and their representations, even if they are not the bodies of heroes, take on special symbolic importance in every human culture of which we know. Durkheim's category of the sacred as that which is set apart, venerated, and protected by taboos from the profane is a helpful tool for interpreting the meanings the bodies of the dead take on in the actions of the living, especially when we understand the binary nature he assigned the category. Sacredness, in Durkheim's reading, could be of two types: pure or impure. One of his students, Robert Hertz, who himself died at a mere 33 years of age on the World War I battlefield in 1915, provided a superb illustration of the content of these two types in a study of funereal rites in primitive Polynesian societies. The dead man or woman becomes a generically sacred object, that is, an entity separated from the profane realm and imbued with an extraordinary energy or power, but the valence of this sacredness varies depending on the particular state of the dead body. The body in the process of putrefaction enters the state of impure sacrality, becoming a transgressive force that is to be feared, capable of defiling, even destroying anything with which it comes into contact. When decomposition is complete and the dead body is transformed into a skeleton, it becomes a pure sacred object, still possessing massive power, but now commanding reverence and respect, even requiring ingestion by family or clan members as a way of harnessing the sacred power. The meaning and structure of Polynesian funeral rites are intimately informed by this set of symbolic transformations in the substance of the dead individual, and while the specifics are limited to these kinds of societies, Hertz suggests, following Durkheim's lead, that the framework of pure and impure sacrality is generalizable as a tool for analyzing the meanings of death.[16]

The deaths of the passengers and crew of Flight 93 differ from the more ordinary deaths Hertz describes in a number of important ways. Not least of these differences is the fact, which I noted in the previous chapter, that the act that resulted in the deaths of those on Flight 93 can be understood as an act of sacrifice. The institution of sacrifice brings other forces to bear on the dead body, but the duality of this sacred power is present there too in the most obvious way. Whether the sacrificed being is human or nonhuman animal, the act of putting it to death is an act that removes it from the realm of the profane definitively. In fact, the process of sacralization of the victim begins before the actual dealing of the death blow. A whole series of ritual processes (bathing, the expression of laudatory praise toward the victim, conferring of gifts of various types on the victim, including sexual favors and edible delicacies) take place "in the course of which the victim is progressively made divine."[17] But the sacred status of the sacrificial victim is complex and neither clearly pure nor impure, for the act of putting it to death is at once a sanctification and a sacrilege. The act of sacrifice, according to Marcel Mauss and Henri Hubert, "can tend to both good and evil" and "the victim represents death as well as life, illness as well as health, sin as well as virtue, falsity as well as truth."[18] It can perhaps even be said that sacrifice puts death to use in the reinvigoration of life.[19]

The status of the sacrificial victims here is of great importance, as this is a case not of purely religious sacrifice, but of the death of the hero in an act of self-sacrifice. In religious sacrifice, the bloody body that brings grace to the community must be present. Congregants may even be required to ingest the flesh and the blood of the sacrificial victim, and the slain victim must be seen, adored, and feared in the physical form. Even in milder contemporary forms, the body of the sacrificed victim is present in cloaked symbolic form, e.g., the host at a Catholic Mass.

How then, if at all, is the hero's lifeless body present in the cult of the Flight 93 heroes? It is present, in symbolic guise, in the form of the flag. In a study of the cultural workings of American nationalism, Carolyn Marvin and David Ingle argue that American patriotism constitutes a civil religion based on the need for blood sacrifice. Borrowing terminology from Durkheim and Bellah, they present a framework for understanding American national identity as broadly comparable to the group identity formed in the totemic societies Durkheim studied. In the American national clan, the American flag is the totem representing the national group. More specifically, the flag is a representation not simply of the national entity, but also of the "the sacrificed body of the citizen."[20] The soldier killed in combat to defend the nation is literally incarnated in the folded American flag always given to the grieving widow and family, and such deaths are periodically required to replenish the vital energy of the totem. This all follows from axiomatic principles concerning religion, the purpose of which is "to organize killing energy" and "[t]he first principle of [which] is that only the deity may kill." In civil religion, the deity is the state, but it has the same prerogative regarding killing and bestows its protection on all those who accept its status and protect it with violence.[21] The "fuel," the "generative heart of the totem myth" in this reading is sacrificial violence and "the borders that a group will defend with blood ritually produce and reproduce the nation."[22] This view might initially seem idiosyncratic or even extreme, but it is thoroughly rooted in a literature in the sociology of religion that traces religious belief and practice historically back to primitive sacrifice, the form of ritual exchange with the gods that centrally involves violence and death, indeed, that may even require the sacrificial death of the god himself.[23] As Bruce Lincoln has argued, religion is fundamentally concerned with the determination of the proper authorities to be turned to for the most serious of human acts:

> Confronted with the disquieting reality of religious conflict, popular wisdom typically comforts itself with the ironist's refrain: "How sad to see wars in the name of religion, when all religions preach peace." However well-intentioned such sentiments may be, they manage to ignore the fact that all religions sanction, even enjoin the use of violence under certain circumstances, the definitions of which have proven conveniently elastic. In similar fashion, academic commentators often regard the religious side of conflicts . . . as relatively unimportant, or, alternatively, they deplore it as a debasement of all that is properly religious. . . . [T]heir analyses rest on an understanding of what constitutes religion that is simultaneously idealized and impoverished.[24]

Viewed from the theoretical perspective of Marvin and Ingle, the American flag becomes a central symbol for use in making meaning of acts of violence and death carried out under the aegis of war. As a totem, the flag thus arouses the greatest emotional attachment.

With this interpretive framework in place, we can look anew at the symbolic work going on at the chapel. The hero's body is indeed symbolically present there (and at the temporary memorial as well) and it is engaged in abundant interaction with congregants.[25] The basic meaning of the American flags present, in original and altered forms, is tied into the sacrificial death and transfiguration of the hero in this optic. The example that perhaps best illustrates the theoretical point is one I stumbled upon during one of the September 11 commemorations at

FIGURE 4.10. 40 totem flag bodies. Photo: ATR.

which I was in attendance. In the makeshift
parking area on the other side of Coleman
Station Road, which is situated just behind
the graveyard that visitors frequently imagine to be the final resting place of the Flight
93 passengers and crew, I noted a large
number of American flags in a mass (figure
4.10). Expecting nothing in particular but
mostly just out of curiosity, I counted them
and came up with precisely 40. I submit
that these 40 flags, mounted in a cemetery,
and also the Angel Patriots described in the
previous chapter that, until September 2011,
flew near the roadside fence at the temporary memorial site, constitute the 40 totem
bodies of the passengers and crew.

FIGURE 4.11. Mascherino's
Thunder Flag. Photo: ATR.

The American flag is a totem also in the stricter and more anthro-
pologically traditional sense in that it represents parts of the natural
world and establishes the link between nature and culture. As a classic
totem animal ties the clan members to the natural world and to one
another in relation to the animal progenitor, Mascherino's Thunder
Flag (figure 4.11), which flies at the entrance to the chapel, is explicitly
related to the four natural elements: earth, air, fire, and water. These elements are in turn seen as the original components of the nation itself,
and thus Americans exist in a familial relation with the natural world,
just as primitive peoples did according to their own totem myths. As
Mascherino wrote on the chapel's website:

The Thunder Flag is composed of the colors symbolic of the four elements of Creation: Earth, Water, Air, and Fire. The red is symbolic of
Earth, native soil, America, God shed His grace on thee, land of heroes
and land of liberty. White, symbolic of Water, the color of heroes, truth,
purity, commitment. Blue, symbolic of Air, the skies of America, oh,
beautiful, for spacious skies, and Stars, depicted here in white, but in the
formal design. Gold, symbolic of Fire, the eternally brightly shining and
infinite stars of the sky, as long as the stars endure, for that long shall

we remember the innocents who perished September 11, 2001. Four stars represent the four places of September 11.

Such symbolic attributions accrue not only to the Thunder Flag, but also to the national flag on which it is based. A document on flag protocol and symbolism published in the midst of World War II by the U.S. Marine Corps did not hesitate to engage in similar anthropological interpretation of the flag's elements:

> The star, a symbol of the heavens and the divine goal to which man has aspired from time immemorial, and the stripe, symbolic of the rays of light emanating from the sun, have long been represented on the standards of nations, from the banners of the astral worshippers of ancient Egypt and Babylon and the 12-starred flag of the Spanish Conquistadors ... to the present patterns of stars and stripes.[26]

On June 14, 1777, the Second Continental Congress, seeking to promote national pride and unity, passed a flag resolution in the following language: "Resolved: that the flag of the United States be thirteen stripes, alternate red and white; that the union be thirteen stars, white in a blue field, representing a new constellation."

So Americans are "born under the flag,"[27] in a deeply structured relation to that symbol and thereby to their imagined ancestral origins in the natural world. This is a useful interpretive frame for understanding flag symbolism at the chapel and at the temporary memorial site, including not only the formal, institutional elements of these two memorials, but much of the folk epigraphy and the gifts deposited as well, as so much of this material also bears the colors and the symbols of the flag. In each of these, the totem body of the hero finds genesis and rebirth. And what precisely do totems do, at the end of the day? They are tools for working out the omnipresent human business of opposition and integration, of creating, organizing, mobilizing, and reproducing the oppositional categories that are the very bases of human meaning-making, whether cosmos/chaos, Eros/Thanatos, or sacred/profane. The national totem eagle, surrounded by its 40 totem bodies/stars, in the red, white, and blue field above the altar (see figure 4.4), now makes better sense. Animals as totems are de rigueur in primitive societies, but Marvin and Ingle note that modern polities embrace them too, and especially the martial, aggressive, carnivorous animals who deal in the death that is the morbid but vibrant fuel that is required to keep the national engine running.

If it appears too much to impute such a ghoulish symbolic concern for the destroyed bodies of sacrificed national heroes to such seemingly innocent processes, we might note that, in the books they have written about them, even family members of the dead heroes have turned their attention explicitly to grim, transgressive speculation on the bodies of their loved ones. Deena Burnett tells us she "wanted to know what was inside [Tom's] casket."[28] Lyz Glick expresses the same dreadful curiosity and goes still further in her speculation about the fate of the physical essence of her husband.[29] Among the objects she was given by the recovery team that were identified as her husband's belongings was a datebook "covered with a fine brown dust" which "made [her] think of the dust from the African mummies when [she] studied anthropology at the University of Colorado. . . . Mummy dust."[30] In a short documentary film about the meeting of Flight 93 families with the actors who played their loved ones in the feature film *United 93* that is included among the extras on the film DVD, Deborah Borza, mother of Deora Bodley, engages in some chilling black humor at the expense of the actress who played her daughter at their initial meeting. She asks her if she has met Deora yet, and after a look of abject horror briefly passes over the face of the actress, she brings out an urn filled with ashes of the remnants of her daughter's body. She then tells a story of another urn of the dead woman's ashes speaking to another family member, in a tone clearly intended as humorous but that touches unmistakably on the macabre.

Mascherino clearly understood the sepulchral nature of the totem myth. He sometimes distributed buttons to children visiting the chapel with their parents that read "Future Hero"—indeed, he gave one to my daughter, personalized with her own name, on one of our visits to Shanksville. He told me that he has seen tears come to the eyes of parents on seeing the words of the button, as the realization of the true meaning hits. That meaning is stunning: the child as potential future sacrifice to the grim symbolic needs of replenishing the blood totem of the flag. He also frequently connected the chapel's symbolic work to the

American military in ways that point with some clarity to the interpretive accuracy of the theoretical vision of Marvin and Ingle. On September 11, 2011, while dedicating a monument placed at the chapel by the Somerset Garden Club as a "a tribute to the armed forces," Mascherino asserted that the chapel had always been "intimately related" to "those who protect us from evil," that is, the military, the job of which is, in Marvin and Ingle's perspective, to create dead enemies, but even more importantly to create dead heroes who can be transformed by their deeds into the clan totem.

We can also now return to Homer's model airplane, Bingham's rugby ball, and Wainio's Christmas dress equipped with this interpretive framework and perhaps make deeper sense of their meaning. The peculiar nature of the sacredness of these objects now becomes clearer. The DNA on them is detectable only with instruments of far more sensitivity than our eyes, ears, nose, or touch, and neither it nor any other merely material trace can serve as the explanatory root of the sacred power of the objects, but their status as the symbolic flesh of the martyred heroes, as sacred relics of the saintly dead, stands out resolutely. We might also note that they connect us to the childhoods of heroes who died as adults, and thereby invoke an ancient symbolic connection between the child and rebirth, or defeat of death.[31] They take visitors back to the pristine moments of the pure, innocent youth of these three passengers and thereby conquer death, although only temporarily and although death is, as the twin of rebirth, also necessarily invoked by them. It is to ensure their status on the side of the pure sacred that they are drawn back to the pristine state of childhood. Like the flag totem, these objects from the childhoods of the heroes recall their sacrificed bodies, but in an apotheosized, symbolic form, rather than in the cruel realism of their obliterated, final state.

Far from being weakened by the tragic fate of the hero, according to Henri Hubert, hero mythologies almost depend on the hero's crushing defeat, his physical destruction and even his failure to fully achieve his goals, for their narrative strength:

> [W]hen the story turns too well, its hero remains a stranger to us, he does not touch us; he is not near or real enough to us. . . . [A] hero is complete only if he meets a tragic end and, more still, it seems, if the society

that sees itself in him has suffered over his disaster. It is astonishing that people take pleasure in commemorating their defeats. The retrospective suffering that they experience here is a source of intimate satisfactions.[32]

Perhaps, then, the symbolic work of the flag totem is not only in its martial, sacrificial value as the fuel for the reproduction of the bond between us and the barrier between us and the totem enemy, but also in its ability to speak to the fascinating desire people have to melancholically reflect on the morbid reality of death, even the deaths of their greatest heroes in the midst of struggles of monumental importance, and cultural defeat. The Flight 93 heroes, it would seem, are not solely Christian martyrs, or civil religious flag bodies, or tragic heroes in an essentially pre-Christian Greek mode; they might well be all of these at once.

Religious Denomination and Division: Civil Religion vs. Religion at the Chapel

Although the basic symbolic thrust of the chapel is clearly civil religious and nondenominational, religious denominational issues with deep roots in American culture are nonetheless present there. Mascherino was still a priest in the Roman Catholic Church when he began the journey toward creating the chapel. His explicit intention, however, was to give it a nondenominational, laissez-faire atmosphere. Frequently, he told me, people using the chapel for weddings, which take place there with some frequency, ask, "What are the rules?" and his response is, "Be respectful and do whatever you want to do." His informal, charismatic manner in the chapel certainly serves as a practical endorsement of his nondenominational attitude. He once cheerfully told me of congregants bringing their dogs with them to Sunday service: "The dogs come in and they lay down on the floor and pray with everybody else." While the body of the congregation is in constant flux and dominated during the events of the annual September 11 commemoration by first-time visitors and other relative newcomers, there is a core group of locals, perhaps numbering as many as 15 or 20, who use the chapel with significant frequency as their regular Sunday place of worship. This includes a mix of Catholics and various evangelical Protestant denominations. In addition to this core group, there are more intermittent but still regular local visitors; Mascherino gave me the example of a family who have a summer home nearby and come regularly during the warm summer months but not at all the rest of the year.

There were, probably inevitably, some significant elements of Mascherino's own religious position in evidence in the conduct of events at the chapel. Mascherino gave a Sunday Mass which is in most ways, in his words, a "right out of the book" Roman Catholic affair, though with the addition of some Leonine prayers at the end, including the prayer to Saint Michael the Archangel. He assured me that many in the regular congregation who attended this Mass are not Catholic and that this never seemed a significant issue. The prayers at the end of the Mass take their name from Pope Leo XII, though the bulk of these prayers (three Ave Marias, a Salve Regina, and a short prayer known as a collect) were added to the Mass by one of his predecessors, Pope Pius IX. They were commonly part of the Roman Mass from the mid 1880s until March 1965, when they were formally suppressed. In describing his Mass to me, Mascherino summarized the history of the Leonine additions, and in so doing clearly aligned himself in an important cultural struggle in the Roman church. The Leonine prayers, he told me, were instituted by Leo XII to "protect the Mass, as a safeguard from intrusion from external sources." It was so protected until the Second Vatican Council, when "they did away with those prayers, and after they did away with the prayers, all these changes started coming into the Mass, and this is what Pope Benedict is trying to undo. He's not trying to turn back the clock. He's trying to reinsert those elements that were so precious in the Mass since the Latin Mass was certified and canonized." In the early 1960s, the first change was made to the Mass since the Council of Trent, Mascherino went on, when the phrase "and her spouse Joseph" was inserted, and then the Second Vatican Council took place and many more changes followed. He spoke in the highest praise of the Lavabo, a prayer just prior to the consecration of the Host in the traditional Latin Mass, wherein the priest symbolically washes his hands in order to cleanse himself sufficiently of his own sin to be able to make the sacrifice. The prayer offered a powerful reflection on the terror of the priest himself, who, Mascherino told me, should feel daunted "as an unworthy minister daring to stand before God," yet it too had been removed from the Mass. It should be reinstated, Mascherino believed, and he invoked Benedict again in agreement when he told me he would be in favor of reinserting at least some Latin into the Mass. When he spoke of this with me, he characterized the Vatican II decision to eliminate Latin in palpably animated terms: "They said, 'This is too cumbersome, too lofty.'" His expression alone made clear his deep disagreement. He then described a passage in Isaiah 6:5–7, wherein the relationship between the holiness of the words of prayer and the status of the human who recites them is made manifest: "The Lord said,[33] 'The words you speak are so precious and so holy, you are unworthy to speak them. Your mouth and your words are filthy from the day you are born. I will cauterize your mouth and your lips before you speak my word.'" There is a prayer, he concluded, in which one calls on this episode and asks "as you did the Prophet Isaiah, cleanse my lips so that I can speak your word. . . . [T]hat's how precious this is." His attitude during this conversation was clearly highly reverent with respect to the tradition of the Church and critical of a number of the Vatican II changes.

But alongside this essentially conservative Catholic attitude to doctrine and structure in the Mass is a much less doctrinal, even radically democratic and, in the view of the Church, borderline heretical attitude to some of the ritual of the Mass. Communion at the chapel is "free and open . . . to anybody who wishes to come." "There are enough things in the Church," Mascherino told me, "and in the world that keep people separated from God. . . . This is not approved by the Bishop, . . . [but] I give general absolution because at other Catholic churches they won't let people go to communion." He acknowledges that this flies in the face of Church dogma but hastens to say "what we are doing here is more important." He constantly stressed to me in our conversations that the participatory rituals of, e.g., lighting the candle or ringing the Thunder Bell are the central aspect of congregational life at the chapel, and that they clearly distinguish the emotional energy of what happens there from what he views as the more prosaic, less intense experience visitors have at the temporary memorial. "Here, we have the plane and God," he argued, "and what else do people need?" In a video on the chapel's webpage, Mascherino told prospective visitors, "The chapel is not meant to be observed, like a museum. The chapel is lived."

Mascherino made the shift from nondenominational minister presiding over the civil religious chapel to Catholic priest officiating at a

FIGURE 4.12. Alphonse Mascherino at the chapel.
Photo: ATR.

Mass in part by donning different costumes. On most days and on the occasion of Flight 93 ceremonies, he wore the casual garb of the Catholic priest, a dressed-down black coat and shirt with a clerical white collar (figure 4.12). When he officiated at Mass at the chapel, he donned the full priestly vestments required for the event.

During the events at the chapel during the Fourth of July ceremony in 2009, I learned of some significant denominational conflicts and rifts that were simmering there. Mascherino related to me that several volunteers had recently left over disputes with him. Two were elderly born-again Christians who routinely spoke loudly during ceremonies and then took umbrage when they were asked to quiet down. Mascherino learned from other volunteers after the departure of these two that they had been saying disparaging things about Catholicism out of his earshot. They had repeatedly hinted to him of their hope that he would have a "change of heart," eliminate the Catholic elements of the chapel ceremonies, and be born again. During this same period, Mascherino learned that a third volunteer, a young member of a Christian motorcycle group who had been spending significant time at the chapel, was attempting to evangelize visitors, preaching to them a "Jesus Christ is the only way" message. Mascherino was visibly perturbed by this position when he related the story to me, reemphasizing the nondenominational nature of the chapel. This kind of fairly open Protestant anti-Catholic bigotry runs against the claims by some[34] that religious conflict and division in contemporary America can no longer be understood by older discourses of denominational conflict but instead must be seen as struggles between orthodox and progressive religious groups of different denominations. Flight 93 Chapel theology and moral positioning is, on most issues, easily as orthodox as that of the evangelical Christianity of some of the groups who make use of the chapel, but this cultural political similarity does not obviate rifts of a more historical pedigree in American society.

The story of Mascherino's conflict with his bishop, beginning with the latter's discovery of the existence of the chapel and ultimately ending in Mascherino's excommunication, offers further intriguing perspective on the chapel's place in the American religious spectrum. Early in 2002, a local newspaper, reporting on Mascherino's purchase of the property, contacted his bishop, Joseph V. Adamec, in order to confirm his standing as a Catholic priest. Mascherino explained to me that he had endeavored to keep his role as discrete as possible and had not even told the reporter he was a Catholic priest, but apparently others interviewed for the story had passed along that information and the reporter had sought confirmation. The story made the front page of the *Pittsburgh Tribune-Review* on March 10, 2002, identifying Mascherino as "a priest in good standing, unassigned . . . with the Diocese of Altoona-Johnstown," and within two weeks, Adamec had called Mascherino for an interview about the matter. The exchange went thus, in Mascherino's account:

"What's this about you buying a church?" "I didn't buy a church, I bought a seed warehouse." "No, you didn't, you bought a church." "It was a warehouse." "It used to be a church, it was a warehouse, now it's a church again, and it's a nondenominational church too. So what are you going to be in all this?" "I'm going to be the chaplain." "I will never understand how a Catholic priest can be the chaplain to a non-denominational church." "Maybe that's because you're too denominational."

Adamec's reaction to the exchange was predictably unenthusiastic, but the official move to excommunicate Mascherino did not begin immediately. Initially, the bishop moved to assign him to a parish at some distance from Shanksville; Mascherino believed the intention was to make it impossible for him to administer to the parish duties and maintain his hand in the Flight 93 Chapel at the same time. When he balked, the bishop delivered an ultimatum: take up the parish assignment or he would initiate the procedure to strip Mascherino of his priestly office and excommunicate him from the Church. Adamec publicly made clear his position in a local newspaper interview: "The chapel is Father Mascherino's personal project. It seems his personal preference would be to be a priest in good standing, but to be [allowed] by the diocese to work in the chapel. That cannot be. . . . Father Mascherino has been quoted as saying he has not left the church or the pope. But by his own choice, he has left both."[35]

In the final analysis, then, should we see the chapel as Catholic or nondenominational, and, in terms of the American culture wars, should it be placed on the orthodox or progressive side? Though much of the symbolic work at the chapel, as I have described above, resonates with a conservative cultural vision, it would not be incorrect to say that in terms of its denominational identity, it takes part in the same movement toward the postmodern, postdenominational positioning that is more characteristic of the progressive side of the culture war binary. Several recent events point to still more complication of the denominational face of the chapel and its founder. In 2006, Mascherino accepted an honorary doctor of divinity degree from an evangelical Protestant seminary, the Midwest Seminary for Bible Theology, after its founder participated in the September commemoration that year and reached out to Mascherino as a token of appreciation of his work at the chapel. In late 2009, the nearly 70-year-old Mascherino began to think hard about how the chapel would carry on after him in the wake of serious health issues. He was diagnosed with a cancerous tumor of the vocal chords, and additional tumors were found in his esophagus and kidney. On September 27 of that year, a ceremony was conducted at the chapel to consecrate Mascherino as a bishop in the Old Roman Catholic Church in North America (ORCCNA), an independent church formed in the early 20th century that is not in communion with the Roman Holy See or the Union of Utrecht that broke with Rome over the doctrine of papal infallibility. Archbishop Joseph Vellone, the leader of this renegade church's California division, had attended several memorial services at the chapel, and this impressed Vellone sufficiently to make the decision to consecrate Mascherino.[36]

However, very shortly after this ceremony took place, Mascherino had a change of heart and broke with the ORCCNA. In October of the same year, he was incardinated in the Catholic Church of the East (CCE) and thereby came under the jurisdiction of CCE Archbishop Ramzi Musallam, Mascherino's close friend. The Catholic Church of the East is a Catholic Church of the Eastern Rite that is in full communion with Rome. Mascherino underwent treatment for his cancer and by late 2010 was nearly back to full strength, but he still felt the pressing need to plan for the chapel's continuity after his death. At the September 11, 2010, commemoration event, he announced plans for the building of a larger facility, perhaps in another location, with the creation of a legal foundation with an executive board and the aid of an architect who drew up a proposal for the new construction.[37] The proposal described about $10 million in expenditures that would be necessary for the construction, and it was not clear how the money could be raised. These tentative plans were dropped, however, when Macherino's health again deteriorated. He finally decided to leave the chapel in possession of his new church, the Catholic Church of the East, with Archbishop Ramzi Musallam as CEO and director. Mascherino died, in full communion with the Roman Catholic Church that had originally ordained him in 1976, on February 15, 2013.

During Mascherino's time as chapel director, there emerged another important religious presence at the chapel. This is the Christian Motorcyclists Association (CMA), an evangelical Christian group with chapters throughout the U.S. and internationally that endeavors to combine their evangelizing activity with their identities as motorcycle aficionados to minister to individuals and communities one might expect to be rather distant from the message of Christian repentance. CMA members frequently volunteer at the chapel, especially around the time of the annual commemoration on September 11, and every year at that time, significant numbers of the CMA gather there for specific events they have organized with Mascherino's approval and assistance. The week before the 11th, they hold an Annual Bikers' Patriotic Day Convergence at the site. Motorcycle groups frequent the temporary memorial as well, and the peculiar mixture of Christian faith, patriotic fervor, and subcultural identity these groups demonstrate makes them a fascinating piece of the Flight 93 landscape. In an ethnography of a similar group, the Black Sheep Harley-Davidson for Christ (HDFC) Motorcycle Ministry in California, Doreen Anderson-Facile examined the obvious conflict in identity positions occupied by the Christian motorcyclist. How is it possible for a member of a subculture with such clear ties to transgression and rebellion against moral authority to claim Christian belief, and often quite conservative, even fundamentalist evangelical belief, and integrate these two identities into a coherent self? The image of the outlaw biker has been somewhat tamed, beginning in the late 1980s when Harley-Davidson "capitalized on the romanticized image of the Harley-Davidson motorcycle rider" to attract "middle-aged professionals."[38] The outlaw biker image was turned into a commodity to be sold to middle-class bike aficionados so they could sip at the outlaw cup, however superficially and inauthentically. The members of the Black Sheep HDFC are in fact far from the biker outlaw in the Hell's Angels tradition; they are actually part of a large group of contemporary more or less middle-class bikers. Anderson-Facile found her biker sample to be Republican Party–identified and politically conservative,[39] and this seems the case for most of the CMA members I have spoken with at the chapel. The Christian biker juggles the two identities strategically:

> In the secular world, the Black Sheep member is able to hide behind the biker costume and bike if they are rejected because they are a Christian. In the biker world, if the Black Sheep member is not accepted as a biker, . . . they are able to hide behind the role of Christian. . . . It is as if these dueling identities are a safety net to secure acceptance or at least some degree of respect in any given situation.[40]

The subculture of bikers has long occupied a seemingly contradictory position in American cultural politics. During the 1960s, as powerfully visually evident in documentaries of the period such as that depicting the Rolling Stones' disastrous Altamont concert in 1969, they were outsiders vis-à-vis mainstream American culture, just as the hippies were, but largely intolerant of the left cultural politics of the hippies. They showed undisguised contempt for countercultural bending of traditional gender roles, pursued alcoholic excesses not for the expansion of consciousness but to show how rough and macho they could be, and vehemently and violently defended their stake in the personal, material property of their bikes (as the hippie crowd at the Stones' Altamont show learned to their dismay). Anderson-Facile suggests the Christian biker desires to sit somewhere between the identity positions "Christian" and "secular,"[41] and, in this framework, the presence of the CMA at the chapel makes a certain existential sense. Here, they find a space where they can be right-wing patriots and rebels, of a certain variety at least, at one and the same time, for the Flight 93 site that receives sponsorship from "respectable" institutions, and most importantly from the government (the congenital enemy of the biker outlaw), is not the chapel, but the national memorial at the crash site. It is in a certain sense appropriate that the CMA, in its complex and even contradictory identity in the field of American religious and political culture, found a home at the chapel, which has had its own complicated position in that same field.

5

The Permanent Memorial

Symbolic Work and Conflict in the "Bowl of Embrace"

A Memorial Contest

Notwithstanding the energy and passion put into the construction of the temporary memorial, planning for the permanent memorial commemorating Flight 93 began almost immediately after the crash. Joanne Hanley and Barbara Black of the National Park Service were centrally involved in the permanent memorial design competition and preparation from the first, and they provided me with a detailed insider history of the trajectory from the first thoughts on the memorial to its currently ongoing construction. Their accounts, together with written records of the process, provide important insights into the cultural narratives and processes that informed the conception of the Flight 93 permanent memorial.

The production of a memorial, like that of a work of art, is a social process involving many actors. Just as sociologists speak of the art worlds that make and use art objects, we can speak of memorial worlds that make and use memorials, and these worlds consist of a number of elements.[1] Among the groups contributing to the work of memorial worlds we can include, in Dee Briton's terminology, the Lost (the recognized dead), the Invisibles (those who might have died in the event who are not recognized as victims), the Bereaved (families and friends of the victims), the Survivors, the Creators, the Interpreters (those who decode the memorial's meaning, including tourists), the Agents and the Perpetrators (respectively, those "supporting . . . [and] those challenging status quo"—chief among the latter are the terrorists), and the Gatekeepers ("those designated by Public Agents to control the production and reception of public memorials").[2] Hanley was adamant about distinguishing the Park Service–sponsored memorial project from the

Flight 93 Chapel of Alphonse Mascherino, referring to the latter as "singular" and emanating ultimately from the efforts of a sole individual, while the permanent memorial idea and project was a collective labor involving the entire community of Shanksville and many others as well. Ultimately, she told me, the Park Service actually played a secondary role, effectively acting only as a mechanism for the elaboration of a general communal will of the locality:

> We worked behind the scenes, worked with the county to have a town meeting in December 2001 to ask the town and county people, "Do you want to have a permanent memorial here?" We actually brought in people from [the memorialization project at] Oklahoma City. . . . [T]hey came and they talked about their process.[3]

By February 2002, rapid progress had been made. When John Murtha introduced the legislation proposing the permanent memorial that winter only five months after the attacks, it passed unanimously in both the House of Representatives and the Senate. In September of that same year, President Bush signed into law the Flight 93 National Memorial Act (Public Law 107–226, 116 Stat. 1345), and thereby authorized the secretary of the interior to administer the memorial as a national park. It had taken only a calendar year from the event to the passing of legislation for a government-backed memorial. The normal course of events involves several years to study the proposal, develop the boundaries, and formulate a final plan to introduce into the legislative process, but this event had proven extraordinary also in the facility of its movement through the bureaucratic and legislative channels. Once the legislation had been signed by President Bush, the Park Service actively began organizing a grassroots, bottom-up coalition to fulfill the mandates of the legislation. This work manifested itself most directly in the creation of a task force of approximately 80 members; one of the first tasks of this group was to nominate 15 members to a Federal Advisory Commission charged with three central mandates: (1) the selection of a design for the permanent memorial by the five-year anniversary in September 2006, (2) the development of a boundary for the national park at Shanksville, and (3) the completion of a general management plan for the park. Along with the Flight 93 Memorial Task Force, the Advisory

Commission, and the National Park Service itself, the Families of Flight 93, Inc., a certified 501(c)(3) nonprofit made up of relatives of those who died on the plane, rounds out the group of four organizations that have been overseeing the process of memorial selection and implementation.

Hanley spoke in a language familiar to those working in the social sciences when she described to me the organic relationship between the large Task Force and the more intimate 15-member Federal Advisory Commission. The normal operating procedure, she explained, would have involved small subgroups of the commission working independently on each of the three central mandates, and would almost certainly have taken more time, but the task force decided on a different procedure. The bulky task force divided itself into committees; there were, among others, a Mission Statement Committee, a General Management Committee, a Design Oversight Committee, a Fundraising Committee, a Temporary Memorial Management Committee, and an Archives Committee. The time the task members spent simply setting up its organizational structure was invaluable in terms of social solidarity. For the first three years of the task force's existence, there were conference calls lasting several hours, three to four nights a week. Hanley was insistent that this process work also enabled members to "form a trust, a backbone" that was indispensable in making possible the broad agreement concerning how to go about selecting a memorial.

As is evident from its name, the Design Oversight Committee was responsible for creating a process for the selection of a permanent memorial design. Two foundations provided a total of a million dollars for this task. Some of this money was paid to professional competition advisors who were to organize the entire process. Donald Stastny, the CEO of StastnyBrun Architects, Inc., and Helene Fried, founder of Helene Fried Associates, had previous experience working together in organizing a competition for a memorial to a terrorist attack; they had served as advisors to the Oklahoma City Memorial project as well. They decided on a two-stage design process wherein all initial entries would be narrowed down to five finalists, then a winner would be determined from these five. Hanley told me that selection of these advisors was in large part predicated on their strong support for the direct involvement of family members in addition to design and architectural professionals on the juries. The design competition formally opened on September 11,

2004, and was advertised internationally. Any group or individual was eligible to present a design with an entry fee of $25. Entrants received a packet of information about the planned memorial site and the competition process. Somewhere in the vicinity of 2,500 registrations were paid, but by mid-December, only a month before the deadline on January 11, 2005, the committee was concerned: only about one hundred designs had been received. It turned out however that a large number of entrants simply needed all the available time to produce their work. By the January deadline, over 1,100 designs had been received, including 565 that came in on the final day alone. Barbara Black spoke of contestants actually running up to submit their designs at the Park Service office in Somerset a few minutes before the official closing of the competition at 5:00 p.m. The response was tremendously diverse, coming from some 48 states and 26 countries outside the U.S. and ranging in quality from the most fastidiously professional to drawings she characterized as from "the kitchen table." In the end, some 50 designs could not be accepted because they failed to meet one or another parameter outlined in the competition booklet, but 1,060 proposals were entered into the first stage of the competition.

All of those initial entries were digitally photographed and publicly displayed in the Park Service's Somerset office. Submissions were made anonymous in the displays and only the competition advisors knew the names of authors of the designs. Black told me even she was unaware of this information during the first stage. Within a month of the submission of the designs, the first-stage panel, a mix of family members and industry professionals, met to winnow down to the five finalists. The Stage I jury was made up of nine individuals. Two of these were family members of Flight 93 passengers: Hilda Marcin's sister, Carole O'Hare, and Honor Wainio's sister, Sarah. The remaining panelists were professionals in the field of design and landscape architecture.[4] According to Black, one of the most important criteria used in this initial stage had to do with the entries' attention to the obvious landscaping requirements for a memorial on the site. As opposed to the memorial design in Oklahoma City, where the space was urban and needs beyond the memorial design itself were limited to the planning of parking facilities and a few other limited factors, the rural hillside in Shanksville called for a relatively elaborate effort to integrate the memorial into the surrounding environment. It was decided by the partner organizations that the boundary of the memorial should include the crash site itself and the adjacent area where human remains were recovered, the land from which the crash site was visible and necessary for visitor access, and "lands necessary to provide an appropriate setting for the memorial"— some 2,200 total acres in all.[5] To fail to account properly for the relationship of the memorial to the surrounding countryside would run the risk, as Black eloquently put it, of plopping an enormous hood ornament down in the middle of the field. Many of the initial entries were rejected on these basic grounds. Serious entrants distinguished themselves not only in their attention to the landscape, but by other means as well. Black told me of several hundred competitors coming at their own expense for a tour of the site. Although a DVD in the entry packet contestants received gave an elaborate description of the dimensions and characteristics of the landscape, physical survey of the site would obviously provide information that evades capture in even the most elaborate photo or video documentation.

During both this initial phase and the final stage, designs were available to public examination and the public was invited to comment. Once the five finalists were selected on February 4, 2005, each was awarded a sum of $25,000 to further develop their design and construct models for the use of the judges in the final stage of the competition. This was in part to help level the playing field, so that firms with more of their own money to spend on the design would have less of an advantage. The finalists toured the site in late February and again in April. They were given until mid-June to submit their final entries, which were to include up to six design boards, two three-dimensional models, a booklet containing a verbal account of the design, and a projected budget. A final jury of 15 convened to select a winning design. This jury[6] included six family members of Flight 93 passengers: Mark Bingham's father, Gerald; Thomas Burnett Sr.; Lauren Grandcolas's mother, Barbara Catuzzi; Edward Felt's widow, Sandra; Andy Garcia's widow, Dorothy; and LeRoy Homer's mother, Ilsa. The weighting of these 15 judges of the final selection was distributed between six professionals working or teaching in areas directly connected to the worlds of architecture, art, and museums; two members of the local community (one from Somerset, one from Shanksville); a director in the National Park

Service; and the six family members. One other family member, Edwin Root, a cousin of Lorraine Bay, served as the nonvoting recorder of the jury. Once the committee's choice had been made, the larger public's opinion was sought. Interested individuals were encouraged to read a preliminary summary of the winning memorial plan posted on the Park Service website during the summer of 2006 and affirm their support or disapproval of the winning design.

The five finalists acquired names during the committee process for easy reference: "Disturbed Harmony," "(F)Light," "Fields, Forests, and Fences," "Memory Trail," and the eventual winning design, which the designers had called simply "Flight 93 National Memorial" but which was identified by the committee by reference to one of its design features, "The Crescent of Embrace." "Disturbed Harmony" was submitted by an Israeli immigrant couple, Leor and Gilat Lovinger of Berkeley, California, where Leor was a graduate student at the UC Berkeley College of Environmental Design and Gilat was working at a local landscape architecture firm. Its key feature was a five-foot-wide, 2.5-mile-long "Bravery Wall," with a varying height, connecting a visitor's center with interpretive materials at the entrance with the crash site. "Fields, Forests, and Fences," the work of Laurel McSherry and Terry Surjan, who were architecture professors at Ohio State and Arizona State, was the outlier of the group insofar as, in McSherry's words, while "[t]he other finalists believe the site should be frozen in time, . . . [w]e felt we wanted to explore something else, a memorial that evolves over time."[7] This minimalist design borrowed the central feature of the temporary memorial, which McSherry had visited in the wake of the crash: the fence. The proposed fence here was even barer and simpler than the chain-link version at the temporary memorial. It was to consist of cedar posts connected by three strands of wire, from which visitors could hang metallic tags on which they engraved messages. A meandering line of hemlock and birch trees would lead visitors from the entrance to the crash site, where tombstones oriented in the direction of each passenger's hometown would mark the so-called Sacred Ground. The cedar-and-wire fence was to serve as a barrier protecting the burial grounds.

Perhaps the most adventurous and experimental of the five finalists was the entry by Ken Lum of Toronto, "(F)Light." The architecture graduate student quoted Marcel Proust in the text of his final proposal to illustrate his design's emphasis on living memory and its rejection of nostalgia. This proposal featured a path recapitulating the flight trajectory of United 93; as visitors walked along it they would encounter text and other interpretive materials. The feature of this design that most set it apart from the others was the use of a luminous, quartzite roof over the flight trajectory walkway in the section titled "The Passage of Collective Memory," just preceding the point in the flight path when the hijackers took over the plane. The roof was to contain text, which would require visitors then to look skyward through the roofscape. After the moment of takeover, the roof would gradually recede until it had entirely disappeared by the point of arrival at the crash site.

The last of the four nonwinning finalists, "Memory Trail," also featured a recapitulation of part of the flight path, as did the eventual winning entry.[8] The lead designer of "Memory Trail," Frederick Steiner, was dean of the School of Architecture at the University of Texas, Austin, and the three codesigners were all professors of architecture. The design's signature feature was an upraised, tunnel-shaped viewing area in the visitor's center that gave a view of the Sacred Ground.

The Stage II jury report of the meetings during which "The Crescent of Embrace" emerged the winner of the competition describes the decision-making process in some detail. Jury members were first given a site tour and a briefing about the memorial mission. There followed three days of examination and discussion of the five final design entries, in the context of the mission statement and the reports generated by the Stage I jury.[9] The general procedure for collective discussion was for one of the design professionals on the jury to present an overview of one of the five designs, followed by free-form discussion and questions.[10] Initially jury members were asked for their statements on each of the five finalists. By the end of the second day of discussions, two entries had been eliminated, though it is not made clear in the jury report which two.[11] G. Henry Cook recalled that these first two entries to fall out of the competition had almost no support from anyone on the jury.[12] Early on the third day, another entry was eliminated, leaving just two; again, the jury report does not tell us the identity of this eliminated entry. A vote was taken on the final two entries: "Ongoing discussion and a final vote by the Jury resulted in one entry receiving a majority of the Jurors' votes. By consensus, the Stage II Jury forward[ed] this selection of the Flight 93 National Memorial to the Partners with the full and unqualified support of each Juror."[13] In an August 2008 joint meeting of the Memorial Task Force and the Advisory Commission, Hanley described the final outcome in similar terms: "The majority of Stage 2 jurors voted for the winning design; the jury report shows that every single juror stated he or she would support it."[14] Tom Burnett Sr., who was on the Stage II Jury, has publicly claimed that the initial vote on the final two entries was nine to six in favor of "The Crescent of Embrace."

In addition to their decision on a winner, the jury issued statements about the merits and problems of the other four entries, and also offered suggestions to the winning team as to how to move forward. One of these suggestions was a call to "[c]onsider the interpretation and impact of words within the context of this event. The 'Crescent' should be referred to as the 'circle' or 'arc' or other words that are not tied to specific religious iconography."[15] The architects decided not to follow this suggestion at this stage, but this makes apparent that there was some recognition on the part of the decision makers of the potentially problematic nature of the very term "crescent" even at this relatively early point, well before the emergence of the significant public controversy concerning this matter that was to come.

In the General Management Plan Summary for the Memorial produced by the Parks Service, a mission statement for the memorial consisting of the following statements is given:

1. honor the heroism, courage and enduring sacrifice of the passengers and crew of United Airlines Flight 93;
2. revere this hallowed ground as the final resting place of 40 heroes who sacrificed their lives so that others will be spared;
3. remember and commemorate the events of September 11, 2001;
4. celebrate the lives of the passengers and crew of Flight 93;
5. express the appreciation of a grateful nation forever changed by the events of September 11, 2001;
6. educate visitors about the context of the events of September 11, 2001; and
7. offer a place of comfort, hope and inspiration.[16]

The plan also provides "preliminary interpretive themes" for the memorial, intended "only as a starting point for the memorial interpretive programs . . . [to be] more fully developed in time as we as a nation gain greater perspective into the tragedy." These themes are intended to "explain the significance of the memorial and help to place the memorial in its national and global contexts." The themes listed are:

Flight 93 was the only hijacked plane on September 11, 2001, that failed to hit its intended target. The crash of Flight 93, which occurred only 20 minutes from Washington, D.C., was the direct result of the actions of the passengers and crew who gave their lives to prevent a larger disaster at the center of American government.

The events of September 11, 2001, revealed the extraordinary bravery of ordinary men and women who, when challenged, responded with spontaneous leadership and collective acts of courage, sacrifice, and heroism.

The first responders, the community, and those individuals and organizations that provided assistance in the recovery and investigation demonstrated compassion and exemplary service.

Knowledge of the events surrounding September 11, 2001, contributes to a realization of the impact of intolerance, hatred, and violence.

The public reaction to the events of September 11, 2001, including the actions of the passengers and crews of Flight 93, led to a strong sense of pride and patriotism and an affirmation of the value of human life.[17]

The Winning Design

The creation of Paul and Milena Murdoch of Los Angeles, "Crescent of Embrace," as it came to be known, featured as a central element a black slate wall bordered by red and sugar maple trees that was to form a semicircle or crescent that conformed in shape to the natural contour of the field where the plane went down. Along with their design materials, the Murdoch team submitted a short poem that succinctly and lyrically summarized their chief goals in the design:

> Timeless in simplicity and beauty,
> Like its landscape, both stark and serene,
> the Memorial should be quiet in reverence, yet powerful in form,

a place both solemn and uplifting.
It should instill pride, and humility.
The Memorial should offer intimate experience, yet be heroic in
 scale.
Its strong framework should be open to natural change
and allow freedom of personal interpretation.
We want to restore life here,
to heal the land, and nourish our souls.
In this place, a scrap yard will become a gateway
and a strip mine will grow into a flowering meadow.
But more than restoring health,
the Memorial should be radiant,
in loving memory of the passengers and crew
who gave their lives on Flight 93.[18]

A memorial is, among other things, a mask. Its primary task is to hide the horror of the event it memorializes; more specifically, it cloaks the destructive effect the event had on the bodies of the dead.[19] In this and other ways, a memorial calls us to *forget* as much as to remember. Chief among the things we are called to forget is the terror of the thought of human bodies being ripped to pieces, instantly, without warning, and with no chance for reprieve or salvation. We are called to forget that some who were once here ceased in a second to be, and we are called to forget that their fate will be ours, perhaps not so dramatically, but just as finally. Catastrophic, mass death is perhaps the single greatest horror in modern life, and we cannot bear to look at it too intently. It reveals the instability of the life of the community, and we must work to forget that in order to regain the sense (however mistaken) of stability.[20] Memorials must studiously avoid representations of the actual nature of the monstrous event itself, and the Flight 93 permanent memorial design certainly does this; indeed, this is true of all five of the final entries in the competition. This requirement is so entrenched in the cultural rules guiding such memorialization that it is next to impossible even to imagine a Flight 93 memorial that would transgress this taboo, for example, by presenting a life-sized replica of the plane, at the micro-second it impacted the ground, front end folding in on itself accordion-like, terror-filled faces of the passengers visible through the windows.

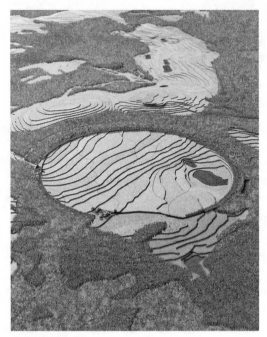

FIGURE 5.1. Three-dimensional model of the bowl figure in the Flight 93 memorial design. Image: Paul Murdoch Architects.

In the first discussion I had with Paul Murdoch about the memorial design, which took place over the phone, he made clear that the most informed conversation concerning its nature would be in the presence of the site itself, or at least with the memorial plans before us. So, I ascertained when he would next be in Somerset and met him there where, standing in the Somerset Park Service offices with several artistic representations of the memorial, including a three-dimensional mold of the land at the site that showed the natural outline of the bowl that is the central topographical feature of the memorial (figure 5.1), he verbally walked me through the memorial design. Tall, lanky, and soft-spoken, with a bushy mustache, Murdoch began by noting that the Flight 93 memorial will be the first memorial project for his design group. The draw of the Flight 93 contest for his team was not only the obvious, i.e., the chance to pay tribute to an act he described as self-evidently heroic, but had also to do with the fact that the intent of the memorial as presented by the four Flight 93 organizations was so well-defined. The mission and the site itself provided the guideposts for their design entry, and Murdoch noted that other memorial precedents were not consulted in his firm's design process as it was so evident that this project offered unique elements that did not lend themselves to being informed by predecessors. It was clear from the first that this had to be a "memorial landscape" and not a mere monument which would be easily dwarfed by the 2,200 acres of the site, which is, he noted, more than twice the size of New York City's Central Park. Because they received the materials after the final precontest official tour dates of the site in December 2004, they had not seen the physical site before producing their initial design, but Murdoch, who grew up in the Philadelphia area, had some previous familiarity with the landscape. From the beginning, the crash site was intended as the focal point: "We were not creating something sacred; that was already created, so we would not preempt that by something we created as a memorial. The focal point wouldn't be something created to represent that, but the actual place."

Murdoch recognized, however, that though the Sacred Ground, which he called "the cemetery, the final resting place," is inevitably, and rightly, the focal point, the memorial still needed to have other elements as well. He spoke of three central "moves" the team wanted the memorial to make: in addition to the focal point at the Sacred Ground, they wanted a memorial element at the entry to the site and they wanted "to recognize the flight path."

The first memorial structure visitors will see, on the memorial's completion, is the Tower of Voices, a curved structure with reflective white glass mosaic tiles on the outside and blue plaster on the inside to allude to the sky.[21] It will rise above the trees to exactly 93 feet in height, which, as Murdoch indicated, is imposing but still small enough not to interfere with flight paths for a local airport. It is intended as a "kind of beacon and welcoming feature," clearly visible from the Route 30 entranceway. The "voices" of the tower will be supplied by white aluminum wind chimes of varying lengths hanging in its interior, one wind chime for each passenger on Flight 93. Murdoch noted that wind is virtually constant at the elevated site, which influenced this element of the design. Symbolically, his desire to include a feature in the memorial that created sound was motivated by the fact that "a lot of the last memories of the passengers and crew are through their voices," that is, through phone calls and the black box recording. He described the tower as "a very unique musical instrument. . . . [W]e want 40 very different chimes, each unique in its dimensions, some as long as 10, 15 feet that will give a kind of subharmonic level of sound. . . . [But] we have to be careful of dissonance, because this was a harmonic action of 40 people."

Visitors will then be directed past this initial feature of the site to car and bike routes leading down through an approach area where the natural landscape will be scrupulously maintained. Murdoch constantly emphasized in our conversations the motivation his team felt to recognize the history of the land at the site in the memorial construction. The distance from the tower to the Sacred Ground is approximately two miles, and Murdoch felt strongly about maintaining some aspects of the "severe quality that characterizes the landscape." He traced the historical periods of the land: once wilderness, then cleared for farming and later mining, still later used as a scrap yard, and finally a burial place for culture heroes and the site of a national memorial. The idea behind the approach to this section of the memorial was the "healing of the land." Accordingly, the natural flora of the area will be allowed to remain here alongside sediment and acid-mine drainage ponds. The whole history of the land is what makes up its nature, and Murdoch was adamant that they did not "want to pretty up that landscape too much. . . . [I]t became clear early that the less we do, the better." The conceptual intent was to achieve a "unity in diversity" of the different landscapes of the memorial. He noted that the meaning of the memorial, and particularly the sacredness of the crash site, would be achieved in large measure by juxtaposition to the other, "more profane" spaces at the memorial site, particularly those that did not include specific memorial features but consisted only of features of the historical faces of the land.

The flight path enters the landform of the bowl headed toward the Sacred Ground from the northwest. It is commemorated in the memorial design by a walkway that cuts through large memorial walls that curve around the bowl and help define its shape. By intersecting the wall, the flight path is "framed . . . in the sky where the plane went overhead and visitors would have a direct connection with the flight." The walkway will extend a short distance into the bowl, giving the visitor a first majestic look at the enormity of the outlined bowl and the Sacred Ground in the distance.

At the end of that walkway will stand a lighted glass plaque bearing the memorial's mission statement, and a visitor center will be nearby with more interpretive elements and materials, including a rotating collection of the gifts left by visitors at the temporary memorial site. Murdoch emphasized the desire to allow the memorial symbols to tell the story of Flight 93 rather than rely too much on textual information:

> You have to be really careful about overprogramming. . . . [T]he only text we have in the memorial is at the end of the flight path near the visitor center, as you move through the two memorial walls. You move through that and you come to a promontory that gives you a first view of the crash site below the hill and you move through these narrow vertical openings in the wall and you come through that and all of a sudden the scale of the field of honor is revealed, so the contrast drives home that heroic scale. . . . [A]nd at the end of that is an inclined glass plane with the inscription of the mission statement preamble "A common field one day, a field of honor forever." . . . [A]nd then the only other place [where one finds text] is down at the Sacred Ground which picks up the flight path again. . . . [A]nd there are two walls that flank the gateway into the Sacred Ground, and the longer of the two walls has the 40 names inscribed in marble and the date, so we've tried to keep the text to a minimum.

In discussing the Sacred Ground more extensively, Murdoch emphasized its distinctness from the rest of the memorial and the unity of the entire site:

> You need some kind of polarity [sacred and profane, in this case] to make existentials, so it's important for articulation in design to draw on those distinctions, but it's equally important to recognize the symmetry between polarity and complementarity. . . . [S]o the continuity of this place that is defined as sacred is continuous with the quality of the landscape beyond the crash site.

The intention of the design is for visitors to be able to closely approach the crash site, which was always somewhat distant and removed from the temporary memorial. For this reason the black wall separating the visitor from the Sacred Ground is only four feet tall, and recedes back toward the crash site, creating a sense of intimacy despite the obvious barrier, which is reinforced with an approximately 12-foot drop from the wall into the Sacred Ground. Murdoch described a typical visitor as desirous of seeing the Sacred Ground first, and the memorial is designed to allow such visitors a relatively unmediated experience of that piece of the memorial, before perhaps retreating to the nearby visitors' center for interpretive material or embarking on a reflective, contemplative walk around the allée ringing the bowl in order to meditate on the experience of the Sacred Ground. The emphasis is not on "messaging" so much as encouragement to quiet reflection on the symbolic power of the experience of the memorial.

Murdoch was reticent to focus too exclusively on the notion of the sacred, a sentiment perfectly understandable in the context of a national memorial of an event around which have raged numerous charged debates concerning religion, not least of which is that between advocates of an unapologetically religious memorial and those who adhere firmly to the doctrine of a fully secular American state. However, the concept of "sacred ground" must be placed in an anthropological context in order to deeply comprehend the meaning and the cultural narrative power of the permanent memorial design. The term "sacred ground" appears in all five of the finalist entries, and presumably in all the Stage I entries. It was proposed by the Advisory Commission in the competition materials distributed to all entrants who paid the $25 fee, along with a basic structural view of the entire park, which was categorized there into constituent elements to be considered by entries. Beyond the Sacred Ground, the other elements of the memorial site given in the competition materials were the gateway, the area of approach to the bowl connecting the bowl to the gateway, and the ridge or high ground surrounding the bowl. It is not then as though Murdoch's team, or indeed any of the entries in the competition, were working from scratch; there was an archetypal framework, as it were, and the Sacred Ground was one of the key elements of the framework. Thus, it can reasonably be argued that the cultural symbolism of sacredness operating in the permanent memorial design winner, though clearly interpreted in ways that differed in some important ways by the five finalists, was more or less inherent in the memorial site as envisioned by the authorities who were given the task to select and implement a memorial.

Sacredness requires boundaries to guard access to the sacred thing or place, and the only means to bypass the boundaries involves ritual cleansing of the profane human being. Participation in the positive cult, i.e., the actual invocation of sacred entities and objects to receive their blessings and powers, requires prior participation in the negative cult, which is simply the prescribed ascetic means of becoming metaphysically able to encounter the sacred without immediately defiling it and greatly endangering oneself. Of course, traditional ascetic rites of the negative cult such as fasting, abstinence, etc. are not enjoined by the symbolic structure of the permanent memorial design, as in our contemporary world such prescriptions would be inappropriate, not to mention inconsistent with law, in a site created by the state. But the Sacred Ground of the crash site is protected from unconsidered, unprepared approach at the same time as, in a recognition of the secular consumer/tourist ethic that will undoubtedly inform a significant number of visitors to the site, the barriers are not formal and can be avoided by those determined to do so. The memorial is not designed to provide immediate, easy access to the Sacred Ground directly upon entry into the park. If one desired only to see the Sacred Ground and skip every other element of the memorial, one would have to drive several more miles after entering the park to arrive at the parking area near the Sacred Ground. It is much more likely that visitors will see the imposing Tower of Voices on entering the memorial and will then park near it in order to approach this first element of the memorial experience. Once that happens, the visitor is then potentially caught up in the other aspects of the park described above and led down the walkways in the direction of the bowl. The implicit attempt seems to be to create something of an ascetic, purifying experience for the visitor, a preparation that is, if not properly ritual, yet still centered on practical action that is profoundly connected to highly charged symbols.

Then, once the Sacred Ground is reached, the visitor discovers that the ground is taboo. No amount of purifying ritual experience can allow the visitor to actually set foot on the Sacred Ground where the heroes lie, as the area is off limits to all except family members of the victims, and even they require special escort into this symbolically powerful area, through a door that aligns with the flight path. The boundary between the worlds of the living and the dead is almost completely enforced here, making problematic the commonly stated belief that this site and the other sites of mass death on September 11 are to be thought of as cemeteries. Though we are generally still in the presence of specific norms that limit our behaviors in ways they are not limited in quotidian profane space when we enter cemeteries today, we nonetheless can enter them at any time we like (so long as the cemetery is not closed) and tread the ground beneath which the dead rest. If the Sacred Ground of the Flight 93 National Memorial is a mere cemetery, it is a strange one in which living visitors are prohibited and spontaneously agree to their exclusion. As I describe in chapter eight, only a very few of the visitors to the temporary memorial site whom I interviewed even dared to express a desire to approach the crash site, and some without prompting offered their perception of being unworthy to do so. If this is a cemetery, then, it is not a cemetery in which mere mortals are interred, and the entities who met their end here are entitled to much greater ritual protection precisely because of the kinds of beings they became in death.

"The Largest Mosque in the World": The Rise of the Flight 93 Memorial Conspiracy Theory

Within a day of the announcement of the winning design, critical responses appeared on numerous right-wing blogs and websites, followed shortly by editorials in a number of local newspapers that echoed the criticisms of the bloggers. The criticisms invoked a cultural narrative for making meaning of the visual form of the crescent. In the view of the critics, the use of the form of the crescent in the memorial amounted to a slap in the face of the heroic passengers and a de facto celebration of the hijackers. How? The crescent moon and star, it was argued, is a traditional symbol for the Islamic faith, appearing on the national flags of numerous Muslim countries including Pakistan, Algeria, Turkey, and Tunisia. Some of the supporters of this reading of the design went to great lengths to make the equation between the crescent in the memorial design and the crescent of Islam, superimposing the images in animated GIFs to show the similarities in the shapes, while others even endeavored to show that the orientation of the crescent at the

Shanksville memorial was toward Mecca, purportedly in consonance with the Islamic tradition of prayer facing the direction of the holy city. The symbolic strategy, it was claimed, was clear: this was a symbolic form dedicated to the ritual celebration of the sacred ideas not of the United States but of its *enemies*, i.e., the Islamist terrorists.

The symbolic universe into which the conspiracy theorists had launched themselves is a complex one. The precise origins of the crescent and moon as an Islamic symbol are somewhat unclear. It is generally understood, though, that these symbolic structures already had cultural and political significance (i.e., appeared on coins, banners, etc.) in parts of the world that eventually came under the sway of Islam prior to that time. The crescent moon has a central role in determining important religious holidays of the Muslim calendar, which is a lunar calendar in accordance with the prescription of the Qur'an. According to Islamic law, a naked-eye calculation of the moment of the waxing crescent moon is the final means for determining the start of a new lunar month, and thus the beginning and end of Ramadan and the proper time for undertaking the Hajj were to be thus determined. So, for example, in the year 2015, which is Islamic year 1436 H.,[22] it is estimated that Ramadan will begin on June 18, but the actual date may change depending on when the crescent moon actually becomes visible to the naked eye.

The National Park Service and Paul Murdoch's team of architects reacted to the criticisms within a week of the announcement of the winning design by pledging changes to eliminate the causes for consternation. Murdoch cited three main elements of the design that he felt were central and not to be altered: the symbiotic relationship to the topography, the presence of the flight path cutting through the central bowl, and the "embracing gesture of the crash site." However, he noted, the manner of achieving these three central elements was negotiable.[23] An altered design was presented in November 2005. Now the language of "crescent" had been removed altogether and the central region of the memorial was referred to instead as a "circle" or "bowl" or, more specifically, as "40 Memorial Groves," after the trees that would be used to close off the formerly crescent-shaped area into a circular form. Crucially, Murdoch addressed the claim that the original crescent shape could be shown to have an orientation on Mecca by extending the circle at the region below the intersection of the flight path.

If one now cared to check the orientation of the broken circle, it was demonstrably changed and no longer oriented near Mecca. But some of the critics remained unsatisfied. They charged that the changes failed to do away with the underlying symbolism and were merely cosmetic. The central advocate of the conspiracy perspective, a blogger named Alec Rawls, denied that the addition of the trees counted as a reorientation of the crescent. Rawls had apparently first seen the analysis of the crescent as oriented on Mecca on another political blog, then checked and refined the calculation himself in the process of becoming the de facto online spokesman for the conspiracy. In an unpublished book manuscript he has written on the subject of the purported memorial conspiracy and its Islamist symbolism, he charged that the flight path wall and the lower tree break point on the circle, the two points from which he had argued one should calculate the line of orientation, were still there, and therefore they still had to be understood as the tips of the crescent. Rawls continued to maintain that the proposed Flight 93 memorial was in fact "the largest mosque in the world."

The National Park Service consulted with architectural and religious experts to analyze the various claims made by the conspiracy theorists, and they were all resoundingly rebutted. The Park Service then convened an open house for discussion of the issue in July 2006, during the same time as it was soliciting responses from the public concerning the General Management Plan for the area. The deadline for public response to the Park Service proposal passed in late August 2006, and the announced outcome of the public responses was overwhelmingly in favor of moving ahead with the Murdoch team's design. This seemed a clear defeat for the conspiracy theorists, but they continued to advocate for their perspective, mostly online via their blogs and webpages, although, as we will see shortly, they were also able to gather some support from elements of the more established right-wing media and political worlds.

A Case Study in American Conspiracy Theories and Theorists: Alec Rawls and the "Crescent of Betrayal"

Although the Flight 93 memorial conspiracy theory has a number of sources and purveyors, one figure has been of particular influence.

Alec Rawls is a blogger and a former Stanford graduate student in eco-
nomics who has been one of the most prolific critics of the memorial
design, writing hundreds of pages online about various aspects of the
case and even producing an unpublished book on the topic. The son
of the renowned political theorist John Rawls, he was also significantly
involved in efforts to lobby the Park Service and other governmental
bodies to drop the plans for the permanent memorial. He has defended
his view in radio and television interviews over the past several years
and, with a few allies, has purchased space in Somerset newspapers to
advocate the position he takes on his blog.

His book manuscript, *Crescent of Betrayal*, was apparently contracted
with World Ahead Publishing, an organization run by two former Pay-
Pal executives that since 2007 has been the publisher of the catalogue of
WND Books, which is the press of World Net Daily, a right-wing web
news service. Representative WND Books titles are *Where's the Birth
Certificate? The Case that Barack Obama Is Not Eligible to be President*;
*The Islamic Antichrist: The Shocking Truth about the Real Nature of the
Beast*; and *Capitol Punishment: The Hard Truth about Washington Cor-
ruption from America's Most Notorious Lobbyist* (the author of the last
is Jack Abramoff, who was at the center of a massive set of lobbying
scandals involving millions of dollars in fraud, conspiracy, and tax eva-
sion). World Ahead Publishing features books on a range of right-wing
conspiracy theories and extremist topics: e.g., anti-Islamism (*Religion of
Peace? Islam's War against the World*), global warming denial (*The Sky's
Not Falling! Why It's OK to Chill about Global Warming*), anti–United
Nations sentiments (*Global Deception: The UN's Stealth Assault on
America's Freedom*), and radical American nativism (*Minutemen! The
Battle to Secure America's Borders*). In the preface to *Crescent of Betrayal*,
Rawls notes that in July 2007 the announcement regarding the outcome of the memorial partners' consideration of the criticisms brought
against the Murdoch design was to appear, and since his book was not
due on shelves before September of that year, the press had agreed to
allow free downloads of the entire text prior to its planned release. The
planned September 2007 publication date has, however, long since
come and gone, and the book remains nonexistent in printed form. On
one of his several websites, Rawls offers visitors a free download of the
entirety of the text, available only "until the print edition comes out in

2009." At the final revision of this chapter in spring 2014, the book had still not been published.

The claims made in the manuscript about the memorial design have received considerable attention from the right-wing blogosphere and from some larger right-wing media enterprises. These claims illustrate a number of the key American cultural fault lines over which all Flight 93 and 9/11 meaning-making is constructed, so the manuscript merits our interpretive attention. Dealing with conspiratorial material frequently runs the risk of giving the mistaken impression that one takes the claims seriously in deigning to discuss them in the first place. But just as socio-logical treatments of, e.g., religious ideas of possession or faith healing do not take any stance or make any judgment on the epistemological status of those claims in studying their impact on the human world, so sociological work on the production of conspiratorial knowledge does not make any statement on the validity of that knowledge or endorse it in any way simply in interrogating the social role such knowledge pro-duction plays and the significant social dangers to which it contributes.

The crescent shape in the original design could not be denied, and indeed no one did deny it. One of the several experts consulted by the Park Service to respond to Rawls's charges even acknowledged an approximate orientation on Mecca, though other experts more knowl-edgeable about Islam noted that a merely *approximate* angle would not satisfy the exacting requirements in the religion for prayer orientation. Another of these academic experts, a religious studies scholar, noted that the crescent is not monopolized as a design form by Islam, nor is the relationship between Islam and the crescent universally recognized. As for the crescent's orientation on Mecca, he noted that the object that traditionally permits Muslims in a mosque to pray in the correct direc-tion, which is called a *mihrab*, is generally a semi-circular niche in a wall. It therefore makes little sense to speak as Rawls does of a *mihrab* lying flat on the ground, as the direction of orientation provided by such a figure, when the crescent is gazed into as one gazes into a niche in a wall, would be straight down into the earth. Further, *mihrabs* have no relation to the crescent moon and star symbolism. The former predate the latter in their usage in Islam by something on the order of about five centuries. Traditionally, *mihrabs* are quite small and it rather surpasses the realm of likelihood that any Muslim would understand a shape as

large as the bowl of the permanent memorial design as a device for ori-
enting prayer.

As I described above, when Murdoch revised the design in response
to the controversy, he dealt explicitly with the claim that the crescent
was oriented on Mecca by changing one of its two points through an
extension of a line of trees that originally ended prior to the flight path
all the way from the Memorial Wall down to the Sacred Ground. This
fundamentally changed the angle of orientation of the object, but Rawls
ignored this and continued to assert that the Memorial Wall must be
the point from which the crescent shape is to be determined, not the
extended line of trees, although it is the line of trees that determines
the shape of the bowl all around its arc.[24] In a discussion I had with
her in late 2008, Joanne Hanley brought a very practical level of criticism to Rawls's abstract attack on the design. She made the point that
all designs change, often substantially, as technical information comes
in and responses to that information are formulated in the design itself:
"As you go further into predesign, schematic design, design drawings,
construction designs, *things move on the landscape.* . . . [E]ven as of last
week, the fence that surrounds the sacred ground, a new survey came
back and showed the fence at a totally different location than where we
thought it was from another survey, so that changes the location of the
sacred ground wall, . . . thereby changing the orientation of the circle."[25]
In other words, there was no reason to believe that *any* orientation of
any object in the memorial design could be fully and accurately pre-
dicted in its final built state from the plans, yet Rawls's argument rests
on this direct, exact correspondence between the design and the finished memorial.

But Rawls's criticism did not end with the claim about the general
shape of the bowl and its orientation. In his vision, the entire design
was saturated in explicit Islamic symbolism. He claimed that the stated
focus of the memorial, i.e., the Sacred Ground, is actually *not* the true
focus; instead, it is, in Rawls's view, a section of the Memorial Wall
above the flight path.[26] The part of the wall below the flight path was to
contain the names of the 40 passengers on separate sections, and Rawls
argued that these names would in fact be on glass blocks mounted in
the wall. On the upper section of the wall, which is, according to Rawls,
the "true focus of the memorial," the design supposedly called for four

additional blocks that allude to the four hijackers (although deceptively and secretly, since they could not actually bear their names).[27]

Rawls's argument regarding the secret dedication of the memorial to the four hijackers rests on his claim that the bisector of the crescent divides the upper and lower sections of the Memorial Wall, and thereby constitutes only the upper section of the wall as the all-important "star" of the crescent. It is here, allegedly, that the four hijacker blocks will be found. On the grand scale of the bowl in Shanksville, if we were to superimpose on the crescent a star of roughly the same size as the typical star on an Islamic crescent and star flag, it would easily be large enough to encompass *both* sections of the Memorial Wall, and therefore the section of the wall containing the passengers' names, which Rawls says is excluded from the star by the Islamic design, would be as much inside the "star" as the upper section of the wall is. Even more importantly, according to both the National Park Service and Murdoch, there were never any planned glass blocks bearing names. The passengers' names are engraved on a series of large marble panels, which are below the flight path on the wall. In the section of the wall above the flight path, which leads into the Sacred Ground, on three other panels the date "September 11, 2001" is laid out. More white marble stretches to the end of the Memorial Wall. Even if one corrects Rawls's glass blocks with marble panels, he had been able to find only these three additional panels above the flight path, and there were *four* hijackers. The fourth block, he claimed, was all the way up at the entry portal walkway, at the point at which the flight path breaks into the circle, which is very far outside of the small area near the Sacred Ground that Rawls claims as the spot of the star of the crescent. So, even in the terms of his own analysis of the memorial as containing glass name blocks it was never designed to contain, Rawls's argument is undone by the fact that the 44 pieces of his "star" are not all to be found at the site he designates as the correct and necessary place to give the memorial the symbolic meaning he claims. Once this part of the argument falls, the whole theory of the memorial as a terrorist memorial crumbles, for "[i]t is the forty-four glass blocks that turn Murdoch's mosque into a terrorist memorial mosque."[28]

Other features of the memorial design are subjected to interpretation from within Rawls's rigid framework. He speculates on the function of the Tower of Voices as an Islamic sundial that would, by its shadow on the surrounding ring of trees, indicate prayer times to the Muslim faithful. More, the tower seems in Rawls's view to have been inspired by the famous minarets of the Shah Mosque in Isfahan, Iran. Why? Because the Tower of Voices has a white exterior and a blue interior, which purportedly models the white-and-blue exterior of the Iranian minarets.[29] He tries to show that not only is the crescent oriented on Mecca, but so too is a semicircle of trees surrounding the Tower of Voices, albeit this is rotated 90 degrees.[30] He even finds a *third* crescent, within the original crescent, marked by the 40 groves. A line drawn from one end of these groves to the other extends, Rawls claims, southeastward to Washington, D.C., the intended attack site of Flight 93, which thus constitutes another terrorist feature of the memorial. Wetlands ponds sketched in the design are "ablution ponds" for Muslims to wash themselves in, and they are even shaped like kneeling, washing Muslims.[31] Even the chance angle at which the plane approached the crash site colludes in the Islamist grand design and makes of the Memorial Wall yet another indicator of the *qibla*, that is the orientation on Mecca for prayer: "It seems Murdoch had a bit of luck here. A *qibla* wall oriented exactly on Mecca would point 35 degrees counter-clockwise from north. The flight path comes down 15 degrees counter-clockwise from north, or 20 degrees off from the ideal orientation. That is plenty close enough to meet the Muhammad-standard for a *qibla* wall."[32]

Rawls engages in vivid speculation as to what he believes will be the practical consequences of these symbols he finds in the permanent memorial design. Groups of Muslims will begin to attend the memorial in order to make Islamic prayer at the requisite times, as informed by the Tower of Voices/sundial, and oriented toward Mecca, with the help of the crescent and the Memorial Wall: "No one should be surprised when imams start delivering sermons from the end of the Entry Portal Walkway, attended by Muslim faithful below."[33] He then goes on to speculate that what will happen next is the exclusion of all non-Muslims from the memorial, since infidels are not permitted in Muslim places of worship.[34]

The conspiracy Rawls envisions begins with the architects who created the design, but it eventually comes to include the National Park Service, high-level political officials, nearly every serious journalist who has reported on the matter, all the scholars who have been consulted on the issue and disagreed with Rawls's reading, and others: "At every critical juncture, another person would step up to run interference for Murdoch: a journalist here, an academic there, higher authorities in the Department of the Interior, a top law enforcement officer, all proceeding on their presumptions about which side they should be on instead of looking at the facts, all of which are trivially easy to verify."[35] The individuals and groups associated with the memorial design and its implementation come in for frequent ad hominem attacks throughout Rawls's manuscript. Murdoch is described as a "master manipulator" and a "willing and able liar."[36] Somerset Park Service supervisor Joanne Hanley is a "[p]oor deluded creature."[37]

It is when Rawls is speculating on the intentions of those he opposes that the circularity of his reasoning is on clearest display: "[W]e already know [Murdoch's] intent. Knowing that Murdoch has intentionally emplaced the central feature of a mosque as the central feature of his design, it is reasonable to assume that further possible mosque elements are also intended as mosque elements. But these possible mosque features also *add* to the evidence of intent."[38] Yet what we know of Murdoch's intent is limited to what he has *said* about that intent, and he has said only that his intentions are consistent with the mission statement of the memorial project. Rawls simply asserts that Murdoch is dissimulating, and then finds other "evidence" of the Islamic nature of the memorial that can only be read as such if we assume malevolent intent on the part of the architect, and then once we do that, the "evidence" returns to reinforce the unfounded original claim of intent. In this manner of assertion, anything can be proven from nothing.

The partially occult interpretive base on which Rawls's exegetical effort is based, and the thing that makes it powerfully persuasive for some readers is cultural Islamophobia. We are told in the second chapter, though it is not clear what it has to do with the argument about the memorial design symbolism, to remember that "the Arab-Muslim world was an integral part of the Axis alliance of WWII" and that the mufti of Jerusalem was sympathetic to some fascist ideas.[39] An effective rhetorical move in the demonization of a foe is to tie him to ultimate evil, in this case, the Axis, i.e., Nazism. Later passages are still more provocative: "Half the religion [of Islam] is a murder cult, claiming to love death. 'You love life and we love death,' says al Qaeda, 'which gives an

THE PERMANENT MEMORIAL | 181

example of what the Prophet Muhammad said.' On this, they have the backing of the entire Wahhabist/Khomeni-ist [sic] Islamofascist mullacracy. They all want to kill everyone who does not love death."[40] Rawls does not tell us how the half of Islam that is purportedly murderous is to be calculated. If he intends sheer numbers here, this would make something on the order of 750 million murderous Muslims around the globe. If we count only every single Saudi (the heartland of Wahhabism) and every Shi'a (the denomination of the Iranian Islamic government) Muslim on the planet, we get a number somewhat less than one quarter of the 750 million, but it is not difficult to find opposition to terrorism within Wahhabist and Shi'a Islam. Despite its logical incoherencies, however, the claim can be relied on to resonate rhetorically with Rawls's ideologically sympathetic readers.

Support for Rawls's and other versions of the mosque theory came largely from the portion of the right-wing blogosphere that is made up of Christian dominionists and anti-Islamic nativists. Right-wing news and commentary sites with more polished online presences and funding but political predispositions not far at all from those of the extremist bloggers also carried the story of Rawls's conspiracy narrative. World Net Daily published a glowing review of the book when it appeared online. Rawls was also given an unencumbered opportunity to air his vision in the online magazine established by David Horowitz, *FrontPage Mag*, in late 2008. There, Rawls directly accused Murdoch of alliance with the architects of the 9/11 attacks: "Why would Murdoch want to build a memorial to al Qaeda's heroes instead of ours? The most likely explanation is that he is on the side of al Qaeda. Flight 93 taught us the nature of our terror war enemies: that they hide amongst us, pretending to be trust-worthy friends. That fits Murdoch's behavior exactly. I would guess that he converted to Islam at some point, became a radical Islamist, and is now acting as a freelance jihadi."[41]

Some higher-profile right-wing figures who gave support to Rawls included G. Gordon Liddy, Michelle Malkin, and radio shock jock Erich "Mancow" Muller. In May 2008, the latter told his audience, with guests Tom Burnett Sr. and Congressman Tom Tancredo listening, that he was prepared to "take a sledgehammer to the abomination," to which Tancredo, who had earlier called the memorial design "an insult to everybody in this country," responded, "I don't blame you a bit," and

Burnett Sr. said, "That's great, I'll join ya!" This discussion was in at least one respect representative of the tenor of the support for the mosque conspiracy more broadly: none of the three men present demonstrated much more than a visceral understanding of the case, and they had embellished Rawls's narrative with even more groundless observations about the structure and meaning of the design. Mancow claimed that the memorial "features symbols that show Tom Burnett Sr.'s son, who stormed the cockpit, and the other passengers being cast into hell, again with Islamic symbols, and the four brave terrorists rising up to see Allah," but did not specify which symbols he believed were doing this work. He also mimed Rawls's ad hominem reasoning in claiming "this project has been infiltrated by the enemy" and accused Murdoch of membership in al-Qaeda.

The question of the influence and dissemination of Rawls's conspiracy theory about the permanent memorial has much more to do with the intellectual and media context of American political culture in the 21st century than with its actual merits. In argumentative terms Rawls is more or less indistinguishable from fringe voices in the radical right of the 1940s and 1950s such as W. Cleon Skousen, a John Birch Society Mormon who has recently been put back into the public eye by the devotion of far-right talk radio jock and television host Glenn Beck. Skousen argued that the American Constitution is fundamentally based on the Bible and that communists had infiltrated the highest levels of American government; he believed, for example, that moderate Republican President Eisenhower was a communist agent. The central difference in the reception of Rawls and that of someone like Skousen has to do with the work right-wing groups have done in the past 50 years to build institutions to give formerly highly suspect, fringe ideas a veneer of respectability. In his time, Skousen was thoroughly ignored by even conservatives of such a pure stripe as William F. Buckley, while Rawls's arguments have received wider attention precisely because of the proliferation of far-right media outlets and other institutions.

Rawls's particular brand of conspiracy theory regarding Flight 93 and 9/11 is not the only such variation. The 9/11 conspiracies await their own book-length study, and in this chapter, I can only brush the surface of this element of American cultural response to the 9/11 attacks. There is a branch dedicated to the examination of 9/11 as a false flag operation, that is, the crash of Flight 93 and other 9/11 events are seen here as orchestrated by the Bush administration, or, in some versions, broader coalitions of governmental and global elites in order to secure mass approval of the War on Terror and its concomitant operations. One of the odder versions of this argument is made by David Ray Griffin, a retired theology professor. In his book *Christian Faith and the Truth behind 9/11*, Griffin argues that the United States is, in purely Christian terms, an "evil empire" that does the work of the demonic on earth, and he envisions the 9/11 attacks as "the chief revelation of the demonic—of the extent to which it has taken control of the American government."[42] This left-wing Christian vision of a nearly omnipotent and objectively evil American juggernaut systematically turning the world away from God and toward Satan almost certainly has a smaller domestic client base than far-right conspiracy theories that see the U.S. government and other elite institutions as potentially infiltrated by Islamic extremists, exemplified here by Rawls.

It is fair to note that, if conspiracy theories are popular and believed by many, this is perhaps at least in part because a few past conspiracy theories have been exonerated as truth. African Americans accused of paranoia when they charge the American government with covert efforts to undercut political activism in the black community need only point to COINTELPRO and the systematic FBI efforts to destroy the Black Panther Party and other activist groups of the 1960s and 1970s. Those adherents to conspiracy theories regarding the Bush administration and 9/11 who are historically knowledgeable might point to precedents in American governmental conspiracies regarding terrorist attacks, for example, Operation Northwoods, in which the U.S. joint chiefs of staff in 1962 proposed a false flag terror attack on U.S. soil to be blamed on Castro's Cuba in order to justify an invasion of our neighbor off the coast of Florida. Some proponents of the view that Flight 93 was a false flag operation do invoke Operation Northwoods as a precedent that they believe gives credence to their beliefs.[43]

It is apparent however that most of the narrowly factual claims (as opposed to murkier claims about, e.g., the pre-9/11 intentions of the Bush administration to exert military pressure on Iraq) made by 9/11 conspiracy theorists are fairly easily dismantled. A well-known example of such an effort here is the March 2005 issue of the magazine *Popular*

Mechanics, which was devoted to debunking claims made by advocates of some of the more popular 9/11 conspiracy narratives. The editors show in a straightforward manner that the major conspiratorial claims do not rise to the level of demonstrable fact. Even though there was no good video footage of American Flight 77 striking the Pentagon, the wreckage of a plane was indeed found at the scene, and jet-fuel-ignited fires can indeed burn hot enough to weaken the steel trusses in the World Trade Center sufficiently to cause structural collapse. It is also uncomplicated, if more labor intensive, to undo conspiratorial claims based, as such claims frequently are, on one utterance by a witness (e.g., an individual interviewed live on Fox News just after the second hit on the World Trade Center claimed to have seen no windows on the plane, and this was subsequently asserted as "proof" that it was not a commercial aircraft) by consulting other eyewitnesses or when, available, video evidence that shows the lone observation to have been mistaken. The *Popular Mechanics* editors also disprove several Flight 93–specific conspiratorial claims, most of which have to do with the idea that the plane was shot down by American fighter jets. It is telling that even Wikipedia, notorious for its relativistic presentation of knowledge, seems to acknowledge the unreliability of 9/11 conspiracy theories in efforts made recently by the site to limit the ease with which Wikipedia pages on 9/11 conspiracies can be accessed via links from more respectable and accurate pages concerning 9/11.[44]

When examined carefully, the broad body of 9/11 conspiracy theories does not even rise to the mediocre level of correspondence with demonstrable fact attained by some other spectacular conspiracy theories of the recent American past. The communist-infiltration conspiracies, for example, of the mid-20th century were fundamentally wrong-headed, as the United States government was not massively infiltrated by communist spies. That there were, however, at least some relatively isolated examples of infiltration in key areas of American society by Soviet agents gave, and still gives, the conspiracy a greater claim to veracity than any of the most common 9/11 conspiracies. What then explains the tenacity to which proponents hold to 9/11 conspiracies, and more specifically to the Flight 93 memorial conspiracy, in the absence of verifying facts? However minoritarian any given conspiracy theories may be, belief in conspiracies is a widespread phenomenon in American society, and significant historical events are frequently the subjects of conspiratorial thinking. The classic example in American history is the Kennedy assassination. A national survey in the early 1990s showed that nearly 80% of Americans believed the Warren Commission had not provided an accurate account of the event and that other individuals not named in the commission's report were involved.[45]

Explanations of conspiratorial thinking along the lines of Richard Hofstadter's classic "paranoid style" essay in *Harper's Magazine* back in 1964 have a degree of utility to this day. Hofstadter argued that proponents of the major political conspiracy visions of the American mid-20th century, most of which revolved around the myth of communist infiltration, were not *literally* paranoid, but rather that the political situation of the American right at that time involved such a radical sense of powerlessness and inefficacy that paranoid reasoning seemed the best means to some partisans of the right to explain the systematic triumph of midcentury liberalism. Hofstadter's paranoid conspiracy theorist is a man of the right, and, although left-wing conspiracies certainly exist in the American framework, and indeed some conspiratorial visions are combinations of left and right political themes, there has long been a tendency for the dominant American conspiracies to emanate from the far right. In the case of the Flight 93 memorial conspiracy, this is clearly the case.

A more broad-based theory of the origins of conspiratorial thinking in contemporary American society has pointed to the profoundly felt need for interpretation and hermeneutics in a world where meaning often seems unattainable because it has become impossibly complex or fragmented, or what one writer calls the "hermeneutics of conspiracy."[46] The rejection of complexity and the desire for total explanation might be read as a de facto rejection of what has been frequently labeled the postmodern nature of the contemporary world. It is certainly the case that many conspiracy theories share an assumption of the interconnectedness of seemingly unrelated phenomena, the belief that "everything is connected" and can therefore be understood in a relatively simple, unified narrative that explains vast amounts of seemingly complex, disparate events and data by recourse to a number of core elements: occult powers that are malevolent and exceedingly powerful, indeed virtually omnipotent and omnipresent. At the same time, though, that we see this hermeneutic of simplicity, we frequently find, as in the case of Alec Rawls, a propensity for conspiracy theories to lose themselves in minute details at the expense of broader issues. Rawls expends great amounts of energy in his efforts to demonstrate that the bowl, the tower, etc. orient on Mecca, presenting calculation after calculation of angles and distances and dimensions, while ignoring larger contextual issues that must be adequately addressed if the minute calculations are to add up to anything in the way of a reasonable analysis. Why would Islamic extremists concentrate as much energy as Rawls believes they have on the sabotage of the Flight 93 memorial, given the fact that the achieved symbolic sabotage is so subtle that it cannot be discerned by anyone except those few who have spent great amounts of time reading the memorial with the intention of interpreting it as an Islamist set of symbols? Is it even remotely likely that large numbers of radical Islamists will come to practically use the memorial as a mosque, as Rawls asserts?

Properly sociological efforts to understand conspiracy theories must look away from purely psychological explanations to a discussion of the structural and cultural facts that serve as prods to such thinking. We might suggest, starting from the preceding look at the role played by one individual in the production and dissemination of the Flight 93 memorial conspiracy, that there may be promise in an individually based approach to the study of conspiracy theories, but one that does not situate itself within the discipline of psychology and instead follows some of the recent breakthroughs in the sociological study of such phenomena as terrorism and membership in deviant religious groups. Much research in the recruitment of individuals into the latter kinds of groups starts from an analysis of the recruit's social context and networks. One of the central relevant facts in understanding who joins new religious movements (or NRMs, the sociologically preferred replacement for the term "cult") or terrorist groups has to do with whether or not the would-be recruit already knows others in the relevant groups. Contrary to the popular idea that NRMs randomly select victims for "brainwashing," the tendency is for recruits to come from the close friends and family members of those already inside the group, as affectively close relations are good conductors for religious conversion.[47] Relatively high educational credentials and a sense of relative, but not absolute, deprivation are contributors to propensity to join such groups. The Lofland-Stark model of conversion to NRMs, based on their research on the Unification Church, posits the following factors in conversion: (1) the convert's experience of enduring tension in his/her life; (2) a religious problem solving perspective; (3) self-identification as a "religious seeker"; (4) encounter with the cult; (5) formation of an affective bond with one or more cult members; (6) reduction or elimination of extra-cult attachments; and (7) exposure to intensive interaction with other converts.[48] Research on terrorist recruitment has revealed some of the same sociological groundwork. Terrorist recruits share social networks and affective ties with current members, and a sense of relative deprivation and membership in institutions where access to relevant ideas and texts is possible are positive contributors to recruitment; e.g., in much of the Muslim world, those who have been in university are more likely recruits to Islamic terrorist groups because the extremist Islamic texts circulate there.[49]

Belief in conspiracy theories might also be studied as a factor of social context and socio-biographical trajectory. It would seem likely that recruitment to the Flight 93 memorial conspiracy might be connected to social networks and alliances. Frequenting of certain political blogs and other webpages where support for the conspiracy is manifest is likely evidence of a certain ideological affinity with the body of ideas generally shared on the far right (militarism, strong nationalism, distrust of government, suspicion or even hatred of Islam and Muslims), and it is clear in the content of the related blogs that many of the bloggers have affective relationships. It would seem to be the case that many of the proponents of the Flight 93 memorial conspiracy, including Rawls, are of relatively high educational attainment and are technologically quite literate. We have substantial data only on the one case studied in this chapter, Rawls, but he seems a nearly ideal typical example of the individual suffering relative deprivation: the son of a world-famous academic (the political theorist John Rawls) with considerable youthful intellectual promise of his own who, for unknown reasons, wound up dropping out of graduate school and being denied the scintillating career path of his father, to instead wind up as a relatively unknown blogger and media activist. What we know about this one case is compelling enough to constitute a reasonable call for further investigation of the hypothesis that the experience of relative deprivation is a common element in acceptance of conspiracy theories.

Islamophobia seems a central trait underlying the propensity to believe in the Flight 93 memorial conspiracy. It has been suggested that in the post–Cold War global political environment Islamic extremism has emerged as the new global enemy for the Western democracies. In important symbolic ways, Islamophobia has taken the place of the fear of communism in the American right's intellectual universe. Although there are limits to comparisons of conspiracy theories regarding 9/11 and Islam, on the one hand, and those having to do with the fear of communist infiltration, on the other, there is also some evident weight to the proposition that Islamic radicalism now occupies more or less the same place in the rhetoric and argument of the far right that was formerly occupied by communism.

The role played by the relatively new communicative technology of the Internet, and the kind of radical democracy it presents in at least some of its incarnations, must also be included in the discussion of contemporary conspiracy theories such as the Flight 93 memorial conspiracy. One of the central debates surrounding new media and communicative networks has to do with whether they contribute to a more educated public or simply allow people to avoid positions they do not like and surround themselves constantly with media that echo what they already believe. There are compelling reasons to see the latter of the two alternatives as closer to the truth, especially when we consider the stunning proliferation of forms of knowledge that are demonstrably false. Blogs require no certificates or degrees; anyone who can master the minimal skills necessary to find Blogger, WordPress, or any of the other free blogging sites online and then follow the easy steps to create a blog and make entries can potentially speak to a larger audience than he ever could previously. Insofar as the vast majority of blogs seem limited to narcissistic inventory of personal observations and cataloguing of life events, the ultimate consequences might seem harmless and even mildly positive in making possible greater connection between individuals. That the Internet still provides little in the way of tools for navigating the sea of information in order to better avoid unreliable and untrustworthy sources speaking to issues of political and public importance, however, means that even those users of the medium who might have a significant interest in avoiding misleading information have a difficult time doing so, and the likely much larger group of users who are interested only in finding support for what they already believe are positively enabled. The rise and nearly complete online victory of the knowledge source described by one writer as "the noble amateur"[50] has inevitably ended up as yet another in a long historical series of heavy blows against expert authority in American society. The online conception of amateurism tends to a naïve vision of the capacity of nonexperts to speak seriously about serious subjects, facile glorification of common sense (which is frequently wrong), and a concomitant denigration of experts and expert knowledge as such. These developments have arguably made the proliferation of even the more patently absurd conspiracy theories about 9/11 online possible.

The Flight 93 memorial conspiracy relies heavily on the populist, antiexpert narrative of the Internet more broadly. Rawls admits he has no formal training in any of the specialized disciplines that address issues of Islamic symbolism and mosque construction, but he shrugs this off as a nonissue and the partisans of the theory scarcely pause a moment for reflection on this fact. Others who have spent even less time with these matters than Rawls eagerly accept the radically democratic claims for knowledge that thrive on the Internet as a justification for their acceptance of arguments that ultimately need not even be argued to garner their acceptance, as their emotional investment in ideologies is what is actually in play. Technological shifts in media mean that claims that in previous times would have been difficult to proliferate can be web-published and disseminated virtually effortlessly.

But Rawls and the other adherents to the Flight 93 memorial conspiracy do not simply embrace the epistemological relativism that could follow from an indiscriminate rejection of expert knowledge and an embrace of amateur opinion. They, like the participants in Hofstadter's paranoid style, at one and the same time reject one set of authorities and posit others to take their places, and they use a discourse peppered with calls for "rationality" and "reasoned argument" even while they make claims with a deep investment in emotionally rooted prejudice and a priori assumption. Rawls is described in the right-wing community that embraces the memorial conspiracy as an authority, by virtue of his lengthy blog entries and his unpublished manuscript. It is remarkable that the Flight 93 memorial conspiracy theorists use exactly the same denigrating terms ("irrational," "emotional," "uninterested in careful argument and facts") to describe their critics as those critics use to denounce them. So it would be too much to say that the discursive world in which the Flight 93 memorial conspiracy exists is adequately characterized by, say, Jean-François Lyotard's now classic notion of the decline of grand narratives and the disappearance of agreed-upon standards for evaluating competing claims and arguments.[51] On the contrary, there is, at least at a superficial level, still an agreement about the superiority of reason and logic. But these have become, for the adherents to the myth of the Flight 93 memorial conspiracy, largely rhetorical rather than substantive standards. It is as though, in a kind of tribute to the Sophism of ancient Greece, they understand that appeals to reason are powerful in American culture, whatever the actual logical rigor of an argument, and so they constantly claim to be proceeding according to dispassionate reason, all the while actually rooting their case in more primordial and dogmatic beliefs about cultural Others and a simplistic morally binary universe of good and evil.

If we cannot follow Lyotard in the part of his argument about postmodernity that concerns the decline of grand narratives, it is otherwise for his sense that agonism becomes the unmasked principle of conflict in the contemporary world. Online, anonymity contributes greatly to the heightening of aggression and the extremity of stereotyping and moral denigration of opponents. This is all, again, seemingly contrary to the constant paeans to reasoned argument, but the contradiction is not dwelt upon in the conspiracy circles. In the same morally charged language as that of the McCarthyist Red-baiters of yore, Rawls et al. uniformly describe all those who decline to accept their claims as, at best, hapless dupes of evil powers and, more frequently, active agents of the violent and murderous enemies of the United States. Much has been said of the ease with which debate and argument turns ugly in new media, and the Flight 93 memorial conspiracy theorists thrive in this new and viciously aggressive realm of discourse.

Rawls and his allies have been successful enough in their campaign to force the Park Service to explicitly respond to their charges in their own online materials. This is arguably evidence of one of the very most troubling of the cultural sea changes that new media has wrought. In the past, although extremist positions existed and were articulated, they had no systematic way to be disseminated, as publishing houses were fewer and operated according to a set of norms that has never been accepted as valid by some of today's publishers of ideological material. Now, in addition to the Internet and the possibility of self-publishing, myriad other means have emerged by which even writers with only a tenuous relationship with the traditional ethos of argument and data can find a way to get ideas out into the world of consumers, and it is undeniable that there are audiences for the kinds of things Alec Rawls and his fellows write. Conflict, and even highly charged conflict, over the design and meaning of national memorials is no new development that arrived in the aftermath of 9/11. It is too often forgotten that the Vietnam Veterans Memorial in Washington, D.C., today widely admired and honored by Americans of vastly different political sensibilities and beliefs about the meaning of the American war effort in Indochina, was initially a flashpoint for a still hot cultural war over that recently ended military war.[52] But what is relatively new, and still developing, is the ability that those willing to do so have to mainstream extreme discourses and viewpoints.

6

The Cultural Narratives of the Books on Flight 93

If the concentrated work of making myth of Flight 93 is mostly done within a few miles of the crash site, another "site" of such cultural labor is to be found beyond Shanksville, in a "location" both far away and yet imminently nearby. In a society like ours, the mass media is the central conduit of most information about most events that are of public note. For the vast majority of Americans not physically present in the locations where the hijacked planes struck, 9/11 is a narrative unimaginable without the news media's real time coverage of the attacks in New York City. For many Americans, the images of the events in Manhattan and the reporting by television anchors describing the images is the entirety of their memory of 9/11, as only a tiny fraction of the American population has visited any of the 9/11 memorial sites, and only a tinier fraction of that fraction has been to Shanksville. Much can be discussed in the cultural narrative of 9/11 using as raw data the mass-media coverage of the events of the day, and one can view that as-it-happened news coverage as a public drama[1] or a social performance[2] with plot lines, characters, mise-en-scène, and audience expectations.

Flight 93 did not play a significant role in the live-action mass media memory of 9/11 for obvious reasons. Although news media did report on the plane's crash and showed images of the tear in the earth it had caused within minutes of the event, this was simply not nearly as compelling a visual phenomenon as what was going on in New York and Washington, D.C., and media coverage stayed firmly focused on those latter two sites, and especially the first, on the day of the attacks and in subsequent days. Eventually, as details began to emerge about Flight 93's last half hour, media narratives emerged, and the work of constructing a heroic myth of the final minutes of Flight 93 got underway with a vengeance on news programs and in the pages of newspapers and magazines. The most concentrated versions of the hero myth would, however, have to wait until the many mass market biographical books on 9/11 began to appear.

The number and variety of biographical and personal narrative books related to 9/11 is impressive. There are oral histories of Manhattanites who witnessed the attacks in New York[3] and of high school students whose school was situated near Ground Zero.[4] There are stories from those who were in the towers and escaped, including a book by a man who carried a wheelchair-bound woman down many flights of stairs,[5] and another by a woman previously absorbed in her corporate career in one of the World Trade Center towers who radically changed her life plan to become a caregiver after the attacks.[6] There is a book by a woman who was dug out of the rubble of one of the towers.[7] There are several biographical books by widows of New York City firefighters and others who perished in the towers.[8] Men who were severely injured at the Pentagon attack and the widows of pilots of the four planes have produced biographical books.[9] There is at least one book that collects stories of the visitation of the ghosts of those who died on 9/11 to their families and friends.[10] In addition to the nonfiction material that relates personal narratives about the experience of 9/11, there are several novels devoted largely or entirely to the topic, at least one of which has now been made into a major motion picture.[11] This is just a sampling, and the number of books of this type continues to grow every year, even more than a decade after the event.

The books on Flight 93 are more manageable in number. There were no survivors at the site, unlike at the Pentagon and in New York, so there are no survivor biographical accounts for Flight 93. What we do have are a number of books, largely by family members, about passengers on the plane, books that both serve to describe what the authors believe their loved ones did during the flight and to provide narratives and details of their lives that frame and account for their actions. These books can reasonably be classified as coherent and only slightly differing versions of an American hero myth. Although, there are significant efforts to refuse to restrict the classification "hero" to a subset of the Flight 93 passengers, it is telling that only four of the passengers have been the subject of such "lives of the hero" books, and these are the four men who emerged in the media discussion in the wake of 9/11 as the central actors in the passenger effort to take back the plane: Todd Beamer, Mark Bingham, Tom Burnett Jr., and Jeremy Glick.

In this chapter, I summarize the important details in the several books that endeavor to tell in biographical mode of the crash of Flight 93 and thereby contribute to the mythology of the event. In the chapter to follow, I will take up the same task with respect to the various films that have been made depicting the events on Flight 93.

The Flight 93 Hero

What precisely is a hero? We talk about them continuously in contemporary America, albeit generally in a fragmented, off-hand way that betrays the lack of a hard, fast definition of the thing. Baseball players who hit game-winning homers in game seven of the World Series, store clerks who foil robbery attempts, doctors who complete difficult operations and enable sick people to get well, and fathers of three who volunteer to mentor children not their own are all called heroes by at least some of us. As I drafted this chapter, CNN was airing its annual special *CNN Heroes*, in which individuals who started charities devoted to such things as providing clean drinking water to communities that lack it are honored as heroes for their deeds. But even here the term is used in an imprecise manner. Celebrity presenters, such as Miley Cyrus, best known for their dubious accomplishments in the realm of popular culture, are awarded the term, in Cyrus's case because of her nonprofit Get Ur Good On. One recipient, Sal Dimiceli, declared in his acceptance speech that the "real heroes" were not the recipients of the award, but the "hungry children" and others they served, a strikingly liberal use of the term in which those who are the beneficiaries of acts deemed heroic are also heroic. This is all evidence, perhaps, not only of how little clarity there is in the culture regarding the definition of the term, but also of how desperately our society feels the need for heroes, however they are defined.

In a formulation at once erudite and populist, Joseph Campbell described the heroic monomyth[12] as consisting of three core actions: separation, initiation, return. The mythic narrative typically runs thus: "A hero ventures forth from the world of common day into a region of supernatural wonder: fabulous forces are there encountered and a decisive victory is won: the hero comes back from this mysterious adventure with the power to bestow boons on his fellow man."[13] Heroes are figures who exemplify the deep meaning of myths by reiterating the acts of the supernatural beings who founded the cosmos in a literal form that normal humans cannot approach. The latter then take their moral lesson from the acts of the heroes, who have mimed the gods. A good working definition of hero is provided by the historian Henri Hubert:

> Without exception, heroes are characters that, at least in the opinion of men, have lived and died, men from a near or distant and legendary past. . . . They are men and yet superhuman; they died and are yet distinguished from the crowd of the dead by the memory that is attached to them and the strength that they are still given. . . . [T]hey are . . . semigods, with a lesser power, limited or temporary, but serviceable to men, to whom they are close, adjoined to them in their recognizable images and certain deaths, in a word, they are divine intercessors. Superhumans or semi-gods, heroes are, in any case, divine; the hero is a *divus*, a species of the divine.[14]

Heroes are models for the lives of the rest of us, "emblems of virtue," even when we recognize that the ideal is too lofty and perfectly realized in the myth for us to realistically do anything more than mark it as the absolute apex of human possibility. The hero should be studied sociologically, Hubert goes on, because a full understanding of the nature of the hero requires a recognition of the social bond between him and the group that makes up his cult.[15] The social group (in Hubert's example, his native France) can even come to see its own origins as intimately informed by its heroes:

> Saint Louis, Joan of Arc, Napoleon have been, or are, heroes for France, but also heroes of the French fatherland, of the French name that we all bear, of the French blood in our veins. The words fatherland and nation, like the word brotherhood, imply kinship. The notion of companionship implies communion. The Greek city was a circle of kinship, like the phratry and the γένος [*genos* = race, stock, kin].[16]

In his study of Saint Patrick, Hubert's student Stefan Czarnowski embellishes this definition. The hero is, in his analysis, "a man who has ritually acquired, by the merits of his life or his death, the effective power inherent in a group or a thing of which he is the representative and the fundamental social value of which he personifies."[17] The case of the Irish patron saint illustrates the hero's frequent insinuation in the life of a certain kind of group, the nation, which Czarnowski characterizes as the "space of recognition . . . [and] site of application of the hero's activity," and the intimate interconnection that can be frequently found in hero mythology between religious and national identities. In Patrick's case, we have a hero who issues from a social-class position that puts him in opposition to the priestly caste of the druids, and thus he is in practice from the very beginning more a national hero than a hero of the Church for the Irish. That his heroic activity does not include final success, as he was unable to completely defeat either druidism or Pelagianism, the two prime enemies in Ireland of the Christian Church of that epoch, illustrates another important element in heroic narrative: defeat can be made glorious, especially in the case of self-sacrifice for the national good.

As the case of Patrick makes apparent, the hero and the nation are tied tightly together. Nations are, among other things, sets of mythical ideas about the characteristics of their members and the genealogies that bind them. Heroes exemplify, in an ideal typical way, the core of the national identity and their adventures demonstrate and help to preserve the unique and generally God-given mission of the nation. One commonly encountered aspect of national hero myth is its tie to national crisis. Heroes are of particular utility, even necessity, when a people feel its identity imperiled. During moments of national cultural crisis, the hero is that exceptional individual who steps into the breach to respond to the crisis and whose action is interpreted as an act of collective affirmation, even if it ends in his death. In such situations, according to Jean-Pierre Albert,

> A national hero is often a "hero against" and his mere invocation designates some "hereditary enemy." More precisely, the tragic contexts that call for heroic gestures can be grouped into a rather simple standard scenario: 1) a group is in trouble, its survival is in question, . . . 2) an unexpected personage rises up and attempts something: an ingenious riposte, an unexpected burst of energy, a last stand, . . . 3) he succeeds or fails, and it turns out in the more or less long term that his action went in the direction of history, in this case that of national affirmation.[18]

Notions of the character of the national hero differ in some substantial ways from society to society, and they change over time even within any given society. One of the key elements in research on national hero traditions and myths in Europe has to do with ways in which heroism has changed from the pre- to post-Enlightenment: the movement is from kings by divine rule as heroes toward secular and democratic revolutionaries, and finally to secular international figures. In the United States, perhaps owing to our comparative youth as a culture, there is some evidence that the trajectory might be somewhat different. Here, the movement is from an initial focus on Enlightenment-influenced, basically secular heroes in the early days after the Revolution to increasingly more religious heroes in the years after: i.e., from Washington to Reagan, the Deist president to the evangelical end times president. It is scarcely possible to imagine an American Panthéon where our equivalents of Zola, Malraux, Voltaire, Victor Hugo, Jean Jaurès, and Jean Moulin would lie. The best approximation of such a site might be the Capitol rotunda, which does feature statues of the early secular founding heroes, but also includes prominent Christian imagery: the paintings *Baptism of Pocahontas* by John Gadsby Chapman and *Embarkation of the Pilgrims* by Robert Walter Weir. The trajectory I suggest for national hero models in American culture is of a piece with the increase in levels of religiosity over most of the lifespan of the country. In this perspective, religiosity in the U.S. is not something always present, as conservative myth would have it, but rather it actually steadily increased from the American founding up until the past decade or so, when we have seen religiosity rates in the country level and even begin ever so slightly to drop. This provides an underpinning for an argument about the direction and change in hero myth in America that differentiates our path from that of Europe.

When we turn our gaze to the more focused relief of hero myth in light of 9/11, we find still more guideposts for our task of placing the Flight 93 heroes. The sociological theorists Jeffrey Alexander and Randall Collins have offered compelling analyses of some of what is in play in the dramatic and ritualized emergence of 9/11 heroism and hero myth. Collins uses his interactive ritual chain theory to look at the ways in which certain objects became charged with significance as a result of ritual-like action that took place around them and then consequently took on symbolic power that they would not otherwise have had. For the firefighters and rescue workers at the World Trade Center site, the "pile" itself became the focus of emotional energy, while, for the rest of us watching from afar, it was the firefighters who became the object of myth and reverence. Alexander looks at the same events with a vision that privileges the narrative and structural elements of meaning. Indeed, in a few pregnant paragraphs in his essay "Performance, Counterperformance and September 11," he presages some of the detail to follow later in this chapter in describing the process by which

> members of [victim groups] were transformed symbolically. They were made innocent and good, were portrayed in a mythical manner that abstracted from their particular qualities of gender, class, race, or ethnicity. The first-place level of transfiguration focused on the victims and participants as archetypal individuals tout court. In the magazine, television, and newspaper elegies that were composed about them, which indeed amounted to commemorations, in the weeks and months after the tragic event, the traders and firemen, secretaries and police became the heroic subjects in sentimental, often heart-wrenching stories about their pluck and their determination. Their highly genred . . . biographies revealed that the strength, dedication, and kindness of the innocents murdered on September 11 allowed each one to build a meaningful and coherent life. The second level of idealized reconstruction focused on the family. Whatever sociological statistics might have to say about divorce and loneliness, absent fathers and latch-key children, abandoned wives and extramarital affairs, the now mythically reconstructed individuals who perished on 9/11 were represented as members of warm and loving families. . . . The third level of transfiguration concerned the economic elite itself. The highly profitable, often cutthroat, and relentlessly competitive business enterprises who rented space in the Twin Towers were represented as decent, entirely human enterprises. They made an honest living, and their industry contributed to the bounty of American life.[19]

The binaries were so rigidly retraced and reinforced here (sacred friends are peaceful, cooperative, honest, rational, ethical, honorable, faithful; profane enemies are violent, antagonistic, deceitful, irrational, dominating, corrupt, cynical)[20] that it became a dangerous business simply to point out the mythological work that was being done, or to make any other kind of analysis of the participants.

The English term "hero" derives from the Greek ἥρως, and some of our ideas about heroes have certainly been influenced, if in a complex and diluted way, by the ways in which the ancient Greeks thought about them. Alexander argues that a central aspect of American heroism in the media coverage of 9/11 owed much to the Greek and Roman model of the heroic citizen warrior and the manly, martial view of the nation to which it was attached. This vision is of a hero whose valor is measured by his willingness to fight for country and his prowess in combat. Alexander cites the front page of the "very liberal" *New York Times* the day after the attacks to show the context within which this hero operates: "U.S. Attacked.... A Creeping Horror.... President Vows to Exact Punishment for 'Evil.'... Onlookers Search for Elusive Safety."[21] One aspect of 9/11 heroism, Alexander argues, as it was interpreted by at least some Americans, and even some of those we might not generally consider among the most bellicose, had to do with the no-nonsense reaction of those who understood the attacks as an act of war and endeavored to respond in kind.

This perspective on the 9/11 hero very clearly emphasizes an attribute of heroism we find in practically every culture: manly courage and aggressiveness. In the contemporary U.S., this attribute tends to take on a specific set of visual forms that are heavily influenced by the body and fitness culture so widespread here. Macho male heroism thus requires an impressive, imposing, and very muscular frame on which to hang. In my teaching, I frequently make use of a comparative example to show students how much more muscular our iconic heroes have gotten over the last few decades by showing them brief clips of two Hollywood films about the Greek defense of Thermopylae. The first, *The 300 Spartans*, was made in 1962 and features Spartan heroes who are physically vigorous but not particularly muscular. The second, *The 300*, was released more than 40 years later, in 2006, and boasts heroes literally larger than life, each one endowed with rippling pecs and massive biceps that a generation ago were the reserve of professional body builders, who were almost universally seen then not as physically admirable and worthy of imitation but as freakish.

The American warrior hero is, in ideal typical terms if not always in practice, a man, and a physically robust, fearless one. According to the basic rules of gender characteristics at work in American culture, this heroic type cannot be attained by women. One might note that it is a cultural model of heroism at some remove, as mythologies often are, from empirical reality, since contemporary American women do serve in the military.[22] But we are in the realm of the mythological here, and the myth is of a hero who is by definition prototypically male. The stories told in the early days after the September 11 attacks of police, or firefighters, or other emergency responders doing heroic things were stories of men.

In the contemporary era, as opposed to the time of classical Greece, wars tend to be matters of technological superiority rather than of face-to-face standoffs between heroes. Where, then, can the physical prowess and bravery of the hero be demonstrated? In American society, the realm of sport has long been one such sphere, where heroes can, in the absence of war, show their powers to best other men in hand-to-hand combat. In some sporting matters, the affair is at least occasionally one of actual life and death; American football players now and then die or are permanently crippled from injuries suffered on the field, and boxing history reveals a list of fights in which one of the participants died that is pointed to by many boxing fans with a strange combination of pride and dread. Sport can be understood in the light of Durkheimian cultural theory as structurally quite similar to religion, with virtually all of the same existential seriousness and collective spirit.[23] In the case of Flight 93 hero myth, which is given flesh in the persons of four male passengers, the heroes were called to war, or a kind of facsimile thereof in the age of terrorism, but, as we will see shortly, their heroic credentials were frequently attested to by reference to their formidable endeavors in the realm of sport prior to the moment of truth on the plane.

In addition to their sporting prowess, the Flight 93 heroes are also characterized as morally pure, indeed nearly saintly, and religious identity and experiences are presented as central aspects of their persons. It is not going too far to say that an archetype of the American Christian warrior-patriot emerges from the descriptions of the Flight 93 heroes, and this archetype tells us much about what Americans are thinking when they consider what it means to be American and what it means to be a hero in America.

The central sources for this chapter are the five existing biographical books about passengers on United Flight 93: *Let's Roll* (2002), *Hero of Flight 93: Mark Bingham* (2002), *Your Father's Voice* (2004), *Called* (2006), and *Fighting Back* (2006). Three of these books were written by spouses of a passenger (Lisa Beamer, Deena Burnett, and Lyz Glick). One was written (like the first three, with the aid of a professional writer) by Lisa Jefferson, the Verizon operator who spoke with Todd Beamer during the flight. The fifth book was written by a journalist and editor at *The Advocate* magazine[24] who did not personally know Mark Bingham, the book's subject.

Sport and the Flight 93 Hero

All four of the Flight 93 heroes were young men, three in their early 30s and the fourth a few years from 40, and physically in the prime of life. In the biographical material both in the books about them and in accounts in the newspapers and other media in the immediate wake of 9/11, their athletic prowess in various sports was a central element in the descriptions of their characters. Sport serves as the initial proving ground of their heroism. Rick Reilly, writing on ESPN.com on the tenth anniversary of the attacks in a piece titled "Let's Keep Rolling," identifies the four heroes with sport at their very core: "And it wasn't soldiers who led the battle. It was four athletes, pushing a food cart."[25] In this mythical light, the heroes are possessed of bodies and wills that are simply stronger than those of the average person. They refuse to accept circumstances and events undesired, and they act decisively to stop outcomes they have not willed from coming to pass. The ultimate evidence of their willful bodily strength and prowess is the formidable deed they accomplished in the last minutes of their lives, but that heroic act is presaged in previous physical heroism in sporting contests.

We learn in the biography that was written by his wife that Tom Burnett was "[f]rom birth, a fighter" who "loved sports."[26] A childhood friend "once described Tom as the kind of guy you gave the football to with five seconds to go in the game. 'Just give me the ball,' Tom would say[,] 'I'll get it in the end zone.'"[27] Todd Beamer's widow makes a similar observation about her husband: "[E]verybody picked Todd first for their team. . . . [He] kept his head in the game, no matter how great the pressure. He remained calm and rarely got flustered. He was often willing to risk something unconventional if it meant he might pull out a win."[28] One of the central tropes picked up early by the mass media regarding Jeremy Glick was his status as a black belt in judo. His wife wrote at length about this in her biographical account, describing his upset of a black belt in a sparring match while Glick was still a brown belt, which made him "a black belt on the spot."[29] She also outlines numerous lessons Glick learned from his sensei, including some that were apparently of key significance to the events on Flight 93: "Sensei taught, . . . [b]e in control, . . . [m]aster your behavior on or off the mat."[30] Her account of an automobile accident in which her husband was involved as a teenager elevates him at that young age to a heroic level to which few can aspire. Glick was driving with a female friend in the front passenger seat when the car was sideswiped at high speed. Incredibly, as the car was in the process of rolling over, Glick used one hand to brace himself and

> grabbed the back of her pants with the other and somehow managed to throw her into the backseat. . . . [I]t was eventually acknowledged by everyone that if he hadn't yanked her from the front seat, she would have been hurled out the window to her death. . . . [H]e had . . . before his eighteenth birthday . . . [saved a human life] with real style, a full-blown snatch from the grave worthy of a judoka.[31]

Perhaps more than any of the other three men, Glick's heroic status and his sporting identity were seamlessly melded together, the one unthinkable without the other. When his wife listened to the cockpit voice recording, along with other relatives of Flight 93 passengers, she believed she recognized his voice in the chaos, and what she heard is the martial hero and the judo star, indissolubly linked: "I heard [Glick's] grunt, his judo grunt, his sound, a trademark. I heard it, amid sharp banging sounds and a fury of cries, I knew right away that I was hearing him fighting."[32] In *Among the Heroes*, we find still more description of Glick the superhero athlete with "an outsized body and an outsized personality . . . bull-rushing his way through life as if it were a judo opponent that could be put into submission with a chokehold."[33] We learn that his parents apparently trained hypercompetitive athleticism into their children,[34] and "[n]one was more competitive than Jeremy, who made everything a contest. He ate the fastest, did more chin-ups, held his nerve the longest down a steep hill before applying the brakes on his bicycle."[35] His father communicated a central message to his children: success requires hatred of failure, and even of coming in second.[36]

Mark Bingham's biography is of a piece with this set of narrative themes. Just as Glick the undefeatable judo expert, Bingham the rugged rugby star became a media cliché in the days after the attacks, and the fact that his biography was not written by a loved one but by a professional journalist was not enough to immunize it from the kind of hyperbole we have already encountered. The book is replete with description of Bingham's incredible exploits on the rugby pitch, winning matches more or less single-handedly and then retiring to the kind of victorious alcoholic excess reserved for the pantheon of great athletes. His disdain for bodily injury is superhuman: "Mark usually played forward, what his friends say is one of the most injury-prone positions. . . . But he loved the game so much he didn't worry much about what it might do to his body—unless you count the times he wrapped electrical tape around his ears so they wouldn't get ripped off his head in the heat of a brutal scrum."[37] In addition to his toughness on the rugby pitch, he was possessed of another requisite skill of the heroic man: at a bar with a shot glass in hand, he could "send anyone under the table." He also, in the words of a former boss, "knew how to respond when faced with the unexpected."[38] He is described foiling an attempt at robbery by two men, one armed with a gun, in the breathtaking language of a Batman comic: "When one of the would-be muggers brandished a gun, Mike [one of two friends with Bingham at the time] immediately threw his wallet on the ground. But an infuriated Mark lunged at the guy, wrestled him to the ground, and wrenched his wrist until the gun flew out of his hand and into the street." As the first mugger fled, the two friends looked back at Bingham, who was "beating [the other mugger] to a pulp." Eventually, the two friends have to convince Bingham to release the man, who takes his partner's lead and flees in terror.[39] Later in the book, Bingham reads Hemingway and then runs with the bulls in Pamplona. "[U]nlike the rest of us," who respond to situations of possible violent confrontation with "shock," we are told, Bingham's "reaction to danger . . . was immediate and head-on."[40]

The preceding matters for reasons that go deep into American culture and history. Even a casual observer will note after only a small amount of observation of American life that sport occupies an immensely important place in it. Henry Steele Commager described the American character as profoundly immersed in moral categories derived from sporting activity, perhaps central of which is the notion of the "good sport" with its connotations that penetrate well beyond the game itself. It meant a considerable amount to many Americans that George W. Bush could throw a strike when he threw out a first pitch. While Barack Obama's delivery from the mound was awkward and weak, he redeems himself through his long-range shooting form on the basketball court, which apparently earned him the nickname "O'Bomber" in high school. Sport matters deeply in American discussions of moral fiber, courage, and heroism, and this despite the frequently encountered trope in the discourse on heroism that would separate "real" heroes from "merely" athletic ones. Sport is one of numerous pieces of contemporary American celebrity culture that is often denigrated as frivolous by cultural critics even as massive evidence indicates how seriously it is taken by large numbers of people and how tremendously it affects parts of the culture outside its own immediate confines. Even some of the biographical writers on the Flight 93 heroes feel compelled to separate their loved ones from the merely sporting heroes that dominate our culture, just before or after going on at length about how clearly the loved one's heroic character could be seen in his own athletic accomplishments and talents. Deena Burnett disdains the fact that "kids these days . . . think how wonderful the lives of movie stars and professional athletes are" when in fact "[t]hese are not the role models our children need. . . . They need men like my husband."[41] Lisa Beamer echoes this contradictory line of reasoning: "David and Drew [the Beamers' children] had always thought of their dad as a hero. . . . But a hero? Like Abraham Lincoln, Jesse Owens, or Michael Jordan? Like John Wayne, Tom Landry, or Billy Graham? Was Todd a hero like them? Most of our American 'heroes' in recent years have been film stars, athletes, or musicians. The term celebrity seemed to apply more appropriately to them than hero."[42] Despite

themselves, or despite the message they have imbibed from serious discourses (perhaps those they have heard articulated in their churches
and religious traditions) about why athletes cannot be real heroes, these
biographers have absorbed a more primordial bit of American cultural
narrative regarding heroes that frames sport as the de facto proving
ground for heroic character most available to most aspirants.

It has been argued that Islamic terrorism is driven in significant
measure by the concerns of some Islamic men about the changing,
increasingly more liberated sexuality of Islamic women. As the Egyptian Islamists who assassinated Sadat saw his marriage to a Western-
ized woman as one of his central crimes, so too, it is claimed, we should
explore the insecurities with assertive female sexuality and obsessive
desire for an uncomplicated, traditional masculine domination of the
sexual realm that can be traced in al-Qaeda and other contemporary
Islamic terrorists.[43] Much was made in certain accounts of the fact that
some of the 9/11 hijackers frequented strip clubs in the days before they
undertook their mission, and perhaps there is something more profound going on here than the mass media sources that took up this angle
of the story can be expected to see. But this sexual lens for viewing male
aggression and violence could reasonably be invoked as a conceptual
tool for viewing the Flight 93 hero myth as well. For here too, a symbolic privileging of hypermasculinized subjects and narratives is noticeable. One of the facts concerning the heroes' biographies that received
little play in the mainstream media narratives had to do with Bingham's
homosexuality. Almost all media coverage of Bingham's character and
role in the events on Flight 93 portrayed him in ways that, even if they
embraced his homosexuality, could nonetheless be easily included in
the heroic narrative I outline here.[44] His biography, written by an editor
at *The Advocate* for Alyson Publications, the magazine's imprint, not
entirely surprisingly reads almost entirely as an account of Bingham's
sexual orientation and various love interests, at the expense of discussion of his alleged role in the events that took place on Flight 93, which
are relegated to a penultimate chapter of just over ten pages. Yet, in
addition to the myriad discussions of his sexuality, we find in Bingham's
biography an athletic hero myth that does not differ in its essentials
from that in the books on Beamer, Burnett, and Glick. His character

is ultimately described in ways that do not challenge "heteronormative assumptions and institutions,"[45] and he could be included in the pantheon of the heroes only and precisely because stories of his conventionally masculine bravery and athleticism fit the traditional image of the hero. Though some gay and lesbian media sources, and even to a fair degree his biographer, sought to turn Bingham into primarily a homosexual man with the goal of politically assisting the social movement of homosexuals, in most media Bingham was described as a "patchwork quilt of identities: gay leader, athlete, Republican Party activist, musician, fratboy, businessman, bon vivant, conservative, surfer."[46] The Pamplona incident was frequently recounted, even exaggerated into a version (which, appropriately enough, seems to have originated in the pages of *Sports Illustrated*) where Bingham was gored and "carried on the horns" of a bull.[47] In this way, his homosexuality could be safely relegated to the margins of the discussion of his empirical identity, and the ideal typical traits of the Flight 93 hero could come to the fore.[48]

The sport Bingham played probably mattered deeply too: rugby is a macho game, requiring mostly raw strength and stamina, marked by its brutal simplicity and martial ferocity, and it is in this way not unlike the combative, violent sports of the other three heroes (judo for Glick, American football for Beamer and Burnett). Seen from this angle, it is easier to start to understand some of the parameters of the sporting hero. To properly embody the aggressive masculine persona of this hero type, only some sports will do. American football, we are reminded by George Carlin in a deservedly famous bit of stand-up comedy, is a sport that mimes war more closely than any other major sport in the American tradition. It is played in places like War Memorial Stadium and Soldier Field. The objective is

> for the quarterback, otherwise known as the field general, to be on target with his aerial assault, riddling the defense by hitting his receivers with deadly accuracy, in spite of the blitz, even if he has to use the shotgun. With short bullet passes and long bombs, he marches his troops into enemy territory, balancing this aerial assault with a sustained ground attack which punches holes in the forward wall of the enemy's defensive line.

Baseball, Carlin goes on, presents rather less macho goals: "to go home and be safe." One wonders if baseball-playing Flight 93 heroes would have been so easily and seamlessly fitted to the narrative that emerged.

Moral Purity and Traditional Values

The Flight 93 heroes are consistently depicted as adhering to highly traditional and conservative visions of values and moral purity. In the case of Beamer and Burnett, this plays itself out in a superpatriotic love of country that takes on the most highly stylized forms. Beamer's wife depicts her husband's parents as "salt-of-the-earth folks" (13) who "raised Todd . . . with a strong biblical value system and work ethic."[49] The details of his moral life read like something out of one of Horatio Alger's dime novels about morally centered subjects achieving material and moral success through their transparent honesty and good nature. The Beamers lived, his wife writes, in a "Norman Rockwell world."[50] "Independence, patriotism, freedom, and the American way of life," she continues "were not trite clichés tossed around lightly in our family. They were highly treasured values."[51] Attachment to family and the Protestant Ethic's call to success in career are the two motivating factors in Beamer's life, and he is so committed to both that there is inevitable conflict between them: "Todd's greatest desire in life was to be a godly husband and father. Yet he was so driven to succeed in his career, he often found the two goals competing against each other."[52]

Burnett's account of her husband's moral sensibility and purity is perhaps still more demonstrative of this conservative, traditional model. She describes her husband's position on the American culture wars in the blunt, unapologetic terms of contemporary far-right-wing Christian discourse, which I will examine in detail in the next section.

We have already seen how the homosexual Bingham was safely recuperated into a traditionalist masculine hero-athlete myth. On the issue of values and moral purity, we find much the same, even though his biography would seem to offer at least the possibility of alternative framings of moral values insofar as his homosexuality is heavily foregrounded in *Mark Bingham*. In both that book and *Among the Heroes*, there is much information that points to Bingham's childhood as morally deviant, even dysfunctional. His parents separated almost immediately upon his birth and his father effectively disappeared, leaving his mother alone to raise him. Alice Hoglan had converted to Mormonism at age 15 and attended Brigham Young University, but while in college she became pregnant, married Bingham's father in Las Vegas, then promptly divorced him a few weeks after Bingham was born because the father would not convert to the Mormon faith.[53] During Bingham's early years, he and his mother moved constantly, and she worked a series of odd jobs, one of which was as a bunny at Miami Beach's Playboy Plaza Hotel.[54] The existence she eked out was precarious. At least once, she and her young son were homeless, living in the back of their pickup truck and eating the fish the boy was able to catch near the campsite they called home.[55] Bingham had originally been given his father's first name, Gerald, but Hoglan regretted this decision after the divorce and began calling him "Kerry," a mixture of his first and middle (Kendall) names. Bingham complained that other boys were saying he had a girl's name, and Hoglan allowed her eight-year-old son to legally change his name to whatever name he preferred, and thus Mark Bingham came to be. All these details, significantly deviant from the traditional conservative moral narrative of American childhood, were however tempered in the books and in other media by the constant reiteration that Bingham had been a successful businessman and a Republican who had campaigned for John McCain in 2000 and who eventually voted in that election for George W. Bush. The fact that he could be squared with other elements of the American hero type (rugby player, fearless and full of willpower, a supporter of conservative boot-strap individualism) made it possible to defang the aspects of his identity and upbringing that potentially complicated a conservative moral framing. That Bingham held to a personal politics that was "patriotic, prodefense spending, militarist, and tough on crime"[56] meant his homosexuality and the morally deviant aspects of his upbringing by a single mother who had worked as a Playboy bunny and who allowed Bingham to change his own name when he was eight could be overlooked. Whatever her failings when compared to the parents of Burnett and Beamer to effectively socialize her son into the morally pure world of the hero-to-be, his mother nonetheless "impress[ed] upon him . . . [t]he 'Protestant work ethic' . . . [that] ensured he would never grow up to be a man who shirked his responsibilities."[57]

Glick's upbringing was much more within the normative, traditional framework than Bingham's, although not so stereotypical of the model as that of Beamer or Burnett. We have seen already the evidence his wife gives of his parents inculcating in him and his siblings a competitive individualism and the "outwork everybody else" ethic that tends to accompany it in American culture. She provides other details of his moral character that further embellish the portrait of him as a morally pure culture hero well before the fateful date of his heroic self-sacrifice. One of the most vivid examples constitutes a variation on a typical American myth about heroically fearless truth telling, the prototype of which is to be found in the story of the youthful George Washington confessing to the chopping down of his father's cherry tree. During a party at the Glick family home during Jeremy's teen years, the family's car was taken out for a joyride and damaged. Glick, going the nation's first president one better, confessed to a crime he had not even committed, but only passively permitted to happen, in order to spare his friends punishment he felt should be his for not acting in the moment to prevent the misdeed. His wife frames the event thus: "[E]ven [Glick's] worst teenage episodes had a strange way of showing how unselfish he was."[58]

Jere Longman's *Among the Heroes* effectively expands the mythical vision of the moral purity of the four central heroes to include everyone on the plane. Not a single passenger is described in the book without several anecdotes or descriptions that reveal him or her as a morally exceptionally pure individual. Some of these stories are the same ones other mass media had run in the aftermath of the crash, but Longman provides one of the richest such pools of mythological source material and covers even the passengers the mainstream mass media mostly ignored. Donald Peterson loaned money and "never charge[d] interest."[59] Deora Bodley was called "Buddha" by some of her friends because of her peaceful, introspective attitude; she apparently also "handed . . . out [little Buddha statues] for good luck."[60] Kristin White Gould let friends use her car and paid their doctor bills, and even "turned an obscene phone call by a desperate, lonely teenager" into a phone friendship of several years."[61] Joe DeLuca brought ice cream to the sick and books to read to his friends' children.[62] Lauren Grandcolas "volunteered at AIDS walks, food distribution centers and adopt-a-kid programs, the United Way and Habitat for Humanity."[63] Bill Cashman loaned large sums of money to needy relatives.[64] My suggestion is not that these and the other endless examples in the book are not true; they doubtless are, and indeed it is likely that more such qualities could be listed for each passenger. But such a list could also likely be put together for more or less any randomly assembled group of 40 people, and a long list of undesirable, egoistic, morally problematic qualities could almost certainly be assembled for that random group of 40 as well as for the passengers and crew of Flight 93. We know that human beings are morally complex in this way, capable of both the admirable and the reproachable and prone to engage in behavior that demonstrates both capacities. That the qualities present in the hero narrative of Flight 93 are uniformly indicative of moral purity and selflessness is more a characteristic of the structural requirements of such myths than it is a fully accurate reflection of the personalities of the Flight 93 passengers and crew, which are inevitably complicated, since they were human.

The Narrative of Christian Hero-Martyrdom

The core thread uniting much of the popular literature on Flight 93 passengers has to do with the emergence of a character we might call the Christian hero-martyr. This figure has a long history in the West. The original Christian martyrs, from Stephen to the apostle James, played an essential role in defining the proper Christian response to persecution. In the traditional mode, the Christian martyr is threatened with torture and death unless he rejects God and gives up his faith, and his brutal suffering and death are met with a stoic refusal to relinquish his belief in the Christian God and a pacifist rejection of violent resistance to his oppressors. The genre represented by the Christian martyr myth is redemptive. This kind of myth rejects the refusal of transcendence in tragedy and sits inside a vision of the world in which human destiny and action are framed by a compassionate God who offers salvation and an end to suffering to those who choose morally correct paths. In this vision, the only morally correct path to choose in the face of the challenge of evil is heroic self-sacrifice.

A key development affecting our case is that the Christian martyr almost inevitably becomes a nationalist on American soil. His faith in Christ is refracted through his equally fervent belief that the United

States is the "last best hope" for establishing the Christian God's ideal in this world, which is a prelude and preparation for the life to come. Further, the Christian martyr in America may die for his faith, but in doing so he refuses to renounce violence or resistance. He violently struggles against the evil opponent and may even righteously annihilate him while not falling out of favor with the Lamb of God. It is not the Christ of the Sermon on the Mount we find here, but rather the storming Jesus in the temple, angrily sweeping away the money changers. The cultural struggle in American Christianity between pacifist accounts of Jesus's message and more militant versions is of old vintage. Dating back at least to the Civil War, there are competing notions of Christian identity, largely centered in the North and South, respectively. In an essay on lynching in the post–Civil War South, Orlando Patterson finds two core stories in the foundational act of Christianity, the crucifixion of Jesus. In one, there is God humbled, brought low by his commoner's death on the cross, and a concomitant sense of contrite empathy with the powerless. In the other story, however, we find the triumphant God standing in righteous and indignant judgment of his enemies and his followers alike. Two stories: God as meek, peaceful servant of the poor, or God as powerful and vengeful master of all. The latter narrative became the template of post–Civil War white Southern culture, as whites who adhered to the notion of the Lost Cause embraced the morally certain and unquestioned strength of Christ the Victorious Judge and Jury and violently rejected the second narrative of the penitent, humble Christ and all its symbolic stand-ins, most centrally the figure of the stoic, punished black. With this interpretive frame, we can even make sense of the symbolism of the racist's burning cross; as the very site of the bringing low of the Christ, the cross must be radically rejected if the white South is to reaffirm its power and its authority.[65] This Christ of the historical post–Civil War white South has become the Christ of contemporary conservative evangelical Christianity and the political and cultural right more broadly. This is a militant Jesus, who does not flinch from violence when it is righteous, who wants his message assertively carried to the four corners of the Earth, and who is not concerned with the multicultural niceties of postmodern pluralism. His follower, the militant Christian martyr, who fights and kills and perhaps dies for his faith and his national group, is the central mythical backdrop of the biographies of Todd Beamer and Tom Burnett, who emerge as Christian soldiers in virtually every sense of the word.

In the three books written about these two men, we find a penetrating focus on questions of religious faith that begins in their very first pages. Lisa Beamer opens by telling of her experience of the morning of September 11, 2001, and by a scant ten pages in, the potentially catastrophic loss of her husband is made right by the Christian narrative: "In that dark moment, my soul cried out to God—and he began to give me a sense of peace and a confidence that the children and I were going to be okay. . . . I felt strongly that Todd's final thoughts and expressions would have been of his faith in God."[66] Lisa Jefferson's book is literally dedicated to God, and the epigraph at the book's beginning reads "God's greatest joy is to be believed. His greatest sorrow is when we doubt Him."[67] Deena Burnett is into the heart of the matter on the first page of chapter one: "Since [Tom's] birth, each time he made the right choice, in light of his experiences and circumstances, God began to build in him the strong foundation of faith, character, courage, and conviction which would enable him—no, compel him—to be who he was on September 11th."[68] Lyz Glick also invokes a religious reality underlying the deeds of her husband on board Flight 93, although it is less denominationally clear than what we find in the other three books. In addressing her daughter with the story of waking up the morning of September 12, 2001, to face the reality of her husband's death, she tells her, "You lay on your back, eyes closed, . . . I cannot explain it, but at that moment I felt the power of something higher pulling me into something bigger than my pain. . . . I think your daddy always suspected he had a higher purpose."[69] Bingham's book is the sole outlier here, opening with a prologue linking Bingham to Oliver Sipple, the gay ex-Marine who wrestled a gun away from the would-be assassin of President Ford in 1975 and was subsequently and unwillingly outed in the press, and never mentioning God.

The Christian hero identity sketched here is resolutely culturally conservative and staunchly orthodox with respect to the American culture wars. Burnett is described as a stereotypically assertive, morally certain man. He rejected "moral relativity" and held to firm, stable definitions of right and wrong that required a certain kind of intolerance of those who chose incorrectly among them: " 'If we don't judge people,' [Tom] said, 'then we lose the concept of right versus wrong and the moral fiber of our country begins to deteriorate.'"[70] The book concludes with a militant call to action in the Christian right's struggle against cultural postmodernism: "For several decades our country has been heading in a moral direction which is wrong. Yet we have been unwilling to admit we are off-course and have justified our actions by muddying the boundaries. . . . The clear difference between right and wrong is founded on eternal principles established by a supernatural God. . . . Those who are willing to do what is right need to stand up. It's time to fight back."[71]

But the moral certainty at which Burnett arrived came, his wife narrates, only after a crisis in faith that is a frequent element in accounts of the religious trajectories of conservative Christians. His wife describes his Christian faith as something he had arrived at not simply as a birthright but after a careful consideration and rejection of secular alternatives. At a certain point in his life, he became more skeptical and, while attending a Catholic university in Minnesota, "sought out the resident monks regularly to debate matters of faith."[72] In the end, he chose religious faith: "[I]f . . . biblical scholars could prove the validity of only some of the Bible stories and scientists could prove only some of their theories, then why not choose to live by that which offered the best, most rewarding way of life?"[73] Burnett's certainty expressed itself, in his wife's account, as a set of classic "culture war" attitudes regarding the current cultural climate in America. He believed the country faced "huge repercussions" because of what he believed to be our progressive turning away from a "Sovereign God."[74] Longman describes Burnett as a man sufficiently dedicated to his religious faith to skip lunch with his family in order to attend daily Mass in times of personal introspection.[75]

Beamer's wife tells a story identical in overall framework if slightly different in some details. The central difference has to do with the lack of even a fleeting acknowledgement of any power in secular worldviews. Beamer is presented as a deeply believing Christian from his youth, largely due to the deep religiosity of his parents, who encouraged their children to read the Bible and put it into practice in everyday life.[76] From early on, "Todd wanted . . . to live the Christian life, not just talk about it."[77] Instead of the hero facing a religious crisis, as in Burnett's case, it is the hero's *wife* who does so here. Lisa Beamer describes a brief crisis in her own Christian faith in the wake of her father's death, which was cured largely by reflection on a Bible passage.[78] Later in the book, she credits God for having prepared her for the ordeal of her husband's death by presenting her first with that of her father's passing.[79] So remarkably strong is Beamer's Christian identity, and so aware of it is his wife, that even the call from the United Airlines contact person with the news of his presence on the crashed Flight 93 does not shatter her calm: "Shortly after United Airlines called. . . . 'Mrs. Beamer, . . . I'm sorry to inform you that your husband was a passenger aboard Flight 93 that has crashed in Pennsylvania.' 'I know,' I replied calmly. I didn't break down crying hysterically. . . . The United representative sounded almost surprised that I was so calm. I didn't fully realize it then, but God was already giving me an incredible sense of peace."[80] Her description of learning of the details of her husband's conversation with Lisa Jefferson is startling. She is so overjoyed to learn that her husband's faith had not wavered in the last minutes of his life that she calls his mother to share this news: "For all of us, even more significant and encouraging than Todd's heroic actions aboard Flight 93 was the knowledge that his faith—and ours—could withstand the ultimate test."[81] The Christian hero-martyr is directed toward only one thing, his God, and all other things—family, career, life plans—pale in comparison. The motivation is the deepest love, and even the evil doers who bring the hero low deserve only his compassion and love; she expressed the belief that her husband was "forgiving the terrorists" in his last-minute prayer.[82] But this loving compassion should not be confused for religious *tolerance*. She is frightened when she hears the cockpit recording and the hijackers' "deluded references to God—not the God of the Bible but a god who would endorse murder and hate."[83] Beamer's father put the matter still more bluntly at the memorial service for his son, noting that he took comfort in knowing that "the hijackers did not have the name of Jesus on their lips in their final moments" and that they must now know that "they didn't only pick the wrong plane . . . [but] the wrong side."[84] It is clear that for Lisa Beamer no account of her husband's actions on the plane that would capture their deepest reality can avoid fully embracing the Christian worldview. She describes her dissatisfaction during the memorial ceremony at the crash site listening to speakers who tried to provide comfort without reference to religion or God: "[I]t struck me how hopeless the world is when God is factored out of the equation."[85] The message of Todd's life is summarized toward the end of the book. The World Trade Center and the Pentagon are symbols of American economic and military power, but they fell. True security and safety can come only from "a loving heavenly Father, who cannot be shaken. . . . For those looking for hope, I recommend grabbing the hand of your heavenly Father as tightly as possible, like a little child does with his parent.[86] Her husband is even described straightforwardly as a surrogate for the original hero-martyr of the Christian religion. Just as the passengers on Flight 93 would have preferred to survive, so too "[t]here was one who came to earth, knowing ahead of time that his most important purpose in living would be accomplished only through his dying, . . . but he really didn't want to die either. . . . Finally he said 'not my will but yours be done.' That was God's plan. I don't think Todd chose to die, but he did choose for God's will to be done in his life."[87]

Lisa Jefferson's book describes Beamer in much less detail than the book written by his wife, given her fleeting acquaintance with the man. Nonetheless, she is effusive in her characterization of him in the same broad terms we find in *Let's Roll!* Jefferson describes Beamer as a "courageous man who boldly bore witness of his faith in Christ," and she expresses the belief that God "scheduled my 'appointment' with Todd Beamer" precisely in order to push her into the same role of service of the faith for which He had chosen Beamer.[88] Theirs was "a conversation between two followers of Christ, both desperately seeking God."[89] She describes fear in the initial moments after taking Beamer's call, but then "[a]n overwhelming sense of peace enveloped me. I knew God was with me and with Todd. . . . In my spirit, I cried out and prayed for God's help."[90] Her book is itself essentially an evangelical effort. Virtually every page contains exhortations of the reader to listen to and follow the Christian God's plans for him or her: "On the morning of that fateful day in our beloved America, God scheduled my role. . . . He may have such a challenge for you—a call. . . . Are you ready?"[91] Beamer's role is defined by his relationship to his (and her) God:

> I believe that God uses situations and circumstances to mold us and to conform us into His image . . . like a potter shapes and molds clay. Being on the spinning wheel can sometimes be dizzying. Sometimes bits of clay

fall off the wheel to the floor in moist clumps of nothingness, and sometimes the pressure of becoming pliable in the Potter's hands is painful—but the end result is a beautiful vessel that can be used mightily by God, to strengthen, to edify, to encourage, to instill hope and trust, . . . and to ultimately bear witness of God's awesome power and wonder.[92]

The Christian hero/martyr myth is noticeably absent in the books on Bingham and Glick. Bingham's biographer has almost nothing to say about Bingham's religious faith or lack thereof. We learn only that his mother was a youthful convert to Mormonism who, in the cultural atmosphere of the late 1960s, left the faith to become pregnant by a man with whom she split up mere weeks after her son's birth. Her subsequent trajectory apparently produced something quite different for her son than the idyllic childhoods the wives of Beamer and Burnett describe their husbands enjoying. Glick's biography is the biggest outlier of the four on religious issues insofar as it is the only one to offer explicitly critical remarks about any religion other than Islam. He was an apparently nonpracticing Jew with a somewhat critical view of religion that is aptly presented by his wife. In one passage, she recounts phone conversations with her husband in which he described his feeling that "we were chess pieces being moved around by the Little Man, . . . [who] put a tremendous amount of energy into his schemes, tried to get us lined up with each other, but he just wasn't the brightest guy and things kept going wrong. . . . Maybe he's been drinking even more than we have. . . . Drunk Little Man, he said, Drunk omnipotent Little Man, I said, Scary, he said."[93]

Premonitions

Though not all of the four central heroes are enveloped in the myth of the Christian martyr, all do participate in another narrative element connected to deep American mythologies about death and the supernatural. The deaths of all four men are described as having been signaled in advance in some form of supernatural premonition or other mystically significant occurrences that demonstrate the hand God had in the events of 9/11. Earlier in this chapter, I described Lisa Beamer's reference to a passage in the Book of Romans as a key part of her emergence from the religious crisis brought on by the sudden death of her father. Later in the book, she writes of two other significant encounters with this same passage in the Bible, and implies that it is not coincidence but God's will that brought the text before her in both cases. First, she is given this very passage in her church as the prompt for discussion in Bible study the week beginning September 10, 2001. Then, still more mysteriously, she claims to have found the same passage handwritten by Beamer in his car after she reclaimed it in the wake of his death.[94]

This is not the sole example of narratives of ominous supernatural intervention in Beamer's book. She also describes her husband leaving Fresno State, his first college choice, to instead attend Christian Wheaton College as a result of a miraculous occurrence. An aspiring baseball player, he was injured in an auto accident and was therefore unable to make the Fresno State baseball team, which his wife classifies as a "sign."[95] In another passage, she tells of one of her earliest experiences of supernatural action in the world: when she was a child, the family cat went missing and then returned after a week, which lead her to "realize . . . that sometimes miracles do happen."[96] Lisa Jefferson tells of yet another such premonition, this one indicating to her the supernatural status of Todd Beamer himself, in her description of her first meeting with Lisa Beamer. She recalls Beamer asking her how she imagined her husband, and Jefferson replies that she sees him in white with dark hair. When Beamer confirms that he did have dark hair and was wearing a white shirt on the plane, Jefferson "knew he was with the angels in heaven."[97]

The trope appears again and again in the biographical narratives. In *Among the Heroes*, we learn that Tom Burnett and his wife apparently shared a premonition that he would die early and tragically; on one occasion, Burnett even tried to double their life insurance policies because the presentiment was so strong.[98] Lyz Glick too is drawn to the supernatural-intervention narrative. She describes a meeting with a psychic in her 9/11 therapy group, during which she was told that "Jeremy's showing me his teeth," which she interprets as mystical advance knowledge that some of her husband's teeth were the only physical evidence of his body discovered in the recovery effort.[99] The psychic also described something "bound in leather" to her, and she reveals that later she retrieved his leather datebook from the wreckage collection.[100]

Longman describes "a bad feeling" Glick communicated to his wife about the 9/11 flight, worrying about a college roommate who had died in a plane crash and wondering if "[l]ightning [might] strike twice in the same place."[101] Mark Bingham's family and friends mention similar premonitions. Matt Hall, the friend who dropped him off at the airport on the morning of September 11, is described as having "a curious vision" of Bingham looking out of the plane smiling as he spoke to him just before takeoff that morning: "How odd. What did it mean? Is this the last time I'm going to see him?"[102] Bingham's aunt Candyce Hoglan purportedly had a dream the morning of September 11 in which a plane went down in a catastrophic crash. She was awakened by a phone call bearing the news that Mark's plane had been hijacked.[103]

Relatives of other passengers on Flight 93 participate too. Waleska Martinez's father had a repeated dream for more than a decade of a plane crashing, believing it was a presentiment of his own fate.[104] Martinez herself had apparently answered a phone call from her mother in the middle of the night on September 10 and came to believe it was "bad luck" to do so, something that emotionally troubled her sufficiently about the flight that she "couldn't stop . . . trembling." Her partner suggested she change her September 11 flight plans, but Martinez replied that she could not do so.[105]

These references to premonitions of the crash or of post-crash discoveries in the wreckage lend still more power to the construction of a narrative of the Flight 93 heroes as individuals chosen by a supernatural power for a sacred mission. Their fate is foretold, and it is as if their true place was never on this earth, with ordinary mortals such as the rest of us. They were always and forever destined to become the sacred objects of the nation that they became.

The Cultural Narratives of the Films on Flight 93

Much has been said about the cinematic nature of the events of September 11, 2001, at least of the part of those events that unfolded in Manhattan. Norman Mailer described the phenomenal level of terror the attacks produced in the American citizenry as rooted in their close resemblance to cinematic nightmares we had already viewed dozens of times: "Our movies came off the screen and chased us down the canyons of the city."[1] But if the events of that day struck many as movie-like in their larger-than-life, mythological nature, film played a perhaps even more important role *after* that day in further mythologizing it.

The four films on Flight 93 (*Flight 93*, *United 93*, *The Flight That Fought Back*, and *Portrait of Courage: The Untold Story of Flight 93*) were produced by different groups of people with varying authorial and commercial interests and goals, but the makers of all four films have one thing in common: each purports to be telling viewers the truth about the events that took place on Flight 93's final voyage. Those who made the films tell similar stories about how they endeavored to stay as close to the facts as possible, and each evinces confidence that the end result was successful. Peter Markles, the director of *Flight 93*, characterized his artistic goal as the production of "something that spoke the truth." Paul Greengrass, who directed *United 93*, exudes a similar confidence about the veracity of his film's perspective; describing a tense scene in the film wherein air traffic controllers are watching a near-miss collision of United Flight 175 and another airliner, he blithely pronounces: "As I watched this being reenacted, you could feel that it must have felt like this." But there is always something more, and different, going on in such tellings than merely the intentions of the tellers. We know this to be true not only of films, but of other kinds of texts too, yet it has been a byword of much media theory and analysis over the years that something about the visual media, and film especially, enable them to communicate at a level more visceral and emotionally powerful, and therefore, for some at least, more truthful, than other media. Cinema speaks a language that approximates the language of dream, of the imaginary, and of myth. Alongside the actual words spoken by the characters who appear on the screen and the mundane thread of the plot, there is an entire apparatus of visual symbolism and archetype that carries viewers in directions that may deviate widely from that provided by the text. We learn important lessons by closely examining the ways in which the makers of these four films inevitably failed to achieve their professed goal of straightforward truth telling and wandered instead into the more complicated, more treacherous, and more fascinating business of myth construction.

Flight 93: The First Cinematic Pass through the Myth

Flight 93 is a ninety-minute film originally aired in January 2006 on the A&E channel, produced in association with Fox Television Studios. I begin my analysis of it with a more or less exhaustive, scene-by-scene description of the film, in order to establish some of the basic elements of Flight 93 cinematography, as the other films use many of the same visual techniques and present a similar factual narrative, although there are also some considerable differences I will note.

In the film's first scene, the central conflict of protagonists and antagonists is established in unmistakable terms. We see first officer LeRoy Homer dressing for the flight, then there is a cut to Ziad Jarrah, the terrorist pilot, as he shaves his face and chest in preparation for what he knows will be his final day on the planet. Pilots Jason Dahl and Homer are seen getting ready for the flight, then we see passengers going through security. We glimpse Lauren Grandcolas reading a book entitled *What to Expect when You're Expecting* in the waiting area as she calls home and leaves a message announcing her changed flight. As passengers board the plane, names on ticket stubs are visible as they are scanned by airline personnel: Rothenberg, Alghamdi, Jarrah, Burnett, Alnami, passengers and hijackers intermingled and, at this point, still undifferentiated except in the ethnic particularities of their names. The hijackers exchange intense looks as they board. The ticket stubs of other passengers are shown as an introduction of more of the film's central characters: Nacke, Grandcolas, Wainio, Beamer, then Nicole

Miller, who is dropped off at the gate by her attentive boyfriend. At this point the characters are no more than a collection of names and a group of faces, with no clear connections between the two. It is easy work, if one is armed with basic information about the individual passengers in advance, to discern who is who, but many viewers of the film likely do not have that information at their fingertips, and so the effect early in the film is a reinforcing of the idea of the passengers as a collectivity, rather than as separable individuals.

At Boston air traffic control, Mohamed Atta is overheard cryptically and menacingly announcing the beginning of the day's horrific turn of events: "We have some planes!" The Boston staff also hears flight attendant Amy Sweeney announce that American Flight 11 has been hijacked. Flight 93 takes off just as Boston hears Sweeney again, now clearly terrified, in the last seconds of her life: "We're flying very low, way too low! Oh my God, we're . . ."

Aboard Flight 93, one of the terrorists goes into the front restroom and takes out what appears to be a bomb apparatus and a box cutter. The visual insinuation made, albeit subtly, is that the bomb is real, for, as the hijacker takes it from his bag, he accidentally almost knocks the object marked "high explosive C3" off the sink and then nervously steadies it. We see shots of passengers' wives at home with children watching television announcements of the first plane hitting the World Trade Center, then gasping in astonishment as the second plane hits on live air. Homer and Dahl receive a message from air traffic control alerting them to the attacks in New York and instructing them to secure against cockpit intrusions. They ask for confirmation of the message before they act on it, which, in the film's narrative, just gives the hijackers the time they need to act. The terrorists brazenly put on red headbands in their seats while passengers in first class watch them curiously; Rothenberg chuckles incredulously, Bingham looks on slightly perplexed. The film's portrayal of the seating arrangements on the plane is inaccurate: a hijacker is shown sitting in the row behind Bingham, which was not the case.

Jarrah hits the assistance button and Welsh responds with a solicitous smile. In a split second, he transforms from an innocuously grinning typical passenger to a violent attacker, grabbing her viciously by the throat, and the attack is underway. Bingham wears a distinct look of terror as the hijackers announce "Stay still, we have bombs and guns!"

The scene is comically staged and hard to read as realistic. The hijackers are strangely calm, which perhaps lends to the air of unreality. Rothenberg steps forward and attempts to reason with them and the calm is abruptly shattered; Jarrah signals to one of the other hijackers and the second man savagely stabs Rothenberg. Bingham, Burnett and the others in first class watch agonized, but do nothing. Burnett touches Rothenberg's body and his hand is stained with blood, which he wipes away, breathing heavily.

In the coach section, the passengers are not yet aware that anything is going on in first class. The hijackers tell Welsh to take them into the cockpit as Jarrah presses the blade of a box cutter to her cheek, drawing blood. She resists initially, but finally knocks on the door. Homer opens for them, and the hijackers immediately slit Welsh's throat and attack the pilots brutally. Homer shrieks, "Mayday!" and the plane starts to plummet. Cleveland air traffic control sees the plane descend on their radar and hears Homer's cry. The hijackers quickly manage to stabilize the plane. Meanwhile, the shaken passengers ask a flight attendant, "What the hell was that?!" and are told it is "just a little turbulence." Dahl's body is dragged from the pilot's seat and Jarrah takes over the controls. He turns the plane violently around to head in the other direction.

At this point, Burnett makes his first call to his wife, and the conversation is right out of the actual transcript. A flight attendant from coach comes up to first class, not realizing what is going on, and is attacked by a hijacker; Bingham cries out ineffectively, "No, please don't!" The portrayal of the passengers to this point is decidedly unheroic. They are shocked and unsure how to react. Deena Burnett calls 911 after talking to her husband. The FBI agent who eventually takes the line seems incompetent, not realizing that Burnett is on a plane still in the air, not in one of the planes that hit the towers. Back on Flight 93, the hijackers force everyone back out of first class and into coach. Burnett and Bingham exchange a knowing look as they are herded noisily toward the rear of the plane, a cinematic signifier of the alliance they will soon form. All move helplessly back as the terrorists scream at them and beat the storage cabinets above the seats. Burnett makes a second call to his wife and is told that other planes are targeting buildings. In a flash, he realizes, in the exact words provided by his wife to the FBI, "My God, it's a suicide mission!" and leans over to tell Bingham: "They're flying planes into buildings all up and down the coast!" Bingham passes the message along to the person next to him. Police arrive at the Burnett home as Deena is on the phone with her husband, but she does not offer them the phone and they do not request to speak to him. A terrorist sees Burnett talking on the phone and yells at him, and he quickly ends the call. Jarrah attempts to announce that they have a bomb on board to passengers but instead patches through to air traffic control. He instantly realizes his error, reacts in anger at himself, and another hijacker reiterates, perhaps to ensure that the viewers have not missed the nuance, "You have pressed the wrong button." Jarrah then successfully makes the announcement to the passengers: "We are going back to the airport, they have met our demands." Female and older passengers react with joy and are happily hugging one another, but the now-emerging central heroes know otherwise. Beamer asks Bingham, "Back to the airport?" and the latter shakes his head with stern certainty: "No way." We are then shown a shot of Louis Nacke with a look of menace inscribed on his face. The symbolic seeds of the rebellion of the passengers are in that scowl.

The most vigilant, aggressive terrorist (beyond Jarrah, it is impossible to distinguish them in the film, given the fact that they are not seated according to the actual flight seating arrangement) prepares to go to the cockpit and tells the bomb-wearing hijacker, who wears a frightened look, "I'll be right back." As though recognizing that the hijacker in charge is not authoritative, passengers now start making calls frequently. The aggressive hijacker tells Jarrah in the cockpit: "They are getting suspicious!" Glick makes a call to his wife, and Bingham too is openly talking on the phone while the obviously frightened terrorist watches them. Glick appears distraught, even fatalistic, telling his wife: "I don't think I'm going to get out of this!" The actor playing him is physically unimposing, substantially less than Glick's actual physical size (six-foot-two, 220 pounds). A plan for retaking the cockpit is underway, and a passenger (presumably Donald Greene, a licensed pilot, although he is not identified) tells the others that he thinks he can pilot the plane if they can regain control of it. Passengers get word from phone calls that the Pentagon has been hit and relay it inside the plane. Burnett is galvanized by now, and has turned from terrified to deadly competent organizer of the rebellion, telling Deena confidently that they have a plan. Several phone conversations are presented in terms consistent with reports of their contents. Beamer asks Lisa Jefferson, the Verizon operator, if she knows what the hijackers want ("Money? Ransom?"). Lauren Grandcolas leaves a message on her home phone, telling her husband, "I love you more than anything," as he showers unknowingly in the background; she then hands the phone to Wainio and tells her, "It's your turn, I know your mother will want to talk to you. What's the number? I'll dial." Wainio tells her stepmother: "Mom, we've been hijacked and I'm calling to say goodbye." Her stepmother responds: "Elizabeth, I have my arms around you and I'm holding you and I love you. . . . We don't know how things are going to turn out, let's just be here in the present, let's look out the window and just breathe and let's take a few deep breaths." As she says this, she looks first at a photo of the two of them, and then out the window behind her at a pristine scene of children riding bikes and playing.

There is a debate among passengers concerning tactics; Nicole Miller asks, agitatedly, "How do you know this is gonna work?" This is a noticeable liberty with what is actually known about the events on the plane, as there is no evidence that she or anyone else opposed the takeover attempt. The passengers vote with a show of hands, prompted by Burnett. All vote in the affirmative, Miller hesitant and crying but still agreeing. All this takes place in plain view of the terrorist with the bomb, a detail that is not established in the factual record (figure 7.1). Another hijacker comes out of the cockpit and tells the first terrorist to return there with him, leaving the passengers unguarded, and they immediately set the plan into motion: "Get some hot water!" Burnett gets out his phone and headset again, looking confident in a decidedly corporate, managerial way. Jarrah's comrade tells him: "The passengers are getting ready, they don't believe the bomb is real." Jarrah responds assertively: "It is God's will, you will fight them!" and one of the hijackers goes back out to face the passengers, while the others remain in the cockpit with Jarrah. Burnett tells his wife: "We're waiting until we're over a rural area, then we're gonna take back the airplane." Deena says: "What do you want me to do?" to which he responds, "Pray, Deena, just pray."

The plane shakes violently from time to time, as though Jarrah is pushing it to a velocity at or even slightly beyond its limits. The pas-

FIGURE 7.1. Passengers vote as hijackers look on.
Flight 93.

sengers gather all the materials for the assault. Military officials are seen talking about how quickly the jets can get there: "So then the fighters are gonna have to engage it inside D.C. airspace?" The jets are 23 minutes away, but Flight 93 is only 19 minutes from Washington. Beamer asks Jefferson: "Lisa, do me a favor. . . . Say the Lord's Prayer with me." She begins and Beamer follows, other passengers (Lyles and Bingham) look on, but no one else joins in. We see cuts to Beamer and Jefferson reciting the prayer, then, at its conclusion, Beamer asks others, "You ready?" He puts the phone down and intones, "Let's roll!" Honor Wainio concludes her call to her stepmother: "I gotta go, Mom, everyone's getting ready to go to the cockpit. I love you! Goodbye!" Her mother responds with a screamed "Elizabeth, no!" and breaks into sobs. Fighter jet pilots are asked about their "readiness status in case you have to shoot down." They reply: "We have 20-millimeters, didn't have time to take on Sidewinders before we scrambled. We may be able to cripple it. I guess if it comes to that, we can always ram it." Jarrah receives a printed message from air traffic control: "Flight 93, land immediately at Johnstown airport via VHF 117." The contents of the message are altered to alert viewers as to the whereabouts of the plane at this point; the actual message sent, according to the 9/11 Commission Report, did not name a specific airport, but only directed Flight 93 to "land asap at nearest UAL airport."

We next see several families watching their television sets as the first tower collapses in New York City, which indicates we are at 9:59 a.m., barely four minutes prior to the crash. The passenger assault begins, as they run single file down the aisle way, yelling and rolling carts toward the cabin. The hijacker wielding the fake bomb sees them and screams in terror. Jarrah rolls the plane after hearing the commotion. Flight 93 barely misses colliding with a small aircraft, which is radioed by air traffic control to "take evasive action and get out of there fast!" This marks the time as approximately 10:00 a.m., which is when Bill Wright, a local pilot reported seeing the plane near the Latrobe, Pennsylvania, airport. The passengers reach the hijacker who is outside the cockpit and overwhelm him easily by pouring hot water on his head. They use the cart to smash through the cockpit door, at which point they are met by knife-wielding hijackers. Burnett is stabbed in the stomach and staggers away from the cockpit with blood on his hands. The film is in the realm of pure speculation here; although a voice speaking English can be discerned on the cockpit voice recording saying "I'm injured," the identity of the speaker is uncertain.

Now we see the plane from the perspective of two men on the ground working in a field, who watch the plane careen just overhead, turning upside down. One man leaps behind a tractor in a harrowing shot, and the plane shoots over a red barn as the older man watches in a shot that recapitulates, albeit prior to the impact, Val McClatchey's iconic "End of Serenity" photograph.

One of the hijackers yells, "Put it down!" and Jarrah responds, "Now!" Both are speaking in English, although the transcript indicates all the hijacker dialogue in the last minutes of the flight was in Arabic. Air traffic control makes a final attempt to call the plane, just as we see the fully realized "End of Serenity" image, aesthetically enhanced to more powerfully emphasize the symbolism of the American rural heartland. Here, the red barn and the second red building are spread more widely across the line of vision, doors wide open, and thereby more fully dominate the image, and we have a tractor and other farm equipment in the foreground, along with the woods and the plume of smoke in the background (figure 7.2). The fighter jets are radioed: "Flight is down." Response: "Down as in landed?" Air traffic control: "Negative, down as in some field." They turn their planes: "Roger that." The camera cuts now to a shot of LeRoy Homer's wife with their baby, and then to the smoking wreckage and crater. Several men are walking around it, and they turn out to be the same farmers who had ducked the plane seconds

FIGURE 7.2. Recapitulation of "End of Serenity" image.
Flight 93.

earlier. Fire engines are speeding down the road toward the crash site. FBI agents arrive and have the following exchange with the firemen: "Is the flight in there?" "We don't know yet." "What do you mean?" "We're still looking for it. First we thought it was in the hole, but there's nothing in there. It must have landed in the woods, but we haven't located it yet." "We're talking about a 757, it's a huge airplane." "Yeah, we know. You can help us look for it if you like."

We then see a series of shots of passenger and crew family homes. Deena Burnett runs out of the house weeping when she hears the news that United 93 has crashed. Lisa Jefferson is told to release the call as she sits expectantly. Homer's family is gathered at their home. Alice Hoglan is given a glass of water by another family member. Hoglan and Deena Burnett dejectedly turn off their television sets.

The camera returns to the crash site, as it is being watered down and FBI agents are in the woods picking up small pieces of debris with handkerchiefs. Then the camera angle swings upward, and we see a majestically beautiful shot of sunlight streaming in around the trees, an archetypal invocation of the mystic manifestation of sacred power. Finally, there is a time-lapse shot of the hole: trucks disappear; snow falls; spring comes; the hole is filled and begins to heal. A text appears on the screen to close to credits: "On Sept. 11, 2001, United Airlines Flight 93 was one of four planes hijacked in midair. Three planes succeeded in hitting their targets. With great courage and resolve, the passengers and crew of Flight 93 prevented their plane from reaching its likely target, the White House or the Capitol Building. This film is dedicated to the passengers and crew of Flight 93, and to their families." The passengers' names scroll by, with a background of the sunlit crash site in spring time, the hole gone, the woods returned to their natural state of grace and beauty.

In the narrowly factual sense, *Flight 93* is largely an accurate account of the timeline of events on the plane. But even if there are few significant editorial digressions from what we know to have taken place on Flight 93 in this film, there is yet much in the way of visual narrative framing to tell a story that exceeds the facts and moves very far into the realm of mythology.

Visual Tropes and Themes in *Flight 93*: Upper-Middle-Class Homes and Omnipresent Babies, and Objective Evil Defeated by a Democratic Vote

The families and homes of the Flight 93 passengers are on nearly constant display in *Flight 93*. This is in marked contrast to *United 93*, where, as we will see shortly, the onscreen action is entirely confined to the plane itself and various air traffic control centers and NORAD facilities. In *United 93*, when passengers talk on their phones to family members, we see only the former, and do not even hear the voices of the latter. In the warmer, brighter, made-for-television product that is *Flight 93*, the family members of several passengers get nearly as much air time as the passengers themselves. Lyz Glick, Deena Burnett, LeRoy Homer's wife, Melodie, Alice Hoglan, Esther Heymann (Elizabeth Wainio's stepmother), and Lisa Jefferson are thoroughly sketched as characters, and we see not only them but the material and social worlds in which they live. They inhabit the kinds of spacious, spick-and-span, elegantly decorated and furnished, indeed, luxurious homes of the American upper middle class. If it is America we are seeing through the families of the passengers, it is a decidedly affluent, comfortable America, and the vibrant images of their elegant homes make the point with visual sharpness.

Classical heroes beginning with the ancient Greeks as a rule issue from the realm of social elites and are unapologetic in their disdain for the *hoi polloi* who can by their very nature never accede to the realm of the truly heroic. By contrast, American heroes are generally depicted as "of the people," even though, paradoxically, social class is almost never foregrounded in American hero mythologies. The very idea of a hero from the upper socioeconomic strata is perhaps something of an oxymoron in a democratic society, for the hero must be representative of his society, and elites face tough obstacles in endeavoring to make that claim in democracies. However, precisely what "representative" means in American society has much to do with which data we consult. Opinion pollsters have long found that most Americans, when asked about their own social class location, claim to be middle class, whatever their actual income, net worth, occupation, and life chances. There are deeply cultural factors behind this fact, not least of which is the general taboo of discussion of class difference and inequality and a default reliance on the idea that everyone, or nearly so, is comfortably in the middle class. If we are all in the same class, after all, how can class difference be a topic of division and conflict? Much hard data has to be overlooked to maintain this widely believed fiction; for example, according to 2005 data an annual income of only $50,000 puts one squarely in the middle of the second quintile of the American class hierarchy, i.e., not far at all from the wealthiest fifth of the population. Peter Markles chose unknown actors for *Flight 93* in order to reflect what he apparently believes to be a fact: that, in his words, "anyone could have had a boarding pass to get on board the plane." But this is patently not so. Airline travel remains largely a phenomenon of the upper middle classes in America, and the demographic represented in the business section of the average American domestic flight is at the extreme upper end of the social class spectrum. According to survey research done by the U.S. Travel Association, from August 2008 through July 2009, only about 48% of Americans traveled by air for either leisure or business, and three of four U.S. domestic passengers were on leisure trips, most at the low-cost and short-distance end of the spectrum.

A brief glance at the educational attainment and occupations of Flight 93 passengers shows what is true of most commercial flights in the U.S.: heavy overrepresentation of those firmly positioned in the upper middle classes by both education and occupation, largely employed in the upper echelons of the corporate world in business and managerial occupations. Of the 33 passengers on the plane, at least 20 had a four-year college degree or higher. Of the 13 remaining, three were in college at the time of death, and five others had occupations that suggest at least a four-year degree, although specific educational data for them was not readily available in biographical material. There were at least three MBAs and three holders of master's degrees, and at least two with law degrees. The current percentage of the entire American population age 25 and over with a four-year college degree is around 19% according to figures given by the 2010 U.S. Census, so the passengers on Flight 93 are distinctly *un*representative on this score: they were at least three times more likely to have such a level of educational attainment.

When one turns to look at occupational data for the passengers, the same kind of picture emerges. Among the 33 passengers, one finds at least three owners of their own companies (a public relations firm, an importing group, and an industrial products supply company), a retired president of an electric company, an executive vice president and two executive directors (of, respectively, a flight instruments corporation, a center for advocacy for the disabled, and the software development arm of a large telecommunications company), an attorney active in international law, the export director of a wine institute, a chief operating officer at a medical products corporation, an environmental compliance manager at a large automobile manufacturer, a retired bank officer, a computer engineer at a middleware software company, a business systems specialist and software designer for a large healthcare and pharmaceutical company, and both an assistant regional manager and an automations specialist with the U.S. Census Bureau. When the focus turns specifically to the four central heroes discussed in the previous chapter, elite social class position is quite evident. Thomas Burnett Jr. was vice president and chief operating officer of Thoratec Corporation, a company that develops and markets medical technologies. Thoratec is based in Pleasanton, California, and operates several facilities in the United States and Great Britain. Mark Bingham was a public relations executive with his own firm, the Bingham Group. The world-class business skills and endeavors of these two are widely featured in all of the media coverage of them, and it is almost certainly safe to say that they both made well into six figures annually. Todd Beamer was an account manager at Oracle, the computer software company, and Jeremy Glick was a sales and marketing executive at Vividence, an e-consulting company. These four men were, in other words, two members of the relatively elite business class and two more very much on their way in that direction, all of them likely making well above the median American income and enjoying life chances quite more robust than those of the vast bulk of Americans. Nearly all the passengers on Flight 93 were, like those on most flights in the U.S., in the top two quintiles of the population in terms of social class.

It may well be that the makers of *Flight 93* so fundamentally misunderstand the reality of social class difference in the U.S. that they do not recognize how unrepresentative the images in the film of passenger homes are of the living conditions of most Americans, and therefore do not quite comprehend the immense difficulties in presenting these characters as "of the people." A truly representative vision of American home life would necessarily include examples of the cramped, cluttered homes of Americans from lower socioeconomic strata, and the modest dwellings of the middle classes. This bit of visual sociology in the film is of tremendous analytical interest in the way it undermines the very mythology to which it intends to contribute.

A particularly poignant narrativization of this mythological bourgeois American home and the idyllic community in which it is situated emerges in the scene wherein Wainio speaks with her stepmother, Heymann. As the latter comforts her stepdaughter, she walks through an ideal typical upper-middle-class home, and behind her, through the large front windows, a street scene straight out of Norman Rockwell (or, perhaps, to update the reference, straight out of Thomas Kinkade[2]) plays out. The contrast between the American dream and the nightmare on Flight 93 is made explicit at the moment when Wainio tells her stepmother she has to go to join the rest of the passengers in their effort to retake the plane, and Heymann, who to this point has been preternaturally calm, finally dissolves into an anguished cry, as children playing in the calm, safe street are framed in the window behind her (figure 7.3).

Family members, and especially infants, are omnipresent as archetypal symbols in *Flight 93*. In one scene, Alice Hoglan's home seems practically overflowing with babies, every adult in the shot holding an identically clad infant.[3] The very first scene of the film, in which LeRoy Homer kisses his wife and infant child goodbye, sets the tone here. If the elegance of the homes invokes American prosperity and middle-class affluence, the many children bring to mind traditional familial mythologies and point to a narrative of a fecund America. The reality of American air travel is, however, rather dissonant with this myth, as many,

FIGURE 7.3. Tragedy with Thomas Kinkade–esque
Americana as backdrop. *Flight 93.*

and especially those traveling in business class, are alone, without family
members or children. There was only one couple, the retired Petersons,
on Flight 93. Every other traveler on the plane was a lone individual,
and most of them were separated from their families by business. There
were no children on the plane.

The depiction of the hijackers is one of the aspects of all the films
that descends most deeply into the subterranean caves of the mythological. Ziad Jarrah, the terrorist pilot, emerges according to much
information about his life (he was, for example, the lone 9/11 hijacker
we know to have had a wife) as a conflicted individual whose commitment to the attack was questioned by the team's leader, Mohamed Atta.
But in *Flight 93*, he is portrayed as wholly morally uncomplicated and
untroubled by doubts. In his cinematic form, he is a truly evil figure, the
personification of malevolence, satanically certain of and committed
to the malign goal for which he has trained. Although we know virtually nothing about the initiation of the attack in its specifics, in *Flight
93* Jarrah is depicted as the clear leader who sparks the other hijackers
into action by violently assaulting Sandra Bradshaw. Just prior to this
attack, all four hijackers have donned red headbands in plain view, with
no effort to hide their actions from the other passengers, who look on
bemused or without reaction. This is a surreal scene. Is it likely, even
pre-9/11, that the sight of four men of distinctively Arab phenotypi-
cal characteristics on an airplane affixing red headbands at the same
time would not immediately elicit alarm? It is also Jarrah who initiates

the stabbing of Mickey Rothenberg by nodding deliberately to one of the other hijackers when Rothenberg attempts to negotiate with them. Later, when one of his cohort informs him that the passengers are planning a revolt, Jarrah ferociously responds that it is Allah's will that they fight the passengers. Beyond the depiction of Jarrah's malevolence, the hijackers are a cipher in this film. They do not speak discernible Arabic, as they do in *United 93*, but instead communicate mostly in broken English, even with one another, which is unlikely to have actually been the case. In *United 93*, the hijackers pray and invoke Allah frequently, and it is a shout of "Allahu Akbar!" that initiates the hijack. Here, on the contrary, they appear to operate according to no obvious logic, and no screamed allusions to Allah or anything else are necessary to set the takeover in motion. They seem to be businesslike professionals with little ideological or spiritual underpinning. Only the scene early in the film of Jarrah shaving his body alludes to the ritual, religious reasons behind the actions.

The fact that this is a made-for-television affair perhaps goes some way to explaining the relatively insignificant role of explicit violence in the film. There is very little graphic footage, and almost no blood. Rothenberg and the pilots are stabbed, and Welsh's face is slightly pricked with a box cutter, but there is nothing approaching the horrific violence of *United 93*. Even when the passenger revolt takes place, no real blows or wounds are delivered to the hijackers; we see Bingham and other passengers dousing the hijackers with hot water and nothing more. It is an antiseptic vision of the conflict on the plane, occupying one pole on a continuum of violence, while *United 93* sits near the other. The coming to awareness and organization of the counterattack by the passengers is also highly visually stylized. From the absurdly calm, knowing look exchanged by Burnett and Bingham as the first class area is being cleared to the iconic vision of spontaneous participatory democracy represented in the scene where passengers gather and vote with a show of hands on the counterattack, while the hijackers look on gloomily as though in recognition that the American democratic spirit has defeated them even before the retaking of the cockpit, the film presents an aesthetic of American cooperative, democratic spirit that at times borders on the cartoonish.

United 93: Vengeful American Ultraviolence and the Cowardice of Europeans

In *United 93*, the effort to construct a realistic narrative of the events on the plane takes on a documentary, ethnographic aesthetic. The shots are aesthetically unpolished, the camera often shaky and uncentered in the manner of many pseudo-documentary films post–*Blair Witch Project*. There is no narration, and the vast majority of the film's action takes place on the plane. A message is being sent to the viewer with each quiver and jolt of the camera's eye: this is how it really happened and how it really looked.

This message is deceptive, but we must be careful about assuming too much of its deceptive power. We are after all a population of media consumers capable of what Mark Andrejevic calls "postmodern savviness, which 'recognizes' behind every promise of truth or authenticity the reality of an illusion."[4] The savvy viewer understands that the effort at realism is always only an effort. It is a surface that masks the machinery of manipulation, and so the viewer is not truly convinced by the attempt at verisimilitude. However, something about savviness produces pleasure at the manipulative effort that tends to immunize the savvy viewer from critical reaction. She is certainly not so gullible as to believe the representations flashing before her. But she is drawn by the techniques that simulate documentary realism into a fascinating interpretive game in which, at the same time that she sees the constructedness of the drama before her, she is also apt to reify a set of conservative assumptions about the possibilities of media narrative. In this reading, the savvy viewer derives pleasure from media texts that purport to be realistic by seeing through that realist ruse and by an adamant postmodern refusal of the possibility of critical realism. "No," the savvy viewer of *United 93* might say, "this film is not realistic, and no realistic film about the event is possible, since these media are fully beholden to the desires of their producers, who want to make money, and their audiences, who want to be entertained and not educated."[5]

United 93 is the sole Flight 93 film released initially in theaters rather than on television. Its run in cinemas began in late April 2006 with a premiere in New York City, a few months after *Flight 93* aired. It was distributed by Universal Pictures and cost about $15 million to make, grossing five times that at the box office. Like *Flight 93*, but even more unmistakably, it sets up a morally rigid dramatic universe of opposing, collective protagonist and antagonist from its first moments. The first audible sound in the film is a voice praying in Arabic. We see Ziad Jarrah sitting on his hotel bed, reading aloud from what appears to be the Qur'an. One of his fellows steps into the frame and tells him, "It's time." In the first minutes of the film, the sole images are those of the terrorists in their religious and ritual preparations. Two bow to the floor in prayer, another shaves the hair from an area of his body below the waist, another glares purposefully into the mirror. The background music is sparse and foreboding, calling to mind the ominous soundtrack of a horror film. A hijacker's hands are outstretched in prayer, then a second later, the same hands grasp, check, and tuck away one of the box cutters that will shortly be employed to slice into human flesh. The symbolic cadence here is obvious: Islamic prayer as the prelude to brutal human violence. Later, there is a powerful reiteration of the trope, after the hijackers have taken the plane and while the passengers are gearing up for their attempt to take it back, wherein the hijackers and many of the passengers are seen praying. At least four passengers, including Todd Beamer, are shown reciting the Lord's Prayer, separately, but with camera cuts that weave their individual lines seamlessly together to create an image of a collective effort in the name of peace, love, and life. As the hijackers pray, however, the camera cuts to the body of Captain Dahl sprawled on the floor. The Manichean juxtaposition is symbolically devastating. When Christians pray, it is for life; when Muslims pray, it is for death.

United 93's opening sequence is striking in its starkness but it is not unique. Three of the four films about Flight 93 contain images of hijackers ritually shaving body hair on the morning of the attack. This visually marks them as culturally foreign to Americans. It is worth noting that we do not know with certainty that this shaving ritual was performed by the hijackers. The instructions apparently given to the hijack teams, three versions of which were recovered (one in a bag checked by Mohamed Atta, the second in a car parked by one of the hijackers of American Flight 77 at Dulles airport, and the third in the wreckage of Flight 93) told them to "shave the extra hair on the body, perfume yourself, and ritually wash yourself."[6] But what is "extra hair"? The answer is not clear, but the makers of these films clearly understand the powerful contribution such images make to Othering the hijackers.

A moral frame is erected in these first few minutes of *United 93*, the work done by the combination of symbols and ominous music punctuated by a banging percussion, with foreign Others uttering what for non-Arabic speaking audiences are eerily indecipherable phrases, human in origin yet outside the world of meaning and surrounded instead by an aura of the unknown. By the time the hijackers have arrived at the airport, the first five minutes of film time have elapsed, the sole communicative material to this point the atmospheric, brooding, malign depiction of the hijackers. This sets the dramatic stage. The antagonist is not a group of human beings with deluded, foolish beliefs about how to achieve political goals; it is evil in its abstract, symbolic form. Director Paul Greengrass intended the story to be framed fundamentally around two characters: Burnett and Jarrah. Early in the film, both make cell phone calls to their wives. But there is a crucial difference that is reinforced by the first five minutes of Greengrass's film in the language of the imaginary: Jarrah's call does not signal love, but rather its barbaric rending and the imminent victory of violence and evil.

As the hijackers make their way to the boarding area, another basic moral narrative is communicated in a fascinating collection of images. Behind them and ostentatiously visible as they walk by toward the boarding area are large, vividly colored advertisements featuring salacious images of young women. In one of these, we see a woman in a pink bikini. In another, a second woman licks a ludicrously phallic popsicle, the phrase "The Bust Issue" printed to her left. In a third, two other women display luxuriant cleavage, one clad only in a bra, and gaze lustily at the camera. Several hijackers are viewed walking in front of these representations of the liberated sexuality of Western women, and as Jarrah passes by, the camera lingers on these objects of carnal desire (figure 7.4). What emerges from this visual code is a statement about the Islamic jihadist's view of the decadent West, where lusty, half-naked, hypersexualized white women taunt onlookers with their "come hither" stares.

Whereas in *Flight 93* scenes onboard the plane are counterbalanced by shots of the homes of family members of passengers and crew, the secondary scene of action in *United 93* is the various air traffic control

FIGURE 7.4. Scantily clad women in advertisements
tempt the hijackers. *United 93*.

and military headquarters and control rooms where institutional decision making about the events of 9/11 took place. As Flight 93 is taking
off, and Jarrah prays under his breath, we see quick cuts between Boston
air traffic control, confirming Atta's "We have some planes!" message
and the NORAD command center in Rome, New York, where a call is
received about Flight 11's apparent hijack: "I got a hijack on the phone
from Boston!" "This is sim?" "No, this is real world, a no-shit hijack,
it's Boston!" Then, as more information pours in, we see the confusion
in air traffic control centers as they struggle to find Flight 11 and lose
transponder signals from other flights. An air of visceral panic material-
izes onscreen. There is a grippingly tense scene when it looks like Flight
175 is going to collide with another flight (Delta 2315), and all the ATC
workers gather anxiously at the screen, then are visibly relieved when
they receive a transmission from the Delta flight that they are okay. New
York air traffic control reports that Flight 175 is "droppin' like a manhole
cover into Manhattan. . . . [A]re you listening to me? This guy is going
straight down into the ground. . . . [T]he target's gone, it's gone."

There follows the single most powerful scene of the film. We see
Newark air traffic control trying frantically to visually locate Flight
175 through a tower window: "There he is, descending rapidly, he's
over the Verrazano Bridge, look how fast he's going, he's going right up
the Hudson River. . . . My God!" As we see the plane hit, the dramatic
music intensifies, and there are cries and profanities from the onlook-
ing controllers: "Ohh!" "Shit!" "Did you see that, sir?" "Jesus Christ!"
"What?!?" They look on at the fireball in the second tower in stunned
horror. Greengrass commented on this scene in his voiceover on the
film's DVD: "That second impact was the moment I think we all became

aware that something terrible was unfolding. . . . I wanted it to to sit dead center of this film, because it marks the moment beyond which this event became unmanageable." The impression of the muddled, confused character of action in these institutional sites is a clear narrative: the institutions responsible for managing and responding to crises such as the events of 9/11 failed utterly. The despair of *United 93* is more radical than that of *Flight 93* precisely because the former describes, in an unmistakable visual language, i.e., the expressions of these experts we count on to know how to handle the unthinkable, the ominous dangers that life in postmodern risk society entails.

The depiction of violence during the hijack and the passengers' attempt to retake the plane is uniquely graphic in *United 93*. In his commentary on the DVD, Greengrass makes this statement on the grounds for his aesthetic:

> I remember talking to one woman, a widow of one of the passengers, and I expressed a worry about the violence in the images I might create. She turned to me and fixed me with a steely look and said, "There's nothing you can do in this film that will match the images I have in my mind and I will have them forever, but I want you to show to everybody else something of what must have happened that day, so that we think on it," and I've never forgotten those words. . . . [T]hese events happened, and they must have looked something like this. . . . [O]ur job was to create a believable truth of what happened on this airplane and what happened on 9/11 because it's still an event that's wreathed in confusion, ignorance, conspiracy, mythology. . . . [T]he truth of 9/11 seems to me to be that we went to war in the space of two short hours against an enemy we never saw and barely understood in a state of confusion. . . . I watch these images and I think, "This is where we are today."

Whereas in *Flight 93* the hijackers seem robotic and professional, killing only as a matter of standard and effective practice, in *United 93* the terrorists kill with bloodthirsty passion, energized with some dark force by the violence and death they indiscriminately ladle out to the passengers. Blood is visible everywhere in this film. We see Rothenberg bleeding to death from the stab wound in his neck. As the slain captain is hauled out of the cabin, his shirt is soaked in gore; the plane's flight plans are even spattered with his blood.

But though it is the hijackers who release the ghost of war in their move to seize the plane, the passengers, converted into righteous heroes by the murderous acts of their foes, deal out their own dreadfully grue-some justice in retaliation. In *Flight 93*, the effort to take back the cabin is depicted in a subdued manner, and the only injury we see inflicted in that final counterattack is to one of the passengers, Burnett. The passengers in *United 93* are depicted as just as blood-thirsty and vicious as the hijackers, although their violence is understood as justifiable retaliation. The most powerful images of the final ten minutes of the film are the bloodied arms and faces of the heroes, the red stains giving witness to their struggle against Jarrah's efforts to throw them off balance and the strong-arm hijackers' use of lunch carts and fire extinguishers to ward them off. While in *Flight 93*, the hijackers are all but beaten after the vote in favor of the counterattack, and the actual combat is wholly anti-climactic, in this film the hijackers fight ferociously in their attempt to hold off the passengers. The service cart is brought into play not by the passengers, but by one of the hijackers as a weapon, and the passengers are doused by a fire extinguisher. We hear guttural cries and screams throughout this sequence ("Come here, you . . . ! Goddamnit!"), and the brutal sounds of bones snapping echo in our ears as Jeremy Glick applies judo holds to the hijackers' arms and necks. The bomb-wearing terrorist has his head caved in with the fire extinguisher one of his com-rades had just wielded against the passengers, and one of the passen-gers grabs the contraption strapped to the now-dead hijacker's body and with a maniacal expression shrieks: "It's a fake!"

The general portrayal of the terrorists in *United 93* strikes a marked contrast with that in *Flight 93*. Here, Jarrah is portrayed in a way that is closer to the complicated image that emerges from what we actu-ally know about him, i.e., as a pensive, even uncertain member of the hijack team, broodingly reflective almost to the point of jeopardizing the terrorists' mission. In *Flight 93*, he initiates the attack by physically assaulting Deborah Walsh, and he is the most aggressive and assertive of the hijackers. In *United 93*, he remains in his seat as the other hijackers nervously fidget and await his direction. Ahmed Alnami[7] even leaves his seat several rows behind Jarrah to take the seat next to him, asking him in Arabic why they are still waiting to begin the attack. It is the kind of move that could compromise their mission by revealing to other passengers that these ostensibly unrelated men are actually associates. We have no evidence to suggest it actually happened. Jarrah agitatedly tells Alnami it is not the right time and to go back to his original seat. His unimpressed colleague responds, "We have to do it now!" They are interrupted by a stewardess, to whom Jarrah responds quietly in English, and Alnami does return to his seat, but not before leveling a stern glance at Jarrah. The meaning is clear: Jarrah is hesitant, and his indecisiveness is a concern to the others on the hijacker team.

Seconds later, Alnami usurps Jarrah's leadership role by giving the visual signal to the hijacker sitting on the same side of the aisle as Jarrah, Ahmed Alhaznawi, who goes to the bathroom to prepare the mock bomb apparatus. He takes a battery and modeling clay from a bag and assembles the fake bomb. As he is in the lavatory working, Alnami and the fourth hijacker on Flight 93, Saeed Alghamdi, are fervently praying, prepared for the mission, while we see a juxtaposed shot of Jarrah, staring ahead nervously. Shortly after Alhaznawi retakes his seat, the fake bomb strapped around his waist under his jacket, Alghamdi nods to Alnami, strides boldly up to Deborah Welsh, and puts a knife to her throat as he shrieks, "Allahu Akbar!" Alhaznawi, who has whipped himself into a fury, then shouts the same phrase and stabs Mickey Rothenberg. As he strips off his jacket and shirt to reveal the mock bomb and strides to join his colleagues at the cockpit door, a look of purest animal savagery is on his face. As Jarrah sits, the other three hijackers indiscriminately pummel passengers, screaming insanely as they move toward the cockpit

FIGURE 7.5. Jarrah prays as Welsh is murdered.
United 93.

FIGURE 7.6. Burnett in command. *United 93*.

and begin herding their victims out of business class. As all of this is happening, Jarrah is still visibly struggling to find the will to act. Finally, in a jolt, he leaps to his feet to demand that Welsh tell them how to get into the cockpit. Seconds later, after they have gained entry and Alghamdi has single-handedly killed both pilots, as Jarrah sits sweating and anxious in the pilot's seat, Alghamdi growls, "We should kill her [Welsh] now! We don't need her!" He then methodically slits her throat, bellowing, "In the name of God!" While Welsh is being murdered, with her gurgling sickeningly audible, Jarrah prays quietly under his breath: "Lord, I have submitted myself to you, given you my faith, on you I depend." It is a stunning juxtaposition: a monstrous, violent invocation, accompanied by an act of murder, of the same God being petitioned in a frightened voice by a man with a conflicted conscience (figure 7.5).

As in each of the other films, Tom Burnett emerges here as the leader of the revolt, but his leadership role is still more visually accentuated in this film. After the hijacker takeover, the camera frequently captures Burnett in stances that evoke authority and command (see figure 7.6), and the dialogue with other passengers and crew shows him as the only passenger with a calm, controlled demeanor throughout the ordeal. At one point in the film, he tells Bingham: "Hey, this is a suicide mission. We have to do something, they are not gonna land this plane. We don't have any other option." Bingham responds with an expletive and hits the seat in front of him, unwilling to accept what Burnett clearly already has. Jeremy Glick is shown crying inconsolably on the phone with his wife at this same juncture in the film when Burnett has already achieved his grim resolve. Later, there is a compelling scene in which Burnett calmly attempts to bring a hysterical Sandy Bradshaw, one of the flight attendants, under emotional control so he can assure her cooperation for the takeover attempt: "Stewardess, listen to me! Are you listening? Go back and get everything we can use as a weapon!" Bradshaw responds despairingly: "What are we going to do?" The determined Burnett tells her: "I don't know, we'll figure that out. But get every weapon you can, we need every big guy." Bradshaw is galvanized by Burnett's leadership and retreats to the back of the plane, where she immediately calls to her colleague CeeCee Lyles to come help her boil water. As Bingham and Glick reluctantly join Burnett at the back of the plane, where, along with some of the flight crew, they form a vanguard of the takeover attempt, Burnett is the unquestioned leader. "You're not listening!" he tells a visibly distracted Bingham; then, when a stewardess tells him someone on board is a pilot, he goes to that passenger to negotiate his role in the takeover effort: "We're gonna get you up there! . . . We're all alone up here, nobody's gonna help us, we gotta do it!"

A final example of mythologically oriented editorializing in the film concerns the depiction of Christian Adams, a German citizen aboard the plane. The uniquely American character of the Flight 93 hero is amply displayed in the myth that has emerged concerning the differences between the responses of the heroes and the sole European passenger. Adams is among the passengers who made no phone calls from the plane, so we have no evidence whatever of his reaction to the hijacking or of his role in the effort to retake the plane. The myth construction undertaken in the various media nonetheless carved out a role for him that is consistent with the requirements of the myth and the characteristics of the hero. In *United 93*, Adams appears in a number of key scenes. First, in the early moments after the hijackers have taken the plane, he is seen telling other passengers, in thickly accented English that identifies him as a non-American, about the infamous Mogadishu hijacking of a Lufthansa flight in 1977: "They will ask for money, then they will let us go." Later, he is overheard saying: "I think we shouldn't provoke them, just do what they want, and they'll let us go and let the police take care of it." From behind him, another passenger, clearly American, challenges Adams: "Shouldn't somebody try to talk to them, do you think we can negotiate with them?" The juxtaposition of assertive American do-it-yourself spirit and passive, irresponsible European reliance on others is communicated effectively and economically in a few words. Then finally, in a climactic scene as the passengers are awaiting the moment of the counterattack, a panicked Adams leaps up and starts screaming in German. He tries to run toward the terrorists, apparently to make his case to them that he should not be included in the act the other passengers are planning. The only discernible thing he screams tells the whole mythological tale: "Ich bin Deutsche!" Other passengers grab him and hold him down, yelling "Shut up!" "Sit down!"

All told, this is a remarkable bit of narrative symbolism with no basis whatsoever in fact. In a *Guardian* article, John Harris notes that Greengrass was directly challenged about this portrayal of Adams in a BBC interview, and he said the German actor portraying Adams had suggested the idea that Mogadishu would have been the relevant framework for him.[8] Harris quotes Greengrass as arguing to the interviewer that a German passenger of Adams's age would certainly remember the 1977 Lufthansa hijacking (when he would have been eight years old) and, while there is no way to know precisely how he reacted, "you have to set the parameters of the film as they actually are and explore it, and in the end, audiences have to make their own minds up about whether that's a credible, believable portrait."[9] In the commentary track on the *United 93* DVD, just after this bit of action in the film, Greengrass says bluntly, without hesitation, "These things happened in our world."

The Flight That Fought Back: "Fallen Camera" Verisimilitude, Stylized Hyperdemocratic Heroes, and Prayer and the Afterlife

The Flight That Fought Back (*TFTFB* hereafter), which aired on the fourth anniversary of the attacks, was the first film on Flight 93 to appear. It was made by a British production company, Brook Lapping Productions, for the Discovery Channel, directed by Bruce Goodison and narrated by Kiefer Sutherland. Like the previous two films, it pursues the goal of verisimilitude through a dramatic recreation with actors of events on the plane, but it also positions itself in territory unapproached by those pictures in that the central substance of this film is interview footage with family members of passengers and crew and various other sources, which is interspersed with a smaller amount of footage recreating the events on the plane. Text shown in the opening sequence claims it is "based on testimony from families and friends of Flight 93 and evidence from official sources and original research."

Like *United 93* and *Flight 93*, *TFTFB* utilizes pseudo-documentary camera techniques during scenes on the plane. But while they all employ jerky, unsteady images intended to testify to the realism of the narrative, *TFTFB* takes the technique to a level unmatched in the other films. The camera angle on occasion tilts to a full 90 degrees to depict action, e.g., during the initial effort of the hijackers to enter the cockpit, after Deborah Welsh has been stabbed and left to die on the floor, and at the moment Captain Dahl is being murdered. In these scenes, the meaning of the camera technique is a miming of the perspective of the dead or dying victim. We are here encouraged to see the action through the unseeing eyes of the victim, at the same time as, paradoxically, we see that victim's sprawled body through the lens. This pseudo-realist effect does not give us a truer perspective on the action; it makes no sense to imagine that, if a camera person were present at such scenes, he would turn his camera to this angle to capture the shot. The goal is purely emotional: to encourage us to experience the violence exercised against the victims more viscerally and consequently to identify still more strongly with those victims. The same visual technique is used in one of the few scenes in the films that graphically depict violence, as one of the terrorists slits Dahl's throat. We watch the gruesome killing at a tilted angle that emphasizes the chaos and anarchy of the moment and, perhaps, also indicates, as in the 1960s *Batman* television series, the moral "crookedness" of the actors we are witnessing in the midst of their evil deeds, in an equally unsophisticated albeit less intentionally campy visual metaphorical language.

Another visual tactic intended to produce verisimilitude that is used frequently in *TFTFB* is the first-person camera angle commonly associated with a genre of video games. The first use of this technique in the film is in recreating the perspective of Mohamed Atta, the terrorist pilot of American Flight 11, as he crashes into the World Trade Center. Here, the towers sway wildly in front of the viewer's visual field as they grow larger with the simulation of the plane's approach. The effect, though quite common in contemporary video culture, still manages to be unsettling. One might even pose questions about the sensitivity of the film's producers to the then still fairly raw emotional wound that might have been rubbed for many viewers by being placed in Atta's subject position. This same tactic appears again toward the

FIGURE 7.7. First-person view and the service cart in *TFTFB*.

close of the film, when the passenger revolt is underway. In this scene, we are positioned atop the service cart that is bearing down on a hijacker (figure 7.7). It is a telling statement about the depiction of violent action in contemporary American visual culture that this exact same camera technique is used in the same scene in *Flight 93*. It has been argued that the first-person perspective in film signifies differently than it does in video gameplay. In the latter, the perspective gives "an intuitive sense of motion and action," while in cinematic uses, the first-person view "effect[s] a sense of alienation, detachment, fear, and violence."[10] Horror films use the perspective with some frequency. We might then see the first-person perspective in the Flight 93 films as a means for viscerally communicating the fearful aspects of the events depicted. It seems equally arguable, though, that the use of the technique in the passenger takeover sequence indicates the gameplay qualities of agency and power. Retribution takes on a video-game-avenger tone in these images, clearly a simplification in the crude terms of contemporary media culture of an event that must in its actual realization have been more complex.

Another technique to achieve verisimilitude in *TFTFB* involves the frequent juxtaposition of visual imagery with text attesting to its veracity. As we see Deborah Welsh's husband in his kitchen, apparently listening to the same recording of her voice we hear on the soundtrack, the phrase "Actual recording" is flashed on the screen. In another scene, as we hear a message left by Mark Bingham's mother on his voicemail and watch her pensively listening to same, the screen shows an audio graph of the call along with the same authoritative phrase, "Actual recording." The latter image is especially curious, as it is not clear precisely what of value the graph of the volume of Alice Hoglan's voice contributes. What the filmmakers clearly believe it communicates, though, is an abstract idea of scientific realism, in which such representations are, regardless of their actual paucity of useful information for the purpose at hand, by definition indications of objective accuracy and truth.

While *TFTFB* pursues the elusive goal of realism, it nonetheless stylizes and aestheticizes unapologetically. Male and female passengers and crew are significantly more "airbrushed" into gendered visual stereotypes than in *Flight 93* or *United 93*. Female protagonists are portrayed as nearly uniformly attractive, while the male passengers are visually depicted as exceptionally masculine and combative. In a series of split screens as the takeover plan is being formulated, the film depicts male passengers simultaneously in the guise of the actors playing them, in a stance of heroic exertion with ferocious looks on their faces, and in still photos of the actual individual passenger in a stereotypically virile pose; e.g., we see two Jeremy Glicks, one rushing the cockpit and the other shirtless and muscular, and two Richard Guadagnos, the first grimly determined to take out a hijacker and the second in denim jacket and baseball cap, confidently cradling a large rifle (figure 7.8).

Although the female passengers are aesthetically idealized in *TFTFB*, they are nonetheless depicted in more active roles during the revolt than is the case in the two films previously discussed. In *United 93* and *Flight 93*, the active roles in the revolt go without exception to male passengers, and more specifically to Beamer, Bingham, Burnett, and Glick. Even if stewardesses are seen in *United 93* boiling water in preparation for the assault, the women stand aside and allow the men to lead the attack. In *TFTFB*, however, we see the women too playing an active part in the attack on the cabin, rushing aggressively toward the front of the plane. Whether this is what actually happened or not, it is in line with the idea that heroes and martyrs, to earn such classification, must have appropriate narratives constructed about their ends. If it is so, as the other films depict the situation, that many passengers stayed in their seats as the assault on the cockpit was taking place (an interpretation likely more compatible with reality, given the narrowness of the passageway between seats and the small size of the area at the cockpit door where

FIGURE 7.8. Male virility. *The Flight That Fought Back.*

any actual fighting would have taken place), then there could only have been a few heroes on the flight. That the families of the passengers recognize this is evident in the bickering that went on in the wake of the making of *United 93*, in which only a few passengers are seen as active in the effort to take back the cockpit, many are not present in the narrative at all, and some are presented as actively opposing the effort.[11]

In *TFTFB*, radical democracy is the aesthetic of the passenger revolt, and all passengers are depicted as pugnacious and spoiling for a fight. There is a moment in the film where various family members wax eloquent about the feisty temperament and fighting skills of their deceased relatives; each is entirely certain of the role his or her loved one played in the struggle to defeat the hijackers:

Louis Nacke's son: "It was not his way to let someone bully him around [or] box him into a corner where he couldn't get out."

Nacke's sister: "He was very, very aggressive. . . . [H]e was never second in anything."

Sandra Bradshaw's husband: "If you made Sandy mad, you better look out 'cause she was a little tornado, she could hit hard, believe me, I know."

Glick's wife: "In a hand-to-hand battle, there was no match for Jeremy. . . . I've seen him break people's arms before in judo matches."

Richard Guadagno's sister: "Richard had to be fit, he was always lifting weights, he could bench press an enormous amount of weight."

One of Bingham's friends: "I can just imagine him going, 'They're not going to get away with it . . . because I'm me and who have I got here, what can we do?' because it's always that team aspect and 'what can we do to overcome this?'"

Lauren Grandcolas's husband: "I also think Lauren was actively involved in coordinating who was going to do what because of her emergency medical training."

Andy Garcia's wife: "He was a pilot. . . . I just have to believe that his knowledge and his experience was used."

Honor Wainio's friend: "I think Liz probably wanted to kick some ass because that was just her, she wouldn't have gone down without a fight."

Louis Nacke's son sums this section of the film up admirably in a description of his father: "He always wanted to be a hero and when it was presented to him, he knew the risks and a hero is always willing to do whatever he can to help anyone else."

TFTFB takes liberties with the basic narrative that are not encountered in the other films. Tom Burnett apparently told his wife in one of his early calls that the hijackers appeared to have a gun, but it is highly unlikely that the hijackers could have gotten a gun past airport security, and none was found in the wreckage of Flight 93. Nonetheless, in the takeover sequence of *TFTFB*, we see a gun wielded by one of the hijackers. Another more substantive departure from the established mythology of the Flight 93 passenger revolt concerns the role of Richard Guadagno, who is presented here as a central actor in the passenger rebellion. In a scene just after the hijack has taken place, Guadagno tells other passengers of his experience working with the U.S. government and assures them that there is a standard procedure in such hijacks. There follows a cut to an interview with his father, who says, "There is no doubt that Richard reacted quickly to this situation." That there was no telephone evidence of Guadagno's participation in the plan is explained by his father, who tells us that he would have been too busily involved in the goings-on inside the plane to worry his parents or friends with a call. In the effort to retake the cockpit, Guadagno is depicted in a leading position; he is the only passenger we see enter the cockpit in the seconds before the crash.

Family members are allowed a fair amount of interpretive authority as to what happened in the final minutes. Although the depiction of the takeover effort is less overtly violent than that of *United 93*, there is significant speculation by family members, presented in the film as fact, about who did what and especially about who handled the grim task of dispatching opposition from the hijackers. The film shows us a shaky, blurred image of Burnett hitting a hijacker with a fire extinguisher, as we hear his wife's confident pronouncement that he would have taken upon himself the responsibility to kill to spare his fellows the grisly deed. Glick's wife is even more graphic in her description of the final moments: "I can imagine Jeremy snapping a neck unbelievably quick and then just beating the guy until he was deader than beyond belief." Family members are also given an authoritative position in interpreting the question of whether or not the cockpit was breached; Lyz Glick and Phil Bradshaw assert their certainty that "just at the final seconds there of the tape, you can tell that the hijackers were not alone."

TFTFB stands out from *Flight 93* and *United 93* in a still more crucial way regarding one of the central elements of the hero myth described above: the recitation of prayer by passengers. It is of note that two of these three films take considerable artistic liberties here with what we know factually. Only in *Flight 93* is the depiction essentially consistent with what we know about the Lord's Prayer story, i.e., we see Beamer and Jefferson praying alone. Others watch as Beamer recites his half of the prayer, but do not join in. It is an act performed by one individual on the plane, not a collective ritual. *United 93*, by contrast, shows Beamer praying the Lord's Prayer, and then cuts to several other passengers praying the same prayer, either in unison with him or spontaneously of their own accord. In *TFTFB*, the scene has expanded still further beyond the available facts. Here, we see a small group on the plane assembled, praying together with a Bible at hand. One of them is reading from the 57th Psalm: "Have mercy on me, oh God, have mercy on me, for you in my soul take refuge, I will take refuge in the shadow of your wings until the disaster is passed, I cry out to God most high" (figure 7.9). The narrator says nothing to describe the scene, which has no evidence whatsoever to support it, as it is taking place.

FIGURE 7.9. Group prayer with Bible. *The Flight That Fought Back.*

The film's assertion of a strong role for religious narrative in the last minutes of Flight 93 can be seen too in a startling black-and-white sequence in which Louis Nacke's brother recounts a dream he had. We see first his vision of the cockpit takeover by the passengers, this time with Nacke instead of Guadagno as the first passenger into the cockpit. Then "a warmth came over me, and then a bright light, and then Joey's [Nacke's middle name was Joseph] telling me, 'I'm okay,' and I said, 'No, you gotta come back, we still need you,' and he says, 'No, no, I'm okay, it's time for me to go.'" We see Nacke open doors to face us, a brilliant light at his back, and deliver a knowing wink (figure 7.10). At the end of the film, Nacke's sister says, "When we go there [Shanksville] now and we look into those hemlocks, we keep waiting for them to come out," and his brother adds, "I always picture him coming out and just brushing himself off."

This is the lone film among the four that points explicitly beyond the crash of Flight 93 to the subsequent war in Afghanistan, and it does so in starkly partisan ideological terms. In a charged scene, Nacke's son, Louis Paul Nacke, who was only 14 in 2001, appears in the uniform of a West Point cadet. With a stern look, he tells the camera: "I want to fight for our country because you took something very dear from me on September 11, something I can't have back, something that can't be bought, sold, something that is given to you, it's a gift, and the gift was stolen from me. . . . I can't take it back, but I can punish the people that stole it from me. I want to finish what he started." The film closes with this statement from Burnett's wife: "Flight 93 gave us hope, it gave us a light on a very dark day, knowing that someone fought back." As her words fade, we see an image of the Angel Patriots, perhaps the clearest emblem of the American civil religion at the temporary memorial site.

Portrait of Courage: The Untold Story of Flight 93: Framing Wild Speculation as Scientific Fact

Portrait of Courage: The Untold Story of Flight 93, which was produced in 2006 for DVD release, is from Grizzly Adams Productions.[12] This company produces conservative Christian films and videos. Taking its name from the long-running NBC television series *The Life and Times of Grizzly Adams*, it has, according to its website, "over the past 30 years produced more than 500 family friendly TV specials, features, series, and episodes for NBC, CBS, PAX, Discovery and other networks." Among the other titles advertised on the company's website are *End Times: How Close Are We?* and *The Case for Christ's Resurrection*.

Portrait of Courage is based in part on Deena Burnett's *Fighting Back*, which presents a decidedly culturally conservative vision of the meaning of 9/11, and so it is not surprising that it is the most overtly partisan of the Flight 93 films in cultural political terms. Unlike the other three films, it contains very little dramatic recreation of events on the plane, instead relying for most of its 60 minutes on interview footage with family members and friends of Flight 93 passengers. This interview footage is broken up with shots of the narrator and brief, stylistically unremarkable dramatizations of action on the plane.

FIGURE 7.10. Louis Nacke's spirit communicates with relatives. *The Flight That Fought Back.*

A move to establish verisimilitude takes place in the film's early moments, when a striking visual is juxtaposed with authoritative-sounding text. We see someone in a white lab coat, with rubber gloves, peering into a microscope, while the voiceover tells us that "the true story of what happened on Flight 93 has taken years of investigation and painstaking detective work to piece together [and] only now are we able to solve some of the mysteries of that flight." This is an increasingly common narrative strategy in much conservative media fare, i.e., an over-the-top rhetoric of scientificity that is nonetheless demonstrably undercut by a clear ideological thrust. We saw in chapter five how even the most outlandish conspiracy theories often attempt to mobilize a veneer of scientific dispassion while reasoning in a patently anti-scientific manner.

The shots of action aboard the plane are much less realistic in appearance than those in any of the other films, probably owing at least in part to what must have been a tiny budget for the film. At the moment of the launching of the effort to take back the plane from the hijackers, the actor playing Beamer's intonation of "Let's roll!" is comically calm, with a wooden look on his face. As the passengers make phone calls to loved ones, the acting is uniformly stilted and unpolished. Several of the actors playing the hijackers look more phenotypically Latino than Arab. The background music veers from overdramatic to lugubrious. The overall feel is of a cheaply made TV feature for an audience understood as aesthetically unsophisticated and undemanding.

The interview footage is rife with unverified and often wild speculation about important elements of the narrative, and this is uniformly framed by the narrator as unchallenged truth. Sandy Dahl, the wife of the pilot, assures us that her husband was not killed immediately in the cockpit takeover, but no evidence is given to support this belief. The Petersons' son, D. Hamilton Peterson, recounts Debbie Welsh's husband telling him she was assertive, and adds that she was more than six feet tall, and thus, without doubt, "she would have tried to stand in the way of the hijackers." Sara Rothenberg, daughter of passenger Mickey Rothenberg, is equally certain of specific details of her father's resistance to the hijack: "my father would have stood up and said, . . . 'Listen, I was right behind that guy in security and I don't think you got a bomb on the plane!' . . . [H]e would not have sat in his seat and said nothing." These are perhaps interesting hypotheses, but strict documentary technique would require an indication to viewers that they are completely unsupported by direct evidence.

The array of "experts" who appear in the film to provide commentary is a curious collection. A journalist with the *Minneapolis Star Tribune*, Gregory Gordon, is given considerable time in the film's narrative, but it is never made clear precisely what his expertise on 9/11 or Flight 93 is. Another individual who speaks authoritatively about the events on the plane is David Dosch, who is identified only as a "757 pilot and a friend of Jason Dahl," the captain of Flight 93. In a highly stylized shot in which he is in full uniform and standing in front of a plane in the hangar, Dosch speculates that Dahl had turned off the autopilot to attempt to foil the hijackers and that the cockpit recording indicated Jarrah screaming at someone (Dahl, in Dosch's interpretation) to stop touching something (the controls, according to Dosch). Nothing more than the claim is presented here. It is not clear how Dosch would even have been able to hear the recording from the plane's black box, as this has not been made available to the public, and the transcript of the recording that has been released contains nothing like the statement to which he alludes. In a later scene, Dosch claims the cockpit recording reveals hijackers discussing whether or not they should bring a pilot back up to help them, indicating that at least one of the pilots was not killed immediately in the takeover. Though the cockpit recording does contain a cryptic comment from one of the hijackers to "bring the pilot back," the precise meaning of this statement is not known.[13]

As in *TFTFB*, much effort is made in this film to describe passengers as capable fighters, aggressive and trained for just the kind of situation presented by the hijacking. Peterson tells the viewer that "it was almost as if somebody handpicked the group that could best carry out an insurrection." Nacke was a "great athlete" who had been training with weights since the age of 13. Guadagno had received extensive "combat training." Bingham, according to his mother, was so aggressive that he was banned from traveling in New Zealand because of a "fracas" he had been involved in at an airport there. Burnett is described as "very athletic" and with "a genius-level IQ." Even apparently frail Hilda Marcin, the oldest person on the plane at 79, "was not one to shy away from conflict—while living in New York City, she chased a would-be burglar out of her home with a billy club," according to the narrator.

The narrative of the passengers as able fighters has a logical, even necessary conclusion, which the film asserts with certainty: the passengers must have succeeded in breaching the cabin and retaking control of the plane, although they were unable to keep it aloft. Many family members are permitted to speculate wildly on what the cockpit recording reveals in order to back up this storyline. Peterson describes it as revealing "the ongoing triumph and ultimate success" of the rebellion. Burnett's wife claims that due to her "experience as a flight attendant" she is "able to visualize where different people were on the plane as we heard them." This esoteric knowledge purportedly enables her to know her husband's voice came from precisely the same location as a hijacker's scream: "You could hear one of the hijackers struggling for his own life and, I believe, being killed. . . . [A]fter that particular hijacker stopped screaming, I could hear Tom's voice and it sounded as if he was right there." She then goes on to theorize that, since the last English words on the recording were "turn up," this must have been the New Zealand–born Alan Beaven telling another passenger in idiomatic Kiwi English to pull up on the plane's controls: "He would never have said that if a hijacker had been in the seat." Guadagno's father later reads a statement from a certificate he received regarding the forensic evidence. It reveals that his son's remains were recovered near the cockpit debris, and he therefore surmises this to be evidence that his son was inside the cockpit and the passengers were in control of the plane at the time of impact.

The film touches on one of the elements of the Flight 93 story that points toward deeply culturally conservative, even reactionary, aspects of the hero complex in at least one of the central figures, albeit in a more or less sanitized manner. As she did in her book, Deena Burnett here reveals her husband's "fascination" with Nathan Bedford Forrest, a Confederate general, noting that he had apparently been reading with admiration about his exploits during the Civil War. He had even given a speech to employees at the corporation for which he worked that presented Forrest's "get there first with the most men" battle strategy as a metaphorical business philosophy for the company to adopt, telling them that "[t]his simple thought, when executed thoughtfully and with passion, is the essence of what is taught in every single military college and business school today."[14] The reference to Forrest likely passes unnoticed by most viewers, forgotten as this figure from the now distant American past is in much of the country. Nathan Bedford Forrest was the first Grand Wizard of the Ku Klux Klan, who committed what would today almost certainly be classed as war crimes during the Civil War battle of Fort Pillow, Tennessee, by massacring unarmed black Union soldiers.[15] In the South at least, Forrest's legacy remains vibrantly alive in right-wing circles. In early 2011, Mississippi governor Haley Barbour was widely criticized in the national press for steadfastly refusing to oppose the effort by his state to release a commemorative license plate with Forrest's name on it. In *TFTFB*, while Deena Burnett describes her husband's admiration for the determination of the Confederate soldiers at Gettysburg, we see an image of Burnett reading about the Civil War; however, the book is not about Forrest but the culturally less controversial Stonewall Jackson. This film is the only one of the four to name the specific and highly controversial Civil War figure with whom Burnett was obsessed as detailed in his wife's book.

While watching another film about 9/11, Nina Davenport's *Parallel Lines*, in which the filmmaker journeys home to New York City from San Diego in the wake of the attacks and films encounters with people across the country, I stumbled into Nathan Bedford Forrest and his legacy again. As Davenport passes through Alabama, on the night before Christmas Eve 2001, she meets two white farmers in Chickasaw. This is just after we have seen her poignant encounter with an elderly black man in nearby Stockton. As their conversation unfolded, the black man suddenly became agitated and told Davenport that he was going to call the police, and in retrospect one sees clearly that his fear had to do with the fact that he is a black man being visited by a lone white woman in the South, where it was not at all long ago that such meetings could easily prove fatal for black men. When she later strikes up a conversation with the two white farmers a bit down the road, the older of the two (they appear to be father and son) tells her not to miss the "Nathan Forrest memorial up there in Selma." With no prompting, and with a frankly terrifying ease, he goes on to the effect that the Civil War was caused by "Yankees [who] was jealous the South was making a lot of money off cotton with the slaves to help 'em work, but if they hadn't been slaves, they'd a been over there eatin' each other, cannibals, in Africa. . . . I got some good friends that's blacks, but you can't trust any of 'em because they're not the trustable kind of people." The younger man then chimes in with even more brutally racist sentiments: "These niggers in the south different than what they are in the north, you just better not stay here long or some of 'em'll be by to visit you! Don't be goin' to Selma tonight, it's some bad niggers up there. . . . [Y]ou don't wanna be in Selma after dark neither, it's a black town, got a black mayor, it's a bad place for a white woman." The older man then tells her he is "not ashamed to say it, I'm a segregationist and always will be. . . . I don't believe in integration, never will." A calculating hatred is etched in the eyes of both men, and Davenport's voiceover as she drives away speaks volumes about the meaning of the historical legacy of men such as Nathan Bedford Forrest: "People keep talking about September 11 uniting the nation. I'm afraid we'll never be united." This sinister connection to American cultural history that is present in Burnett's fascination with a historical figure such as Forrest remains hidden in *TFTFB* and the other films on Flight 93.

TFTFB concludes with hyperbolic culturally conservative reiterations of mythologies we have already examined in earlier chapters. The narrator summarizes: "What does it mean to be a hero? On September 11, the word 'hero' was recast, perhaps back into its original mold, and suddenly the uncommon valor, self-sacrifice, and amazing bravery of people most Americans had never heard of became the ruler by which all others are measured." Nacke's brother elaborates: "If you're worried about who led the charge, or who was most important, you're very foolish because it doesn't matter. . . . [I]f you look up the word 'American' in Webster's dictionary, you should see 40 people and they all were from Flight 93." Though the data is frustratingly incomplete, the narrator goes on, "some things we do know." Peterson finishes the thought: "Good can and must prevail over evil." In the extra interview footage on the DVD, Peterson relates another story that solidifies its mythological elements. Virtually everything on the plane was "vaporized" by the crash, he says, but one mysterious object survived the impact "virtually intact": his parents' Bible. This is, he tells us with great seriousness, "absolutely consistent with their lifelong faith and commitment to God and how they carried themselves every day." This story is even further mythologically embellished in Longman's *Among the Heroes*. There, one sentence after we learn of a "dog-eared, . . . damaged, . . . but . . . still readable" Bible found at the crash site, we find the Christian's symbolic enemy there too, destroyed by the mythical deed of the heroes: "A snake, sunning on a rock, was seared with its body coiled, its mouth open to strike."[16]

The Cinematic Contribution to the Flight 93 Myth

It is perhaps in the films on Flight 93 that the mythical elements of the hero narrative are at their most viscerally compelling. There is a great deal of consistency in the contours of the basic symbolic language and the story they are used to tell in the various manifestations of the Flight 93 myth we have examined in the book to this point. Yet the heroic stature of Beamer, Bingham, Burnett, Glick, and their fellow passengers and the abject evil of the hijackers is most powerfully felt in the visual medium. The coherence of the symbols and their positioning in a particular plotline with definite parameters is also perhaps more striking in the films than in the autobiographical books or in any of the physical memorial sites, if only because the nature of film as a medium makes it possible to bring to vivid life even the most gut-wrenching or fantastic elements of the myth, e.g., the battle scenes of good against evil aboard the plane, or the messages communicated from the beyond by the hero-martyrs. In a sense, the films on Flight 93 have had to do some of the work in visual cultural meaning-making that was done for the part of the 9/11 events that took place in New York City by live, onsite television footage, and we should not be surprised to find viewers who see in documents like *United 93*, *Flight 93*, *The Flight That Fought Back*, and *Portrait of Courage* testimony of essentially the same level of veridical power.

8

Myth in Practice

Visitors at the Temporary Memorial Site

During the summer and fall of 2009, I conducted interviews at the temporary memorial site in order to get a sense of how the various elements of the Flight 93 narrative and memorialization process were understood by those who visited the site. As I have indicated elsewhere, in order to mean anything, it is not enough that signs be *produced*; they must also be *consumed*. I wanted therefore to gather some understanding as to how the signs at the temporary memorial were actually interpreted by those who came there.

The fruits of interviewing are frequently invaluable to an understanding of the meaning of phenomena such as the crash of Flight 93, but interviewing itself is hard work. While the work is not as physically demanding as some other more onerous varieties of labor, it makes its considerable demands in realms other than the physical. Such research requires a very high tolerance for repetitive activity and the boredom that often accompanies it. For every minute I passed at the temporary memorial talking to visitors to the site and learning how they experienced the memorial, I easily spent 20 waiting for someone to arrive, slowly roasting in the sun or shivering in the wind or both. Even once I had interviewees, I discovered that they frequently said essentially the same things I had already heard from others. Many were terse or inarticulate, perhaps owing to the emotional power of their experience of the site. There are other hazards to the trade that are brought on by technical malfunctions and glitches. In addition to the wind-caused degradation of the recording quality of the device I used, which frequently made recordings all but indecipherable except under the labor of repeated and carefully attentive listenings, I also simply lost some number of audio recordings of interviews because the recorder failed and stopped working altogether, without warning or clear reason and before I could save the files to my computer. It is difficult to describe the frustration of looking in the folder on the device where close to a dozen interviews were stored and finding it inexplicably empty. It may be that after the fact such experiences can potentially make for added piquancy in the written final results, but in the moment they can only honestly be described as dreadfully disheartening.

Having acknowledged the value of interview data to a project such as this one, I must yet say a word about the limits regarding what interviews can tell us. There exists in some corners of the social sciences a certain romanticization of what is called fieldwork (when I first heard the expression, the impression given was of exhausting agricultural labor requiring heavy equipment or at least a few oxen) and its resultant data which, as any other form of intellectual self-congratulation and hubris, cries out for as much critical scrutiny as can be mustered. It is perhaps so that, at least some of the time, when sociologists and anthropologists say they are "letting their subjects speak for themselves," they are knowingly engaging in something metaphorical or rhetorical. Yet I cannot count the number of times, while attending job talks and other public communications of research projects that rely on ethnography or interviews, that I have heard colleagues use this phrase with clear relish and wide-eyed enthusiasm, and I cannot help but think that at least some of them literally believe what they are saying. Writers and conference participants who do not let us"hear the voices of the people studied" have failed, they insinuate, in some profound way, both professionally and, one senses, morally as well. But the stubborn reality is that we never really hear from the subjects, or at least we hear from them only through a moderator, and that moderator necessarily changes what they say, if only because the context of their utterances, so crucial for the meaning of their speech, is gone in reporting it to us. The moderator, or researcher, hears what the subject has said to her and records it in some way, perhaps with a device like the one I used, perhaps by taking notes by hand or keyboard as the subject is speaking. In the latter case, the moderator is already editing as she is collecting the notes, as no social scientist I know is capable of seamlessly capturing in real-time notes everything the subject says, while still maintaining the required (pretense of) presence in the interview as an interlocutor. But even if she emerges from the interview with a nice sound file of everything the subject said (everything at least that did not disappear in the wind or that was not rendered inaudible by some other fact of the physics of sound recording), short of simply transcribing all that material and placing it unedited into a chapter titled "What My Interview Subjects Said," the moderator radically modifies that content in reporting it to the broader audience. She codes the material, making decisions about what is and what is not important, what can and what cannot be discussed in the format she has been given (book, article, conference presentation, etc.). There is no established such format in the scholarly world today wherein a moderator can simply dump raw interview material on unsuspecting readers and, given the overwhelmingly tedious nature of much unedited ethnographic materials, this is almost certainly a good thing. It is expected that the researcher will "work it over," or in the more frequent phrase that indicates in archetypal language the improvement thereby made on the raw material, "work it *up*" into something more coherent, more palatable, more comprehensible to an audience that desires much of the interpretive work on that material to already be completed before they open the book. Even when the "real words" of the subject are presented, they are inevitably chopped up, made to fit into some interpretive box or other, and, as already noted, they are always and in every case surgically removed from the context of their utterance.

This latter point is of tremendous importance. How many times in everyday conversation is something we say or hear someone else say dependent on contextual cues and structures for its meaning? The wry grin or downturned grimace that accompanies a phrase makes all the difference in what is intended by the speaker and what is received by the listener. Some varieties of sociological research, for example, much of conversation analysis, attend with great precision to these extraverbal cues and signposts, but the most astute of those researchers realize it is a losing battle. Only by *being there* does one gather the full context, and even then only potentially, and on condition of many other requirements. When the words are disembodied and placed on the page that necessarily annihilates the bodies and the space that produced the words, it is not the meaning of the bodies and the space that is communicated. Something new is. That something new can inform us, to be sure, and it can be invaluable for a number of tasks. But posturing naïvely, or disingenuously, about "letting the subjects speak" should be eschewed by those who would like to avoid deliberately misleading readers. We who produce the books in which "the subjects speak" have much to say about what they speak of.

The goal of this chapter is simply to present impressions of visitors to the site in their color and tone. The time and other resources I had to dedicate to these interviews were not sufficient to make statistical claims of a representative nature regarding their content.

Impressions of the Temporary Memorial and the Permanent Memorial Design

My plan of attack in pursuing memorial visitors for interviews was greatly informed by the physical layout of the site and its general manner of access by visitors. There was one entryway through the fence surrounding the memorial, toward the back end of the parking lot, and I stationed myself there as inconspicuously as possible during hours of operation. I would smile and sometimes join the police officer who was posted there in greeting visitors as they exited their cars and entered the site. Then, when they were exiting the memorial, I would approach them, introduce myself as a sociologist at a nearby university, quickly explain what I was doing at the site, and ask them if they were interested in talking to me for a few minutes about their impressions of the memorial. Visitors frequently arrived in sizable groups, sometimes in tour buses, and in those cases interviewing was difficult, since all of them would typically exit the memorial at about the same time and I would therefore have enough time to interview only one or perhaps two before the group was ready to depart. Given the nature of the site and the clear emotional impact it had on some visitors, I was viscerally aware of the need not to take up exorbitant amounts of the visitors' time and tried to conduct interviews expeditiously. In general, an interview would last no more than 20 minutes, and many were significantly shorter than that. Much depended on how eager subjects were to speak. When they were animated and interested in continuing to talk even after answering the questions I had prepared for them, I tried to keep them talking for as long as I could, and a good deal of interesting information came of these extended sessions.

In addition to trying to elicit responses from them that would help me to get a sense of the meanings they read in the memorial, I tried too to gather what I could in the way of interpretive material from observation of their behavior at the site. The demeanor of the overwhelming majority of visitors was demonstrably respectful and serious. Even visitors who arrived in groups were generally not effusive in their conversations with one another as they walked around the site. The affect was of quiet meditation for the most part. Perhaps the most outstanding feature of this attitude, and the one that makes the most pointed rebuttal to the argument that visitors to this memorial site can adequately be described as tourists, had to do with the surprising absence of photographing and videotaping. By and large, visitors to both the temporary memorial and the Flight 93 Chapel seemed markedly less interested in photographic mementos than is characteristic of tourists, who are defined by their desire to bring back evidence of their presence at the tourist site. At the World Trade Center site, more typical tourist behavior is omnipresent, i.e., photographing and videotaping are highly visible modes of visitor interaction with the site.[1] Nearly every time I have been at the WTC site, someone has asked me to photograph them with the site where the towers stood as the backdrop, and this despite the fact that I am often busily snapping pictures of my own. In Shanksville, to be sure, some visitors do take photos, and you can even find numerous videos of the temporary memorial site that visitors have posted to YouTube, but I noted long intervals at both the chapel and the temporary memorial in which significant numbers of people were present and no cameras appeared. I sometimes had the sentiment at both sites that I stood out like a sore thumb among other visitors as I frequently occupied myself with my own camera to take the pictures that appear in this book. It may be that something as simple as the different kinds of people who visit the Shanksville and New York City sites explains this distinction. Visitors to the Flight 93 temporary memorial were typically significantly older than those who visit the World Trade Center site, and they almost certainly came from a much more limited range of points of origin, largely centered in Red (and Purple) State America around the crash site: western Pennsylvania, Ohio, Indiana, West Virginia, and other locations in the vicinity. The younger, more cosmopolitan, and more typically touristic population one finds at the WTC site tends to manifest a much less reverent attitude toward the site than is broadly found among Shanksville site visitors, especially with respect to the free use of cameras.

I asked visitors about the specific aspects of the temporary memorial that struck them, their impressions of the permanent memorial design (which most of them had been introduced to during an Ambassador's presentation), and their own ideas for what ought to be included in the permanent memorial. An idea expressed by a good number of those I spoke to had to do with the desire to keep the memorial site simple and to retain the personal elements they saw in the objects left by other visitors. Their language was austere and personal, emphasizing the necessity of memorializing the human dimension of the events on Flight 93. These visitors believed that the bareness of the site's geography and its isolation from the noise and bustle of an urban environment lent itself to a simple memorial. One respondent succinctly summarized her experience of the minimalism of the temporary memorial in words that were echoed by others: "If someone told me this [i.e., the temporary memorial] was the permanent memorial, I would be very impressed." Another, after expressing concern about his understanding that "they are taking land for the permanent memorial and that some of those folks were unhappy,"[2] told me that "my original thoughts were: 'Do you need it that big?' Some of these folks who are losing their property, they've had the land in their families for hundreds of years. I understand it's a great thing, but maybe they could make it a little smaller." His wife then echoed his sentiment: "To me this [pointing to the temporary memorial fence] is special, just keep it like it is." Several visitors expressed a feeling that "a tombstone" was sufficient as a memorial, and that the permanent design was "too extravagant." One particularly eloquent interviewee drew a direct comparison to the memorial at the site of the battle of Gettysburg:

We wanted to make [their visit to the memorial] an educational experience for our daughter. We took her to Gettysburg and we talked about the importance of duty over yourself, and how you fight for your country. . . . That was a poignant experience; just an empty field in which people gave their lives for their country, whether it be North or South, . . . and this is almost the same instance except in a more modern time. People gave themselves for their country, once again, in just an empty field, and the field is really the monument to me. It doesn't need much more than that. Just to stand in the place where people gave their lives, knowing you have yours to live and because of them you have your family to stand here with you is more important and more poignant than any monument can portray. . . . You almost want to leave it untouched. That's one thing about Gettysburg: the field is untouched, but just in town, everything's a monument, and this person's standing here and that person's standing there, and that's great, but it's almost a commercialization of a historic national monument and that kind of takes away from it. . . . I know this isn't an official grandiose monument but to me just the empty field and a few trinkets is almost the best thing in the world. It's more visceral, it's more intimate, and it's less commercialized. It is what it is, it's genuine. . . . I kind of like it the way it is.

This feeling that the simplicity of the temporary memorial constituted a de facto defense against crass commercialism was a common element in the responses of the visitors with whom I spoke. One man put it in the following vivid language: "I like that there's not a zillion signs and a zillion people hawking shirts."

Most of those I spoke with who preferred keeping as much of the temporary memorial as possible intact in the construction of a permanent memorial spoke respectfully of the permanent design, but some were directly antagonistic to its scale. One told me he believed it was

a perfect disgrace that they're gonna take this down and put a marble and concrete thing up that won't mean a hill of beans to anyone. This is people's patriotism, this is people's love. They should put a building all around this, glass all around it, all weather, so that people can come here and see what counts. . . . Leave it be. . . . It bothers me that they're gonna take away everyone's patriotism. This should be [the permanent memorial]: a bench for everybody, and an angel for everybody, and everybody's thoughts and love.

Another visitor expressed his desire for something more permanent than the temporary memorial "but maybe not [a memorial taking up] 2,200 acres." A small but vocal number of visitors expressed some disappointment with both the temporary memorial and the permanent design. One group of friends visiting from Texas were particularly outspoken exemplars of this perspective. In contrast to those visitors cited just above, they told me they were "depressed" by what they saw as the significant "commercialism" of the site and expressed disdain for the Ambassadors for "promoting their project" for the permanent memorial. One member of this group said he had formed a "negative attitude" in advance about the permanent design, having heard a bit about the land dispute, and he and others in the group declared that they much preferred the Flight 93 Chapel, which they had visited just prior to coming to the temporary memorial site.

Many others, however, in numbers roughly equal to those who desired to keep the temporary memorial or some similarly simple commemorative site, were impressed with the permanent memorial design, which had generally been presented to them in its basic details by an Ambassador at the conclusion of the presentation. A number indicated specific elements of the memorial that they saw as attractive or highly appropriate, for example, the Tower of Voices: "I loved the wind chime idea, that's beautiful. . . . I'm a designer myself, when I saw the wind chime idea, I really thought that was significant." Another visitor spoke affirmatively about the "awesome" flight path walkway that allows one to "walk right up to the sacred ground." Many respondents felt strongly that there should be photographs of the passengers somewhere in the permanent memorial in addition to textual biographical material, convinced of the visceral power of images of the dead heroes while still alive. The idea that the permanent memorial should aesthetically emphasize "peace" and serve as a "place of comfort" was echoed in many visitors' comments. One made an explicit comparison on this topic to her experience at the Vietnam Memorial in Washington, D.C: "[It should be a] place where people can sit quietly and reflect . . . [at the Vietnam Memorial] people are chit-chatting, and then you get to this wall and all of a sudden there is silence, people don't want to talk, I envision that [here]."

One particularly fascinating idea that emerged in the comments of a very small number of respondents was a desire to have the plane, and even the crash itself and moment of impact, explicitly represented at the memorial. A man visiting with his wife spoke vividly of "having a plane, the exact size, *flying upside down*. . . . [A] replica would show the people exactly what they were into, so they could picture that. . . . [T]hat would give the individual the feeling [the passengers experienced]." Another was even more precise and dramatic, relating the following to me with tears in his eyes and his voice occasionally breaking:

> What's my vision of the memorial? If I was doing it, what would I do? . . .
> [O]n the Sacred Ground, I would have a concrete floor, shaped generally like a fuselage. There would be exactly 40 people [pause and sobbing], and they would all be standing because I think that's the way they died. They were told, "Sit still, don't worry, nothing's going to happen," but in the end they were all standing to save our country, to save people like me [voice breaking]. So I would see it, the fuselage, 40 people standing up and looking to that cockpit, to that pilot, to those razor blades.

As I noted in earlier chapters, in a certain sense, this desire is extremely transgressive of the broad historical cultural mission of memorials of such events. Generally speaking, there is a powerful collective emotional investment in not depicting the catastrophe itself, as this, it is believed, potentially turns the minds of visitors too traumatically toward realities (i.e., the fragility of human bodies and the massive destruction wrought on them by accidents involving high velocities, and the terrible fact of death itself) that are, when studied closely, exceedingly difficult to bear. Yet here I found evidence that there are some few members of the culture, at least, who will unguardedly express, to a complete stranger, what is perhaps an unexpressed, even unconscious and suppressed transgressive desire felt by many more of us.

Frequently, visitors described their excitement at the prospect of returning once the permanent memorial is finished: "[The permanent memorial] was well thought out. . . . [W]hen it's done, we'll be back, and we don't ordinarily go back to the same site twice, but I think we will be back here"; "We'll be interested in coming back [when the permanent memorial is built], it's gonna be nice." The excitement to see the memorial finalized was sometimes mixed with a critical perspective on the timeline for its construction: "I think they could speed it up a little. It's taking too long. It should have been done a long time ago." One elderly visitor expressed an idea present in the remarks of others regarding the fragility of memory and the difficult work to be done by a memorial, whatever its design and size: "[They should] make it as available to the public as possible, particularly to have somebody to explain it to younger people because it's passing in time already and a lot of young people don't understand what happened."

When asked about their favorite features of the temporary memorial, visitors gave a variety of answers, but far and away the most frequent response had to do with the gifts left at the site by other visitors. People were effusive in describing the emotional power they felt when they saw objects left on the fence and elsewhere throughout the memorial space:

> The wall where people have shared something personal, and you can just feel that energy, . . . little monuments that people took their own time to make. . . . [I]t's incredible.

> The little trinkets and things people leave behind are kind of interesting. . . . [W]hether it's the kind of people that left the objects or the kind of objects that represent the people that died, either way, it's pretty interesting.

> All the little trinkets that people have left. There's just such a variety, it's just moving to me to see all that, I guess, love that people have left. . . . It's just anything of a personal nature.

> The variety of mementoes that people left behind. I'm sure many of them have significance for the people who left them. People left patches. I think there was a patch for the fire department near where we used to live.

> Everything is so personal. Everything here [on the fence] is from basically a family or just people, I wouldn't say random people, but people who want to give thanks.

> The mementos left on the wire fence. Very touching, interesting in their diversity and what people chose to leave, they had personal meaning.

> The fact that people have come from all over the country and left little mementoes. People leaving things that, I guess, mean something to them.

Very impromptu people left bracelets, necklaces, license plates off their cars. They didn't plan on leaving something, but they did in the end.

That wall over there is bound to affect anybody. . . . I saw things over there from California. It's amazing because this is such a small town and area.

Some visitors described their initial sense of confusion at the presence of the gift objects at the memorial. One woman told me she first interpreted the fence from a distance to be a souvenir stand: "As I pulled in, I thought, 'Ohmigosh, I can't believe they have souvenirs for sale!' I thought, 'Ohmigosh, we sell everything in America!'" Another respondent expressed "surprise" that "people don't pick things up, coins and stuff." Other aspects of the temporary memorial that were noted frequently as particularly affecting were the Angel Patriots, the benches with the passenger names inscribed on them, and "that very moving lone flag out in the field" that marked the crash site. I was struck by the fact that almost no visitors to whom I spoke called attention to the lone obviously religious item at the site, the cross, despite the fact that straightforwardly religious interpretations of the event by visitors were not uncommon. Some idiosyncratic responses were of note. One elderly woman told me of how one piece of the memorial had actually caused her to have a change of heart regarding a personal prejudice: "I liked the motorcycle club plaques. . . . I was surprised because I always see a group of those people as someone to be afraid of but they're not. . . . I've been finding out from others telling me and then what I saw just confirmed what I've heard. They're very kind and generous and have big hearts."

A significant minority of visitors made clear, sometimes quite explicitly, at other times in more careful if still easily understood terms, that they were unhappy with what they believe to be the Obama administration's lackadaisical efforts to prosecute the War on Terror. One older white male responded to my question regarding the meaning of the events of September 11, 2001, in terms that were terse and disdainful of the current administration: "We have to keep our guards [sic] up and not let it down like they're trying to do now. . . . [T]hey're trying to tear the country apart now." A younger white male was somewhat more circumspect in his criticisms of developments in the Obama administration's handling of terror suspects, though the attitude is still plainly discernible: "We really have to be viligant [*sic*] with what we're doing. I'm all for stomping these terrorists out wherever it [*sic*] is. We can't wait for them to come here again. I don't like what's going on a little bit now. Our former president, even though he didn't do everything I like, these guys, you can't just say, 'Hey, we'll take you to court.' . . . I think we go get them, we can't wait for them, why would we do that?" A bit self-consciously, he finished with "That's *my* opinion, but I'm a hillbilly!" and laughed aloud.

Almost entirely absent in comments from visitors were criticisms of the War on Terror. In several weeks interviewing at the site, I spoke with only one visitor who expressed such a position. This was an elderly man who self-identified as a veteran of World War II and offered these words of caution: "The world is in terrible shape. . . . [T]hat was a tragedy, but look at the tragedies now. We're in Iraq, and we're in Afghanistan, and we're in Pakistan, and boys are getting killed every day. To me it doesn't make a lot of sense. I wish it did. I'm a veteran of World War II, but I don't think these wars make much sense to me. If I was the president, I'd be figuring ways to get out."

Thinking about Religion and the Crash of Flight 93

I asked interviewees a number of questions about their sense of the role religion played in the events of 9/11, and specifically of the crash of Flight 93, and their aftermath, if any. Many of the responses touched on ground whereupon religion and nationalism meet, or are at least only a few steps away from one another. There were a small minority of responses best described not as civil religious, nor as religious, but as expressive of a straightforward, bellicose nationalism, e.g., those that consisted of phrases such as "You may laugh now but we'll have the last laugh" and "We can beat anything that these other nations bring our way." Many more who did not speak in that unadulterated nationalist language nonetheless invoked concepts of the nation that are intimately connected to religious symbols and narratives. A great number reiterated basically the same version of the mythological tale of passengers praying en masse that we have already encountered in media accounts and in the narratives at the temporary memorial and the Flight 93 Chapel. One typical such response described it thus: "They got in a little group and said a prayer and held hands." Another insinuated that he had first heard the myth from the temporary memorial Ambassador during his visit and noted the emotional impact of this piece of the narrative: "It just gave me chills to hear that they all prayed together before they made their decision. . . . [T]hey all agreed and they all prayed, and then 'Let's roll.'" The Beamer catchphrase is neatly tied in to the collective prayer here. Others who did not discuss the mythological collective prayer were nonetheless certain that the passengers as a group acted with Christian faith in their hearts: "The story [of Flight 93] is these Christian people who felt compelled to act. . . . I don't think they were concerned about themselves, from the stories I've read, most of them believed in the hereafter and they weren't afraid to die for it." Still others spoke of the event as creating a religious response not only in the passengers, but in the rest of the country as well: "It brought people together, brought people out to churches, brought people together in prayer, and united our country more."

There were also examples of varieties of religious extremism and fundamentalist fervor in the responses. One young girl, visiting the site with her mother and siblings, summarized the meaning of the event as evidence that "the Devil is alive." Another man ended his comments to me by signaling his belief that 9/11 was "probably one of the signs of the end of times." He then cited a number of Bible passages on the end of the world and the necessity for preparation for the imminent event before he headed back to his car. This kind of extremist religious expression was expressed by only a small minority of my respondents, but the visitors who held to such ideas were unanimously confident and relatively unrestrained in their assertions. In any event, I got no impression that they were weighing their words more carefully with me than they might have in more intimate company.

Much more common were responses that indicated a belief that the events and the aftermath of 9/11 and the crash of Flight 93 were part of some larger plan on the part of God. The Baylor Surveys of Religion have found consistently that large minorities of the American population believe that supernatural forces have acted upon them personally or on the world. One fifth of Americans believe God has spoken directly to them, one quarter believe they have witnessed a miraculous physical healing of illness, more than half (55%) believe they have been protected from harm by a guardian angel, and between 25% and 37% believe places can be haunted, the physical world can be influenced through telekinesis, and/or some UFOs are spaceships from other worlds.[3] In the context of these data, it is not hard to understand how so many of those who visit the temporary memorial site believed that God was exercising his power in allowing or even causing the events of 9/11. The most common of these scenarios involved a belief that it was God's intervention that allowed the passengers to take the plane down where they did, in an area that was relatively unpopulated and where therefore there would be no casualties outside of the people on the plane. One emotionally intense man told me in no uncertain terms that "the Lord wanted it to happen. He did not want the White House taken, so He took these courageous men and women, everyone on the plane" as his tool for protecting the White House. An elderly woman echoed this sentiment: "I think once again God protected our country—that would have been such a disaster to have the Capitol hit. . . . What would have happened to the function of the government? . . . [This would have produced] a lot more turmoil." A middle-aged woman visiting with her husband provided perhaps the most colorful version of this basic narrative. Only minutes after telling me she thought there was no religious meaning to the events of 9/11, she reversed course abruptly and radically: "I'm sure there was a higher power that put the plane down here rather than in a city. I imagine a plane flying upside down with a huge hand of God guiding it to this field." After this description, she paused and cracked a nervous smile. "I'm getting crazy!" she half-apologized and laughed self-consciously. Some who were struck by the aesthetic beauty and tranquility of the countryside surrounding the crash site expressed a belief that God had put the plane down there precisely to give the passengers a particularly idyllic and peaceful place of rest and visitors an agreeable experience at the memorial He presumably knew would later be erected there: "I do think the place where it happened is significant, how solemn and how peaceful and how quiet it is here, I think God had a hand in that." The man who spoke these words was then questioned by his wife: "But you don't think God made the flight go down?" to which he quickly responded, "No, but I think the place, there is something special about the place. . . . [I]t's holy ground. It could have hit a major populated area and it went down here so far away from everything. . . . [S]omething let it land here." This satisfied his wife, who remarked, "Okay, I see where you're going with that." Another older couple expressed the same belief ("I think the Lord had a hand in it to save more people"; "The Lord kept it from going down in Washington where it could have taken more lives") just before indicating their sense that the struggle on the plane represented a larger struggle between Christianity and Islam: "It seemed almost like a Christian-Muslim thing: the hijackers were Muslim, . . . and most of the people on the plane . . . I think were Christian."

This last remark points to one of the topics of central interest in my interviews with visitors. I wanted to discern how much of what visitors understood about Flight 93's meaning, and the meaning of 9/11 more broadly, might be connected to negative conceptions of Islam and Muslims. The question of the consequences of 9/11 and American responses to the attacks for American Muslims and U.S. relations with Muslim peoples around the world has been widely discussed and hotly contested in the years since September 11, 2001. I found that a small but vocal minority of visitors to the temporary memorial were willing to speak of the meaning of the crash of Flight 93 and the events of 9/11 by invoking Islam in pointedly negative, accusatory terms. A still smaller minority of these did so by alluding to the conspiracy theory concerning the permanent memorial as a mosque, which is discussed in chapter five. One woman, after telling me she had heard something about a controversy surrounding the charge that the permanent memorial design "worship[ed] Muhammad," asked me if I knew how the controversy had been resolved: "Did they keep that in?" When I told her in the most objective way I could devise that the design had undergone revisions that were intended to respond to the criticisms, she seemed unsatisfied with my explanation and said bluntly, "I think they should change it more than just a little bit." Another visitor, who also expressed his dissatisfaction with the Obama administration's prosecution of the War on Terror, described his sense of the meaning of 9/11 in uncomplicated terms: "You have another religion, radical Islam, coming after us." Two men who described themselves as military veterans, visiting the site with their wives, were among the clearest representatives of the most pointed articulation of this anti-Islamic sentiment. In the view of the one who did most of the talking, while his friend nodded and chimed

MYTH IN PRACTICE | 273

in enthusiastically with short additional comments, the United States is currently in a clear struggle of good and evil and we cannot afford even the recognition of the humanity of the opponent:

> I have no empathy for the hijackers or their families, none whatsoever. I don't want them memorialized here or their names or anything like that, they're just cowardly criminal people. . . . I heard they were debating whether to put their names on plaques,[4] but I think it's bullshit. . . . [W]e're dealing with a whole 'nother ball game with these people. . . . [U]ntil a Muslim mother loves her child more than she hates a non-Muslim, this is never going to end. If you put a bomb on your kid to go blow something up, there's something wrong with you. It's a mental illness.

A much smaller number of visitors I spoke with endeavored to make the same separation between "correct" Islam and the "perverted" Islam of the hijackers that has been championed by two American administrations desirous both of prosecuting a war on Islamic terrorism and avoiding a broad-handed condemnation of all of Islam. One visitor to the site ably summarized this perspective thus:

> We all have one God no matter what we call it. . . . [F]rom the comments on the voice recorder, these people [the hijackers] are just plain idiots [his wife adds "cowards"]. . . . They're fanatics [his wife interjects: "They prayed to Allah, they prayed to God, and God would not at all say, 'Do something like this.' God's act is what the people sacrificed, that was God's will"]. . . . It's against their own religion, it's against their own religion. Their religion doesn't practice that. They're not whatever they want to call themselves, they're just terrorists, that's all [his wife again: "True cowards"].

A clear majority of visitors articulated some place for religion in meaning-making concerning the crash of Flight 93, even if it was simply in a sense that the events of 9/11 had increased their own religious faith. A man told me that "the crash made my faith in God much more profound," though he was also clear that "I don't see them pushing any type of religion here, I mean, I see a cross and I see the gravestones and I think that's fine." A woman described how her comfort about the fate of the passengers came from her religious faith: "I'm very thankful there's a Lord, so they could go to heaven." One mother, traveling with her two teenage daughters, articulated a theme, pointed to also by others, of the unfathomable ways of God as a framework for attempting to put in order what otherwise seems senseless: "I think it makes you question God. I'm a Christian and sometimes we only want to see God in the good, but God is in the bad too, you have to weigh both and realize there's a bigger meaning, we may never know it, but that's what I think." She was openly weeping by the time she finished her statement, when one of her daughters added, "You can see that God can give people hope even from things that are bad."

But in the sea of religious responses, there was yet a significant minority of visitors who either refused to invoke fundamentally religious terms to make sense of Flight 93 or took a religiously pluralist interpretive angle on the event. There were many variations on the pluralist perspective:

Regardless of what religion they were, they all came together and done a job.

On the terrorists' end, it might have been religion, but on our end, that depends on the person.

I'm sure there were so many different religious views, and in the end it didn't matter, they all ended up the same.

Most religions just came together, looking around here, there's rosary beads and different things, they came together.

Some clearly framed their interpretation of the events of 9/11 in the language of religion, but they did so invoking a now classic distinction in the popular American religious lexicon between "religion," understood as church-based, collective worship of one or another established cult, and "spirituality," which is a more idiosyncratic, individualist notion of religiosity. One woman there with her children provided a particularly apt version of this perspective:

I'm not a very religious person. I'm a very spiritual person, and in reading the transcripts, in there, it's very disturbing where it says in the name of Allah, our only God, and all of that. Personally I just want to throw up my hands and go, "This is why I'm not a religious person" [laughs]. That's the absurdity. I don't want to be disrespectful to any religion and certainly not Islam, but those statements, it's just absurd.

Religion that relies on collectively held tenets, traditional texts and doctrines, and dogmatic beliefs is here presented as incomprehensibly wrongheaded. The cultural liberalism of the perspective is palpable ("I don't want to be disrespectful to any religion"), but there's also something of a disdain for religious worship in the communal forms Durkheim, Bellah, and others have described as the very base of religious experience. The woman just cited went on in the language of the culturally pluralist, individualist religious bricolage worldview that is probably the single fastest growing religious perspective in contemporary America, especially among younger Americans: "I have young children and I told them I want you to feel it, I remember when I went down to some of the Mayan ruins in Mexico and I had [an] experience there, I felt the energy of the place and I just told the kids I want you to try to feel the energy of the place, I believe there is a special energy to places like this."

Some visitors spoke of sacredness in a language that was not explicitly religious but more apparently civil religious, in a way that parallels the use of the language of sacredness in the permanent memorial design, where the crash site is explicitly designated as "sacred ground" but without any mention of the supernatural or God. An emotionally expressive male visitor told me: "The sacredness of it [the crash site] also says to me that I will never be able to walk on that ground, and I'm okay with that. The sacredness makes it okay. I don't qualify."

One other fact that emerged from my interviews at the temporary memorial site is that an overwhelming majority of the visitors there had neither visited nor even heard of the Flight 93 Chapel. Given my own method of discovery of the chapel, this did not greatly surprise me. I did not know of its existence prior to my first visit to Shanksville, but saw small, homemade roadside signs once we were in town reading simply "Flt 93 Chapel" with an arrow and located it after we had visited the temporary memorial site. Although the chapel has for some time been advertised in visitor information pamphlets available at local hotels and businesses and has had a webpage for a number of years, it certainly still receives considerably less media attention than the crash site and memorial, especially once one is out of the immediate Shanksville/Somerset area. Father Mascherino's sense that Park Service staff were deliberately discouraging visitors from dropping by the chapel, however, was almost certainly mistaken. It may be that he was not incorrect in perceiving antagonism to the chapel among some Park Service personnel, but the widespread ignorance of the temporary memorial visitors concerning the very existence of the chapel was the main reason so many did not visit it. A few visitors I spoke to who had heard of the chapel mistakenly thought it was located on the same site as the temporary memorial before their arrival.

The Role of the Ambassadors in Shaping Visitor Response and Interpretation

Visitors to the temporary memorial did not assign meanings to what they saw there in complete autonomy or in a vacuum. As we have seen, they certainly brought much with them in the way of premade American cultural mythology about heroes and national identity, and they may well have come into contact with some of the media material on Flight 93 described in chapters six and seven. Once at the memorial site, they also received specific information and more implicitly communicated cultural cues from the Ambassadors. Many of the visitors I interviewed described factual material that they had learned about during the brief presentation given by the Ambassadors during their visit. For those visitors who came to the site with little knowledge of Flight 93 beyond the very most basic, this included even fundamental knowledge such as how many people were on the plane and the fact that they made phone calls from the plane and discovered what had happened in New York and Washington, D.C. The position of the plane at approach and impact (it was flying almost upside down and struck nose and right wing first) was noted by several as a particularly stunning revelation.

I observed perhaps a dozen Ambassador presentations to crowds of visitors during the time I was interviewing at the site. The way in which they took place was generally informal. As visitors milled about the site,

Ambassadors would wait until there was something of a critical mass of at least ten or 12, though on slower days and times I saw Ambassadors addressing groups that were smaller than this. The Ambassador would go from one small group or individual to another, announcing that a presentation on Flight 93 was about to begin. In the event of the arrival of a busload of tourists, the Ambassador would sometimes have a brief conversation with the bus driver or director of the tour group, who would him- or herself then round up the group for the presentation. The Ambassador would begin a narrative of the last flight of United 93, starting with the boarding of the plane, proceeding to the crash and then to a description of the subsequent memorialization work, usually including information on the permanent memorial plan (some design images were for some time posted in the small visitor center at the site). For the most part, visitors were quiet during the presentation with the exception of gasps, discrete crying, or other expressive gestures at the description of particularly dramatic facts. Exceptions to this informal rule frequently illustrated a principle I have noted in other aspects of collective memory-making. At one presentation I observed, as an Ambassador was describing the moment of the hijacking and the subsequent diversion of the plane back to the east, an older woman responded that a friend of hers had seen the plane "do a 360-degree turn in Ohio." This bit of folkloric knowledge is highly unlikely to be true, given the fact that flight data records show us that the plane was at that point, early in the hijacking, some 5,000–6,000 feet above its normal flight elevation of 35,000 feet and therefore would have been a less than obvious phenomenon to someone watching from the ground, and especially someone in a public that, at that moment, was not even aware that there might be a hijacked plane flying somewhere in the vicinity, since there had yet been no media announcement of this flight as a hijack. Yet it does demonstrate a recurrent theme of the memorialization work concerning Flight 93. In much of that work, individuals who are objectively quite far removed from the actual events that took place on September 11, 2001, on board the plane and on the ground in Shanksville nonetheless endeavor fiercely to connect themselves in some personal way to those events. Whether we are observing a visitor to the chapel or the temporary memorial leaving a personal memento or hearing someone relate his or her own real or perceived connection to the flight and its passengers, the force at work has to do with the desire to experience the most direct contact possible with the sacred objects and persons involved, even if one must play fast and loose with facts to do so.

The language of sacredness is explicitly invoked by Ambassadors, who now address visitors to the still-incomplete permanent memorial, though I have no reason to believe this is systematic or explicitly directed by the Park Service. Rather, spontaneously albeit frequently, Ambassadors intermingle their own emotive language of sacrality with the bare recounting of the facts of the crash. One Ambassador I witnessed described the crash site in powerfully sacred language: "Our fellow citizens are buried out there. . . . You and I are not allowed out there. We don't need to go out there. *That's holy ground.*" Imbedded in this description is the idea, which I presented earlier, that the crash site is a cemetery, but not an ordinary one. The message communicated by the Ambassador, which is, as we have seen, the language too of the permanent memorial design, is that this is a cemetery in which individuals who are not like us are interred, and they are of such a rarefied substance as to deserve protection from contamination by the merely human. This is precisely the language of Durkheim on sacredness and profaneness. If someone insufficiently ritually cleansed comes into contact with a sacred entity or item, great danger arises. The status of the sacred thing is compromised, and significant evil can come to the profane desecrator and the community as a result. In most ritual frameworks, there are individuals who by definition cannot remove their profane status (in primitive societies, frequently, women) and who therefore must simply be banned from contact with the sacred. The Ambassador is here informing visitors that they are, with respect to this sacred object, profane by definition and without recourse, and therefore cannot under any circumstances tread the sacred ground where the remains of the passengers of Flight 93 lie. The permanent prohibition was effectively made by the arrangement of the temporary memorial site itself, and the permanent design builds it in too, although the latter permits visitors to get quite a lot closer to the crash site than the former. So the structure is already there, and what the Ambassador does in this communication is provide an explicit symbolic universe to the visitors for making sense of that structural fact.

Ambassadors also use a language saturated in cultural categories of morality and religion, even though they are careful to avoid nakedly ideological statements or pronouncements of their own personal religious beliefs. Simple moral categories of good and evil are put to work here, as at the chapel, although one has to listen more carefully to find them. "That's what this is about," said one Ambassador to a group. "These people stood up to Evil. What would you do in their place? At some point, you have to stand up for what's right, I don't care about politics." The idea that there is an implicit cultural politics of a fairly specific variety inextricably involved in Manichean categories of Good and Evil apparently eluded this Ambassador, but he was not alone. The position of the Ambassador is arguably one of someone endeavoring to tread over quicksand. An objective, neutral account of the event and of its relation to ideas about the nation and religion is in practice immensely difficult to achieve. Almost inevitably, an Ambassador will take one or the other of two positions: he will articulate a religious framework for Flight 93, or he will speak of the event in purely secular terms. Both positions have advocates among visitors, and both have opponents, and both rely on broad mythologies about the origins and meaning of America for their sensibility. It is likely too that the frames the Ambassadors use to describe what happened on Flight 93 matter significantly in the local process of the production of collective memory.

I often felt a great deal of kinship with the Ambassadors as I watched them go about their work, at the precise moment that I was going about mine. As they interacted with visitors with the intent of aiding them in their visit to gain understanding and, perhaps, emotional peace, I too was interacting with the visitors with my own set of objectives. We were both caught in a game in which complete neutrality was an impossibility from the start, however much we might have felt ourselves tied to it as an ideal or a rhetorical device or both. I hoped fervently and constantly that I was not leading interviewees in directions they would not have chosen of their own volition, but I ultimately do not and cannot know that this hope was realized. Many Ambassadors expressed to me their similar desire not to impose anything on visitors that they would not willingly choose to accept. The complexity of the mutual interactions between Ambassadors, visitors to the site, and those like myself who wanted to describe the actions of both is neatly summarized in something I saw take place several times during the presentations of Ambassadors. The leaving of gifts at the site by visitors is, as I described in chapter three, one of the core collective practices in Flight 93 memorialization and collective memory, and indeed, as I noted, the phenomenon has become something of a more or less universal response to disasters over the past few decades. I observed an element in some Ambassador presentations that enriches our consideration of the motivations of the visitors who leave such personal objects at the site. For, in a reflexive twist that is the very stuff of social life and the effort to study it, the process by which the gifts are collected and catalogued was frequently narrated to visitors as part of the description of post-crash memorialization, and visitors were even, in some cases, directly invited to leave things. As one Ambassador put it: "Nothing [of gifts left at site] is thrown away. It's all collected, stored, catalogued. . . . So if you want to leave something, find an empty space and put it there." How much gift leaving has been prompted at least in part by this motivation? We cannot know, and I have no doubt that much of that activity has been motivated by something at work on visitors before they arrive at the site. Yet I can scarcely think of a better statement about the deeply interpretive work the Ambassadors performed over the ten years of the temporary memorial's life and its effects on the thoughts and actions of visitors. They have been important players in the construction and preservation of the Flight 93 myth.

9

What Flight 93 Tells Us about America

In a certain sense, the construction of the mythology surrounding the crash of Flight 93 tells us little about the American people, American society, or American culture that fully distinguishes them from other peoples, societies, and cultures. There is perhaps nothing completely unique in the things people in Shanksville and elsewhere have done since the plane struck ground more than a decade ago to produce a commemorative narrative about the fact, and I have endeavored to show some of the common patterns in ritualization and memory-making around events of mass death that are exemplified by aspects of Flight 93 memorialization. One could defensibly assert that this simply serves as an example among many others of a well-established fact about our species, which has to do with our eagerness to create and then immerse ourselves in fanciful stories of the marvelous origins of our people and the ways in which we can master death through heroism and selfless sacrifice to the group.

But, if the mythic notions of national history and heroic endeavor are aspects of human belief not unique to American culture, it is yet the case that the *particular* forms of those myths as they are found in the United States and their relationship to ongoing cultural political conflicts and debates here are revealed in some detail in the symbolic work that has gone on around the crash of this plane. The evidence we see in the Flight 93 myth demonstrates that the American civil religion is alive and well, and it continues to operate in the morally complex ways that Robert Bellah described nearly a half century ago. This set of mythical narratives and symbols about American identity continues to drive much cultural work and meaning-making, and especially that which is evoked by events of mass catastrophe and death such as those of September 11, 2001.

As I noted earlier in the book, there are some who would assert that the Flight 93 myth, and perhaps also the American myth into which it

taps so strongly, can be reduced to the reactionary politics of the Tea
Party or some other segment of the contemporary American political
right. This kind of claim demonstrates nothing more clearly than the
inability of many American intellectuals in the humanities and social
sciences to even begin the work necessary to bracket the taken-for-
granteds of their own left academic lifeworlds and try to understand
the mode of generation and the power of this kind of popular cultural
mythology. One does not, I have tried to show, have to believe that the
myth is literally true in order to understand and even experience it personally as moving and meaningful. These intellectual critics of the Flight
93 myths have their own myths, which tend to be just as unexamined
and uncritically accepted as the Flight 93 myth is by reverent visitors
to the memorial sites. So any criticism they might make of the Flight
93 myth is flawed by the fact that, in making it, they purport to operate
from a position completely free of the grasp of myth. The implicit claim
made is "reject this myth (theirs) and accept another (ours)," but the
express mode of justification of the criticism obfuscates the real relativism involved in the business of asserting fundamental worldviews.

It may be true not only that myth is inescapable for human beings,
but also that we cannot even effectively understand the relationship of
past, present, and future without it. In a book on the mythological form
of the American Western, Will Wright argued against perhaps the greatest contemporary scholar of myth, Claude Lévi-Strauss, on the place of
myth in modern societies. Whereas Lévi-Strauss believed such societies
as our own had no myths but only history, Wright countered that it is
impossible to approach the past unless we are armed with both history
and myth. While unemotional historical narrative produces our understanding of the past, it does not permit us to act in the present based on
recognition of our current relationship to that past. Only modern myths
provide us the capacity to envision the relationship of past and present
and thereby to act in accordance with that understanding.[1] Primitive
societies differ from us in that they understand the past and the present
as one in a mythical eternal moment, but, while we reject that notion,
the modern world is yet not rigidly convinced that the past is something
relegated to a realm forever separated from our own. In our myth, we
see the problems of the present already addressed and resolved in their
past incarnations, and through our absorption of mythical narratives,

we find practical ways to move toward resolutions of our current conflicts and dilemmas that are not offered by purely empirical history.[2]

In its depiction of God-fearing patriotic hero-martyrs who confront danger by selfless sacrifice of life in the interests of God and country, who thereby illustrate the chosen status of America in the eyes of God, who are worshipped in their martial heroism as flag totems by those who continue to reproduce in their own lives the same rigid bounds of national tribal identity the heroes died protecting, and who even aspire to be chosen themselves to die and kill for the totem that is the flag, in all this, the Flight 93 myth inevitably participates in fundamentally culturally conservative patterns of belief and thought. Its function is to preserve certain venerable narratives about America and Americans by referring current events to these traditional symbols and beliefs. In the work Flight 93 memorialization does to hide the reality of catastrophe and death and to turn the tragedy of loss (and its grim opportunity for reflection and humility) into sanitized paeans to culture heroes and national triumphalism, it reinforces a set of attitudes toward human mortality that might be characterized as misguided, even dishonest by some. It is certainly a view that sanitizes brute realities and stylistically embellishes material that might otherwise force us to think harder about certain basic aspects of our existence in the world.

Yet, at the same time, the myth of America that emerges in the efforts to narrate the last moments of United Flight 93 is a myth that encloses and comforts those who recognize themselves in the tribe that is described in that myth. The chaos and terror engendered by death, and especially by the kind of lightning-bolt mass death represented by terrorism and other mortal dangers of risk society, may well be too horrific to be gazed upon unadulterated, at least for most of us. Myths like those about the American nation and people that undergirded the collective story telling about Flight 93 provide existential protection for culture members that is just as primordial and powerful as that provided by any purely religious myths of eternal life and celestial realms beyond the grave. So mythologies such as those we find in the American civil religion function, in a secularizing age, precisely like those of more properly religious myth did in the past: they provide a consoling set of narratives of eternal life in the body of the collectivity (the nation and its ascended heroes) to wield against the eternal fear of death and chaos. That American civil religion finds a way to enshrine freedom, a fundamentally individualist value, as the core value of the collective civil religion is not a contradiction. Individualism is one of the core shared values that defines American culture, and Americans are, perhaps somewhat paradoxically, nowhere more like one another than in their deep, prerational affirmation of individualism and individual freedom as unchallengeable principles.

It may be that we simply cannot have one side of the Flight 93 and American myths (the protection from existential angst, the stable sense of identity, mission, and collective belonging) without the other (exaltation of in-group over out-group and brusque rejection and even demonization of the latter, blindness to inconvenient or uncomfortable realities). Jonathan Haidt, writing in the *New York Times* on the mass celebrations that took place in the U.S. in reaction to the killing of Osama bin Laden, tried to assure readers that those who assert in-group solidarity in effervescent acts[3] such as these celebrations are doing something fully distinct from the out-group rejection that can be found in, e.g., the anti-Muslin sentiments I heard expressed by some visitors to the Flight 93 temporary memorial. Tellingly, however, he offers little evidence to support his assertion about the neat distinctness of the two collective sentiments, and there is much to indicate that they might be inevitably linked together in the same evolutionary history that he likes to cite. The comfort and protective shell provided by cultural narratives of the elect status of our group and our heroes may well require a lowering of other groups and actors seen as antagonists and the exclusion from participation in the in-group of anyone who bears too many characteristics of the out-group. The desire to separate two differently valued moral behaviors (in this case, in-group validation and out-group vilification) is perhaps understandable here, but the truth's complexity may well once again frustrate our simpler moralistic desires.

The American cultural effort to propagate a mythology of national identity and heroism of the sort evident in the Flight 93 memorialization work faces not only the age-old enemy of death and disappearance but the more modern one of uncertainty and the failure of rational planning in the face of advanced technological threats and undependable technical systems of protection. In asserting the willful efficacy of the action of the Angel Patriot heroes in the face of danger, the Flight

93 myth occludes some of the more powerfully existentially troubling aspects of the deadly events of September 11, 2001. We have already discussed the massively increased technological risks imposed by a society in which huge machines with tanks full of jet fuel hurtling through the air at speeds greater than sound can, through the skillful efforts of determined killers and unreliable security systems, turn into huge bombs aimed at skyscrapers in heavily populated cities. The failures in the technical web of protections relied on by all of us in our everyday lives that made the event possible go well beyond those that took place on the day of the flights. Months before, on April 26, 2001, Mohamed Atta was pulled over for erratic driving in Fort Lauderdale. He had no American driver's license and claimed to have left his Egyptian license at home, but the county officer who detained him gave him a break and did not arrest him. He was told instead to appear 30 days later in court to produce the license. When he did not appear, a warrant was issued for his arrest, and this should have been available to every police computer in the state of Florida. But on July 5, in Delray Beach, Atta was stopped a second time. He had since acquired an American driver's license, which he produced for the officer. When his information was plugged by the officer into the police computer record system, the warrant for failure to appear in court should have come up, and Atta should have been taken into custody. But, inexplicably, it did not, and he was not arrested, instead escaping with a minor traffic fine and the freedom to continue working on the plot that was then barely two months from fruition. If the security net of electronic surveillance upon which we automatically, and generally confidently, rely for protection from those with bad intentions had worked as it is supposed to work at that point, the 9/11 plot would have been at least postponed, and who is to say what might have been discovered and prevented if Atta had been taken into police custody and questioned more closely?[4] The failure of that technological safety net created a situation in which thousands were instantly made desperately vulnerable to lethal attack, and this despite any efforts they may have made through their own willful planning to avoid such risk.

Unpredictable sequences of events unamenable to manipulation by individual willful agency not only allowed the attack to happen; they also had a part to play in determination of who would or would not be at the site of mass death at the moment at which it struck. One man overheard in the History Channel's *102 Minutes That Changed America* tells someone that he was on his way to work in the World Trade Center when the South Tower collapsed, and that he was 15 minutes late for work because of his late-night television watching the night before. Ecstatically, and in stunned incomprehension of the fact, he shouts: "Monday Night Football saved my life!" The sheer inability to foresee, control, and manage our vulnerability to mind-numbing horror and chaos is difficult to bear in the extreme, but it is impressed on us as a reality by myriad events like these from the September 11 attacks. The myth of Flight 93, and the American myth on which it relies, perhaps makes it more bearable by shielding this fact of the ultimate insignificance of our agency and our rational schemes of protection from our sight and turning our gaze instead to mythical, powerful Angel Patriots in the sky.

Ultimately, the intent of Flight 93 mythologization is not to help us remember, or at least not to help us remember the aspects of September 11, 2001, that cannot be reduced to the contours of the American hero myth, but rather to help us forget our vulnerability and our weakness and to thereby return as quickly as possible to our normal lives. This kind of work can certainly be criticized by those who would prefer more critically and rationally based historical narrative, but the critics ought also to be required to shoulder the responsibility of coming up with an alternative form of cultural therapeutic work to handle such catastrophic events. How will merely critical or empirical historical efforts around Flight 93 do the work done by the existing Flight 93 memorials and narratives, which is not inappropriately referred to as 'healing' by some? Should the memorial effort turn instead with fixed gaze to the horrible, the anxiety-laden, the dreadful, which is arguably the chief objective feature of the day's events? Should it, instead of cultural hagiography, perform progressive left political criticism of the United States and its demonstrable role in creating a world situation likely to provoke such attacks? And are these sustainable cultural forms of self-conception and memory, or are they merely the dreams of some intellectuals, themselves in many cases so profoundly alienated from the most basic frameworks of the culture of the society in which they live that they have lost sight of the difference between the possible and the fanciful?

Recently, as I was driving through a small Pennsylvania town not unlike Shanksville, I stopped at a red light behind a pickup truck bearing a peeling and weathered window sticker that read "9/11/2001 Never Forget." It was a remarkable experience precisely because I could not recall the last time I had seen such a public declaration here in the very red central part of the state. In the first few years after the attacks, such public pronouncements were omnipresent in this part of America. The reality announced by the fact that now, scarcely more than a decade after the event, such stickers have worn off their bumpers, or been replaced by others, with such inevitable predictability is that we are already forgetting 9/11, and it will not be long before the only sites wherein one can encounter the collective memory of Flight 93 will be those described in this book, and in those very sites we are moved to recall things that will help to distance us from the most stunning and inscrutable parts of the events of that day.

Robert Bellah passed away in July 2013, but there is no danger that the utility of his thought will fade soon. Flight 93 mythologization is clear evidence of the relevance and continuing interpretive power of the concept of civil religion. Some will embrace it in all its aspects, including those that construct narratives of individualism and American nativism that erect rigid boundaries of insider and outsider and fuel exclusion. Others will reject it altogether in the name of a critical progressive position that is ignorant of its own reliance on myths and prerational symbols. Bellah's more complex attitude toward American culture, informed by his own intricate understanding of its nature but also by particular cultural struggles it was undergoing at the time he wrote *The Broken Covenant*, presents a third alternative. He spoke of his relationship to the American civil religion as a "tension—*odi et amo*—of affirmation and rejection": "Of all the earthy societies I know this one is mine and I do not regret it. But I also know through objective observation and personal tragedy that this society is a cruel and bitter one, very far, in fact, from its own highest aspirations."[5] My sense of this, my country, is essentially the same, and my reaction to the myths described in this book is heavy with indecision and confused sensibilities. When I hear people speak of the American founders as demigods and the American Constitution as a sacred object, untouchable by mere humans, perfect and pristine, I remember my junior year in college, in

1987, when the university I attended celebrated the 200-year anniversary of the completion of the Constitution with a series of vivid and charged debates about whether this document was or was not a fundamentally democratic one, whether it might even have been at least in part concerned with protecting the interests of the powerful against the masses, and whether it should or should not be significantly amended to make it better fit our contemporary situation. I cherished those debates and the critical attitude they evinced toward the country's founding documents and individuals, and I do not believe they made me admire the Constitution or the Founders any less.

And yet, in July 2009, when I was working on the last stage of interviews at the temporary memorial and staying with my family at the Flight 93 Chapel guesthouse, I lived in another emotional space, a space in which I found it easy and obvious to rely on other ways of understanding the nature of America and my relationship to it. On one particular night that month, I was driving through Shanksville from the memorial on my way to the guesthouse. A full moon shone overhead, the peaceful night sky was serenely quiet, everything that passed outside the car window as we drove out of town and into the countryside—the trees, the barns, the cornfields—seemed familiar and welcoming. I thought of the people I had met at the chapel, especially of my friend Alphonse Mascherino, and of people I knew from the temporary memorial, especially some of the Park Service Ambassadors with whom I had so cheerfully chatted about myriad things during my days there. I thought too of the symbols that surrounded me daily as I worked at both sites. I gazed up at the huge moon atop the hill as we unloaded the car beside the chapel, which shone nearly as bright as day in the shimmering moonlight, and I felt a spontaneous, overwhelming sense of rootedness and belonging.

NOTES

CHAPTER 1. FLIGHT 93 AND 9/11

1. Chermak et al., 2003, p. 4.
2. As is made apparent in this first chapter, Robert Bellah, whom I consider an intellectual descendant of Durkheim at least in part, is also a key source on which I rely. Many works in the contemporary field of collective memory are also referenced throughout the book, although I would hesitate to call this a study in collective memory, as the framing I prefer—a study in contemporary civil religion and mythology—is broader and more inclusive.
3. Eliade, 1988, p. 17.
4. Ibid., p. 18.
5. Barthes, 1972, p. 122.
6. "The Fat Plateau," *Economist*, January 23–29, 2010.
7. Morin, 1956.
8. Friend, 2006.
9. Bellah, 1975, p. 1.
10. Ibid., p. 153.
11. Bellah, 1976, p. 172.
12. Bellah, 1975, p. 12.
13. Amis, 2008, p. 3.
14. Gitlin, 2006, p. 128.
15. Schudson, 1992, p. 3.
16. Longman, 2006.
17. Vaughan, 2006.
18. *New York Times*, April 25, 2011, updated online info file.
19. The single most complete summary source on the number of calls, who made them, and their duration is contained in the prosecution's presentation materials from the case of *U.S. v. Zacarias Moussaoui*, criminal number 01-455-A, in the United States District Court of Virginia. At the time of this writing, these materials could be found on the webpages of the court at http://www.vaed .uscourts.gov/notablecases/moussaoui/exhibits/. It would seem the sources of this data are the actual United Airlines documents cataloguing calls made during the flight, which were also consulted by the 9/11 Commission in the completion of its report. I use other indicated sources for substantive content of the phone calls.
20. Kean and Hamilton, 2004, p. 13.

21. American 11 had just over a half hour between hijack and crash, Flight 93 just a few minutes more, perhaps 35, and American 77 was in the air the longest from the time of hijack, approximately 45 minutes.

22. The Moussaoui prosecution team does not explicitly claim to be documenting all calls made from the plane, but the number provided there would seem to be more or less complete, as I have been unable to find any press coverage of any substantive calls that are not included in their total, with the exception of one call from Thomas Burnett Jr. that is discussed below.

23. The two cell phone calls were the last two placed from the plane before the crash, both at approximately 9:58 a.m., by CeeCee Lyles and Edward Felt.

24. Kean and Hamilton, 2004, p. 21.

25. Longman, 2002, p. 128.

26. Ibid., p. 161.

27. Ibid., p. 162.

28. Ibid., p. 172.

29. Ibid., p. 177.

30. Ibid., p. 176.

31. Barrett, 2002, pp. 144–45.

32. Longman, 2002, pp. 132–33; Barrett, 2002, pp. 156–57.

33. Jefferson and Middlebrooks, 2006, pp. 34–36; Longman, 2002, p. 199.

34. Jefferson and Middlebrooks, 2006, p. 42; Longman, 2002, p. 199.

35. Jefferson and Middlebrooks, 2006, p. 44; Longman, 2002, p. 200.

36. Jefferson and Middlebrooks, 2006, p. 47.

37. Ibid.

38. Longman, 2002, p. 200.

39. This was reported in a number of media outlets in the immediate aftermath as well.

40. Jefferson and Middlebrooks, 2006, pp. 47–48.

41. Ibid., p. 52.

42. Ibid., p. 53; Longman, 2002, p. 203.

43. Jefferson and Middlebrooks, 2006, p. 53.

44. Ibid.; Longman, 2002, p. 204.

45. Glick and Zegart, 2004, p. 189.

46. Ibid., p. 190.

47. Ibid., pp. 190–91.

48. Ibid., pp. 191–92.

49. Ibid., p. 191.

50. Longman, 2002, p. 147.

51. Glick and Zegart, 2004, p. 194.

52. Ibid., pp., 193–94.

53. Ibid., p. 194.

54. The Moussaoui prosecution materials indicate that Burnett used a seatback phone

for all three of the calls it catalogues, but his wife claims that some of the calls were placed using his cell phone, as she saw it on her own phone's caller ID (Burnett and Giombetti, 2006, p. 61).

55. Burnett and Giombetti, 2006, p. 61; Longman, 2002, p. 107.

56. These are the times provided in the records of the Moussaoui trial; Deena Burnett claims the second call came at 9:34 Eastern time (she was in California at the time), although her account of the times of the other two calls matches those given in the Moussaoui trial.

57. Burnett and Giombetti, 2006, p. 64; Longman, 2002, p. 110.

58. Burnett and Giombetti, 2006, pp. 65–66; Longman, 2002, pp. 111–12.

59. Burnett and Giombetti, 2006, pp. 66–67; Longman, 2002, p. 118.

60. National Transportation Safety Board, Flight Path Study, February 19, 2002.

61. Ibid.

62. Kean and Hamilton, 2004, p. 22.

63. Simons and Chabris, 2012.

64. Halbwachs, 1992, p. 53.

65. Ibid., p. 59. In *Falling Man*, Don DeLillo presents us with a fictional version of a phenomenon that must have been well represented in New York City in the first years after the attacks. He writes of New York children, too young to have been made privy to the official details of the events by their protective parents who have invented their own private, familial mythology of the 9/11 attacks. They spend time looking out windows with binoculars, in search of more planes on a trajectory toward tall buildings, and speak mysteriously of a "Bill Lawton" (bin Laden) who flies planes, speaks 13 languages, and has the power to make food poisonous (DeLillo, 2007, pp. 72, 73, 74).

66. Halbwachs, 1992, pp. 61, 119.

67. Ibid., pp. 116, 85.

68. Ibid., p. 73.

69. Ibid., p. 40.

70. Clavandier, 2004, p. 151.

71. Abrams, Albright, and Panofsky, 2004, p. 201.

72. At this writing, the video could still be seen on YouTube (http://www.youtube.com/watch?v=_NhpqMaAjEw&feature=relmfu).

73. Clavandier, 2004, p. 142.

74. Snodgrass, 2011.

75. Ibid.

76. A basic fact that is fundamentally altered in every American memorialization effort of this event: there were not 40 bodies, but 44. The four hijackers are inevitably excluded from the count in the mythological narrative of the sacredness of the earth where the bodies are interred.

77. Balzac, 1977 [1831], p. 41.

78. Schudson, 1992, p. 14.

CHAPTER 2. DEATH, HORROR, AND CULTURE

1. Becker, 1973.
2. Fagan, 1984, pp. 160–61.
3. Paz, 1993, p. 63. All translations throughout the book from non-English sources are my own.
4. Lomnitz, 2008.
5. Ariès, 1977, p. 21.
6. Ibid., pp. 18, 26.
7. Ibid., pp. 294, 296.
8. Ibid., p. 398.
9. Ibid., pp. 573, 574.
10. Sudnow, 1967, p. 61.
11. Ibid., p. 37.
12. Ibid., p. 171.
13. The source is Kagan's course on death in the Open Yale Courses Series online. As I was finishing this book, Kagan's lectures were published in book form (Shelly Kagan, *Death*, Yale University Press, 2012).
14. Clavandier, 2004, p. 22.
15. Picardie, 1997, p. 129.
16. Heidegger, 1962, p. 282, emphasis in original. We can crudely translate his notoriously difficult concept *Dasein* as "human being."
17. Ibid.
18. Ibid., p. 284.
19. Ibid., p. 281.
20. Ibid.
21. Ibid., p. 297.
22. Ibid., p. 302.
23. Ibid., p. 298.
24. Morin, 1970, p. 36.
25. Ibid., p. 126.
26. Lomnitz, 2008, p. 58.
27. Stannard, 1977, pp. 38–39.
28. Ibid., p. 65.
29. Ibid., p. 66.
30. Ibid., pp. 157–60.
31. Ibid., pp. 173–74.
32. Ibid., p. 185.
33. Ibid., p. 189.
34. Elias, 1985, p. 35.
35. Mauksch, 1997.
36. Lawton, 2000.
37. Kaufman, 2005, pp. 28–29.
38. Green, 2008, p. 192.

39. There is a much more detailed description of Baudrillard's effort to think through death in contemporary societies like the United States in Riley, 2010, pp. 151–59.

40. Baudrillard, 2003, p. 5.

41. Giddens, 1990, pp. 102, 124–31.

42. Rozario, 2007, pp. 112–13.

43. Brunsma et al., 2007, p. 1.

44. Clavandier, 2004, pp. 233–34.

45. Rosenblatt, Greenberg, et al., 1989.

46. Clavandier, 2004, p. 43.

47. Ibid., pp. 26–27.

48. Ibid., pp. 28–29.

49. Ibid., p. 149.

50. Ibid.

51. Ibid., p. 38. I will have much more to say on this dual notion of sacredness in chapter four.

52. Clavandier, 2004, p. 60.

53. 2008 study by the National Consortium for the Study of Terrorism and Responses to Terrorism, pp. 2–6.

54. Ibid., pp. 43–45.

55. Mark Harris, "The Movie Trailer from Hell," *Entertainment Weekly*, October 9, 2009, emphasis in original.

56. I will look in chapter seven at how this technique is appropriated in several of the films about Flight 93 in the interests of capturing precisely this effect.

57. CameraPlanet archive on 9/11, http://www.youtube.com/watch?v=x4sRi5stG10& feature=fvw.

58. I do not make such descriptions lightly or for mere effect. That the dust from the disintegrated towers was understood as a relic of the human bodies that were in it at the time of destruction is evident in the urns of the dust that were given by then mayor Giuliani to families of the dead in a memorial ceremony at the WTC site just after the attacks in October 2001 (Sturken, 2004, p. 313).

59. CameraPlanet archive on 9/11, http://www.youtube.com/watch?v=gJbGm7GE1tA &feature=channel.

60. Murphy, 2002, pp. 152–53.

61. See, e.g., "Falling from the Twin Towers," at http://www.youtube.com/watch?v= 2d3KoQuXL24.

62. The entirety of *102 Minutes That Changed America* can currently be found online: http://www.youtube.com/watch?v=Y3FjhEwNo1M&feature=related.

63. Both calls can at the time of this writing still be found on YouTube: Doi's at http:// www.youtube.com/watch?v=2QsdUevUQgk, Cosgrove's at http://www.youtube .com/watch?v=RLWojKKRXMo.

64. Longman, 2002, p. 260.

65. Glick and Zegart, 2004, p. 208.

66. Prothero, 2002.

67. J. Taylor, 1998, p. 129.

68. "Demographic Data on the Victims of the September 11, 2001 Terror Attack on the World Trade Center, New York City," *Population and Development Review*, Volume 28, Number 3, September 2002, pp. 586–88. The exact numbers are 2,100 men and 2,064 whites among the victims.

69. Linenthal, 2001, p. 224.

70. Ibid., p. 226.

71. Ibid., pp. 227–29; Clavandier, 2004, p. 150.

CHAPTER 3. THE SACRALIZATION OF SHANKSVILLE

1. Craig Smith, "Shanksville Area Showing Strains of Living in the National Spotlight," *Pittsburgh Tribune-Review*, September 4, 2011.

2. Kashurba, 2002, p. 11.

3. M. Taylor, 2009, p. 176.

4. Robb Frederick, "The Day that Changed America," *Pittsburgh Tribune-Review*, September 11, 2002.

5. McClatchey would not grant permission to reproduce the image in this book. It can be easily found online, however. In chapter seven, the reader can find a still image from one of the films on Flight 93 of a cinematic variation on this iconic image.

6. Durand, 1999, p. 44.

7. Marx, 1964.

8. Chermak, Bailey, and Brown, 2003, p. 57.

9. See, e.g., http://flight93photo.blogspot.com/2006/07/val-mcclatchey-photo-more-smoking-guns.html.

10. Morin, 1971.

11. The Anti-Defamation League produced a 2003 report on anti-Semitism in 9/11 narratives that highlights some of the key elements in those narratives and the groups and Internet sites that propagate them (http://www.adl.org/anti_semitism/9-11conspiracytheories.pdf).

12. Linenthal, 2001, p. 119.

13. Kashurba, 2002, p. 81.

14. Sather-Wagstaff, 2009, pp. 170, 171.

15. Santino, 2006.

16. Margry and Sánchez-Carretero, 2011.

17. Kashurba, 2002, p. 51.

18. Ibid., pp. 91–92.

19. Personal interview with Barbara Black.

20. Elizabeth Gaffron, *Daily American* intern, in Flight 93 Somerset County Visitors Guide 2007, p. 7.

21. I discuss visitors' perceptions of the fence in detail in chapter eight.

22. The length was chosen to represent the 40 passengers on the plane—the four

suspected hijackers are not included in the count of 40, a symbolically significant act in itself.

23. Personal interview.

24. As I will note later, some Ambassadors explicitly informed visitors that they were welcome to leave objects should they choose to do so, and it is not clear how many such acts were caused by this suggestion rather than spontaneous and individual decision making on the part of visitors.

25. Document preserved in the Somerset, Pennsylvania, office of the National Park Service, Flight 93 Archival Collection, August 13, 2004.

26. Ibid., August 17, 2004.

27. Ibid., June 6, 2007.

28. Ibid., August 15, 2004.

29. Ibid., November 7, 2004.

30. Ibid., November 30, 2004.

31. Ibid., July 20, 2008.

32. Ibid., May 5, 2007.

33. Ibid., June 6, 2007.

34. Ibid., November 30, 2004.

35. Ibid., July 3, 2008.

36. Ibid., July 5, 2007.

37. Ibid., July 3, 2008.

38. Ibid., August 2, 2002.

39. Ibid., July 20, 2008.

40. Ibid., July 14, 2002.

41. Ibid., October 21, 2004.

42. The Park Service also made available at the site a "Junior Ranger Storybook for Younger Children" featuring Zoomer the Softball, which was left at the site by a child as a "tribute" to the passengers and crew, who "made their plane come down in a field instead of where a lot of people live or work." Zoomer explains to young readers why people leave tributes ("to remember, honor, or thank someone") and describes a number of the elements of the temporary memorial, including many of the flags flying atop the fence and the Angel Patriots discussed later in this chapter. "Superheroes are pretend," the reader is told, "but there are real heroes too." The pamphlet concludes: "Remember September 11, 2001, Honor the heroes of Flight 93, Choose to make a difference, Hope for tomorrow." The hijackers and terrorism are not mentioned in the narrative.

43. Document preserved in the Somerset, Pennsylvania, office of the National Park Service, Flight 93 Archival Collection, undated.

44. Linenthal, 2001, p. 114.

45. Personal interview.

46. In some conservative discourses, this is required precisely because of the sins of contemporary secular American culture.

47. Mauss, 1990.

48. Mauss, Hubert, and Hertz, 2009, pp. 48, 67.
49. Mauss, 1969, p. 593.
50. Durkheim, 1995, pp. 111, 112.
51. Ibid., pp. 114, 115.
52. Ibid., pp. 123–25.
53. Ibid., p. 119.
54. Ibid., p. 124.
55. Ibid., pp. 120, 121.
56. Ibid., p. 131.
57. Ibid., p. 130.
58. Ibid., pp. 133, 135.
59. Ibid., p. 136.
60. Ibid., p. 191.
61. Ibid., p. 201.
62. Ibid., p. 208.
63. Ibid., pp. 212, 213.
64. Ibid., p. 221.
65. Ibid., p. 222.
66. Although, as we will see in the next chapter, collective effervescence is to be found in abundance at the Flight 93 Memorial Chapel.
67. Collins, 2005.
68. They were at the site long enough to have weathered sufficiently to be replaced at least once; one sun- and rain-worn set was in a box in the storage facility in Somerset when I visited in the summer of 2008.
69. Personal interview. See too Glessner's account of this time in Elizabeth Gaffron, Flight 93 Somerset County Visitors Guide 2007, p. 8.
70. I discuss this last belief in detail in chapter six.
71. Personal interview.
72. Bingham supported McCain's 2000 bid for the White House "because the senator's maverick style appealed to him" (Barrett, 2002, p. 169).

CHAPTER 4. FLAG BODIES
1. This poster board can be seen in figure 3.2.
2. Mascherino was unwavering in emphasizing a distinction between the commemorative effort at the temporary memorial and his own work at the chapel. He speculated frequently on the likely incomprehension, or even hostility, that Park Service personnel would feel about the free mingling of church and state at the chapel; occasionally, he even suggested to me that perhaps Ambassadors at the temporary memorial were actively discouraging visitors from coming to the chapel. I saw no evidence of such deliberate antagonism to the chapel among the Ambassadors, though, as I describe in chapter five, it was clear that at least some Park Service officials and staff were just as eager to separate their efforts from Mascherino's as he was.

3. The bald eagle became the emblem of the U.S. in 1782.

4. Exodus 19:5–6, New American Bible.

5. Exodus 19:9–11.

6. Exodus 19:16–20.

7. Exodus 19:4.

8. Durand, 1999, p. 123.

9. Ibid., p. 129.

10. Morin, 1956, p. 14.

11. Sturken, 2007.

12. Schuler, 2004.

13. Sturken, 2007, p. 6.

14. This section is a composite ethnographic summary of several different commemorative events that took place at the chapel on September 11 and other dates between 2006 and 2011. Under Mascherino, much of the September 11 ceremony was repeated from year to year, with relatively slight variation.

15. Goffman, 1959.

16. Mauss, Hubert, and Hertz, 2009.

17. Mauss and Hubert, 1981, p. 30.

18. Ibid., p. 60.

19. Morin (2002 [1970], p. 130) defines sacrifice as "the systematic and universal magical exploitation of the fecundating force of death."

20. Marvin and Ingle, 1999, p. 63.

21. Ibid., p. 10.

22. Ibid., pp. 64, 66.

23. Mauss and Hubert, 1981.

24. Lincoln, 2003, p. 73.

25. We might note too that at least one of the Flight 93 passengers, Thomas Burnett Jr., was given a military funeral, although he was not a member of the armed forces, and his wife was presented with the flag totem that all families of soldiers killed in combat receive.

26. "How To Respect and Display Our Flag," Camden, NJ: Alpha Litho, 1942.

27. Marvin and Ingle, 1999, p. 21.

28. Burnett and Giombetti, 2006, p. 214.

29. Glick and Zegart, 2004, pp. 136–41.

30. Ibid., p. 208.

31. Morin, 2002 [1970], p. 127.

32. Mauss, Hubert, and Hertz, 2009, p. 75.

33. Mascherino's recollection of the passage was inexact, as Yahweh is not the speaker here. It is Isaiah who bemoans his unworthiness to gaze on the Lord, and one of the Lord's seraphs cauterizes his lips.

34. See, e.g., Hunter, 1992.

35. Mary Pickels, "Flight 93 Memorial Chapel Founder Gets Higher Calling," *Pittsburgh Tribune-Review*, September 26, 2009.

36. Ibid.

37. Mary Pickels, "Plans to Move Flight 93's Somerset Chapel on View Today," *Pittsburgh Tribune-Review*, September 11, 2010.

38. Anderson-Facile, 2007, p. 5.

39. Ibid., p. 43.

40. Ibid., pp. 87–88.

41. Ibid., p. 90.

CHAPTER 5. THE PERMANENT MEMORIAL

1. Britton, 2007.

2. Ibid., pp. 24, 26.

3. Personal interview.

4. Kashurba, 2002, p. 234.

5. General Management Plan Summary, p. 7.

6. The nonfamily members were Julie Bargmann (professor of landscape architecture at the University of Virginia), Robert Campbell (an architect and architecture critic for the Boston Globe), G. Henry Cook (president and CEO of the local Somerset Trust Bank), Dr. Gail Dubrow (dean of the Graduate School and vice provost at the University of Minnesota), Charles Fox (member of the Flight 93 Memorial Task Force and Historic Site and Museum Administrator for the Somerset Historical Center), Connie Hummel (principal of Shanksville High School), Jonathan Jarvis (regional director of the Pacific West Region of the National Park Service), Laurie Olin (professor of landscape architecture at the School of Design of the University of Pennsylvania), and Thomas Sokolowski (director of the Andy Warhol Museum in Pittsburgh).

7. *OnCampus*, Volume 38, Number 13.

8. This idea of tracing the flight path as a crucial element of commemoration extends beyond the formal design of memorials. When I was interviewed by a local radio station host to talk about the ten-year anniversary of the crash in August 2011, the interviewer informed me that a local pilot apparently had recently recapitulated the precise Newark to Shanksville trajectory Flight 93 took on September 11, 2001, as a tribute.

9. Flight 93 National Memorial International Design Competition Stage II Jury Report, September 7, 2005, p. 2.

10. Ibid., p. 3.

11. Ibid., p. 4.

12. Kashurba, 2002, p. 239.

13. Flight 93 National Memorial International Design Competition Stage II Jury Report, pp. 4–5.

14. August 2, 2008, Joint Meeting Notes, p. 18.

15. Jury Report, p. 13.

16. General Management Plan Summary, p. 15.

17. Ibid., p. 16.
18. Paul Murdoch Architects, p. 13.
19. Clavandier, 2004, p. 144.
20. Ibid., p. 149.
21. The tower will be one of the last memorial features to be built, according to the present National Park Service construction phasing plan.
22. The "H" is for "Hijra," which is the journey the prophet Muhammad took from Mecca to Medina in 622 C.E., or year one in the Islamic calendar.
23. Paula Reed Ward, "Designer of Flight 93 Memorial Receptive to Changes," *Pittsburgh Post-Gazette*, September 16, 2005.
24. Rawls, unpublished manuscript, p. 35.
25. Personal interview.
26. Rawls, unpublished manuscript, p. 53.
27. Ibid.
28. Ibid., p. 55.
29. Ibid., p. 77.
30. Ibid., p. 61.
31. Ibid., pp. 89–90.
32. Ibid., p. 88.
33. Ibid., p. 78.
34. Ibid., p. 79.
35. Ibid., p. xvi.
36. Ibid., pp. 48, 142.
37. Ibid., p. 148.
38. Ibid., p. 80, emphasis added.
39. Ibid., p. 45.
40. Ibid., p. 85.
41. "Crescent of Betrayal," interview with Jamie Glazov, *Frontpage*, September 8, 2008.
42. Griffin, 2006, p. 181.
43. E.g., R. Morgan, 2006, pp. 158–59.
44. Noam Cohen, "On Wikipedia, Echoes of 9/11 'Edit Wars,'" *New York Times*, September 12, 2011.
45. Goertzel, 1994, p. 731.
46. Fenster, 1999, p. 93.
47. Stark and Bainbridge, 1986; Dawson, 1998.
48. Lofland and Stark, 1965.
49. See, e.g., Jerrold Post, Ehud Sprinzak, and Laurita Denny, 2009; and Juergensmeyer, 2009.
50. Keen, 2008, p. 39.
51. Lyotard, 1984.
52. Wagner-Pacifici and Schwartz, 1991.

CHAPTER 6. THE CULTURAL NARRATIVES OF THE BOOKS ON
FLIGHT 93

1. Monahan, 2010.
2. Alexander et al., 2006.
3. Damon DiMarco, ed., 2004, *Tower Stories: The Autobiography of September 11th*. Lewisburg, KY: Revolution Publishers.
4. Annie Thoms, ed. 2011. *With Their Eyes: September 11th—The View from a High School at Ground Zero*. New York: HarperCollins.
5. Michael Benfante and Dave Hollander. 2011. *Reluctant Hero: A 9/11 Survivor Speaks Out about That Unthinkable Day, What He's Learned, How He's Struggled, and What No One Should Ever Forget*. New York: Skyhorse Publishing.
6. Leslie Haskin. 2006. *Between Heaven and Ground Zero: One Woman's Struggle for Survival and Faith in the Ashes of 9/11*. Ada, MI: Bethany House; 2007. *Held*. Carroll Stream, IL: Tyndale House; and 2009. *God Has Not Forgotten about You: . . . and He Cares More than You Can Imagine*. Ada, MI: Bethany House.
7. Genelle Guzman-McMillan. 2011. *Angel in the Rubble: The Miraculous Rescue of 9/11's Last Survivor*. New York: Howard Books.
8. Alissa Torres. 2008. *American Widow*. New York: Villard; Marian Fontana. 2006. *A Widow's Walk: A Memoir of 9/11*. New York: Simon & Schuster.
9. Brian Birdwell, Mel Birdwell, and Ginger Kolbaba. 2004. *Refined by Fire: A Family's Triumph of Love and Faith*. Carroll Stream, IL: Tyndale House; Cheryl McGuiness and Lois Rabey. 2004. *Beauty beyond the Ashes: Choosing Hope after Crisis*. New York: Howard Books.
10. Bonnie McEneaney. 2010. *Messages: Signs, Visits, and Premonitions from Loved Ones Lost on 9/11*. New York: William Morrow.
11. Karen Kingsbury. 2003. *One Tuesday Morning*. Grand Rapids, MI: Zondervan; Jonathan Safran Foer. 2011. *Extremely Loud and Incredibly Close: A Novel*. New York: Mariner Books; DeLillo, 2007.
12. The latter term is taken from James Joyce's *Finnegans Wake*.
13. Campbell, 1949, p. 30.
14. Mauss, Hubert, and Hertz, 2009, p. 42.
15. Ibid, p. 40.
16. Ibid. p. 48.
17. Czarnowski, 1919, p. 16.
18. Albert, 1999, pp. 16–17.
19. Alexander et al., 2006, p. 106.
20. Ibid., p. 98.
21. Jeffrey Alexander, "Power and Performance: The War on Terror Between Sacred and Profane," RSCAS Distinguished Lectures, European University Institute, Florence, Italy, January 2007.
22. The mythic archetype nonetheless seems still to be reflected in the reality of differences in what American male and female soldiers actually do, i.e., combat is

reserved for men alone, and the overwhelming majority of American casualties in both the Iraqi and Afghan theaters are men.

23. Riley, 2010.

24. The author, Jon Barrett, had initially written an article in the magazine announcing Bingham's selection as their Person of the Year for 2001 and subsequently took up the book project.

25. Another ESPN story about Jeremy Glick bore the following title: "Glick Lost His Life, but Won His Final Bout" (Adrian Wojnarowski, ESPN.com, September 17, 2001).

26. Burnett and Giombetti, 2006, pp. 10, 11.

27. Ibid., p. 296.

28. Beamer and Abraham, 2002, p. 29.

29. Glick and Zegart, 2004, p. 121.

30. Ibid., p. 17.

31. Ibid., p. 45.

32. Ibid., p. 145.

33. Longman, 2002, p. 144.

34. Ibid., pp. 144–45.

35. Ibid..

36. Ibid., p. 150.

37. Barrett, 2002, pp. 12–13.

38. Ibid., p. 91.

39. Ibid., pp. 97–98.

40. Ibid., p. 168.

41. Burnett and Giombetti, 2006, p. 96.

42. Beamer and Abraham, 2002, p. 220.

43. Friedland, 2005.

44. King, 2009.

45. Ibid., p. 5.

46. Ibid., p. 12.

47. Ibid.

48. King notes that themes of homosexuality were at least occasionally invoked, albeit not in mainstream but in more marginal media, in a negative light to rhetorically denigrate the hijackers; e.g., a 2001 *National Enquirer* story headlined "Mohamed Atta and Several of His Bloody Henchmen Led Secret Gay Lives for Years" (ibid., p. 19).

49. Beamer and Abraham, 2002, p. 16.

50. Ibid., p. 41.

51. Ibid., p. 55.

52. Ibid., p. 25.

53. Barrett, 2002, pp. 26–28.

54. Ibid., p. 29.

55. Ibid., p. 34.
56. King, 2009, p. 15.
57. Barrett, 2002, p. 67.
58. Glick and Zegart, 2004, p. 44.
59. Longman, 2002, p. 14.
60. Ibid., p. 32.
61. Ibid., pp. 230, 231.
62. Ibid., p. 159.
63. Ibid., p. 127.
64. Ibid., p. 73.
65. Patterson, 1999, pp. 218–24.
66. Beamer and Abraham, 2002, p. 11.
67. Jefferson and Middlebrooks, 2006, p. 9.
68. Burnett and Giombetti, 2006, p. 9.
69. Glick and Zegart, 2004, p. 7.
70. Burnett and Giombetti, 2006, p. 15.
71. Ibid., p. 246.
72. Ibid., p. 12.
73. Ibid., p. 11.
74. Ibid., p. 13.
75. Longman, 2002, p. 116.
76. Beamer and Abraham, 2002, p. 15.
77. Ibid., p. 31.
78. Beamer and Abraham, 2002, p. 83.
79. Ibid., pp. 175–76.
80. Ibid., pp. 165–66.
81. Ibid., pp. 187, 188.
82. Ibid., p. 213.
83. Ibid., p. 193.
84. Ibid., pp. 225–26.
85. Ibid., p. 234.
86. Ibid., pp. 300–1.
87. Ibid., pp. 301–2.
88. Jefferson and Middlebrooks, 2006, pp. 89, 100.
89. Ibid., p. 51.
90. Ibid., p. 44.
91. Ibid., p. 18.
92. Ibid.., pp. 109–10.
93. Glick and Zegart, 2004, p. 49.
94. Beamer and Abraham, 2002, pp. 149–50, 274.
95. Ibid., p. 30.
96. Ibid., p. 52.
97. Jefferson and Middlebrooks, 2006, p. 88.

98. Longman, 2002, pp. 116–17.
99. Glick and Zegart, 2004, p. 105.
100. Ibid., p. 207.
101. Longman, 2002, p. 20.
102. Ibid., p. 29.
103. Ibid., p. 141.
104. Ibid., p. 240.
105. Ibid., p. 166.

CHAPTER 7. THE CULTURAL NARRATIVES OF THE FILMS ON FLIGHT 93

1. Cited in Simpson, 2006, p. 94.
2. Thomas Kinkade, who died in 2012, was a contemporary commercial artist who claimed to have his work hanging in more American homes than any other painter. He worked in an idiom perfectly described as pseudo-nostalgic, ultra-patriotic kitsch, specializing in the symbols and images from a mythological "days of yore" in American history that arguably never existed.
3. The shot, though stylized, is modeled on reality. Hoglan's brother Vaughn and his wife, Kathy, were the parents of five babies by surrogate mothers, four of them delivered by Alice, including triplets born six months before the crash of Flight 93 (Longman, 2002, p. 129).
4. Andrejevic, 2004, p. 133. He is elliptically borrowing from Todd Gitlin.
5. Andrejevic, 2004, p. 135.
6. McDermott, 2005, p. 249.
7. Unlike *Flight 93*, *United 93* correctly replicates the hijackers' actual seat positions, so their identities in the film are discernible on that basis.
8. John Harris, "Skating on Thin Air," *Guardian*, May 25, 2006.
9. Ibid.
10. Galloway, 2006, p. 40.
11. According to Jere Longman, writing in a *New York Times* review of the film ("Paul Greengrass's Filming of Flight 93's Story, Trying to Define Heroics," April 24, 2006), there were significant levels of disagreement and discomfort among the Flight 93 families regarding how democratically heroism on the plane should be depicted: "It's not that other victims' families discounted or resented the valor of those men [Beamer, Bingham, Burnett, and Glick]. But the families resisted early attempts by politicians to honor only these four. There was concern that bravery aboard United Airlines Flight 93 not be made into a kind of Olympic sport, where some passengers received a gold medal for gallantry while others had to settle for silver or bronze." Hilda Marcin's mother expressed the more democratic perspective ("You don't want to cause problems between families, but I don't understand the thinking that someone should be highly elevated from someone else. What is to be gained? . . . Why diminish everyone else? They're all dead"), while Bingham's mother represented the more elitist vision of heroic depiction ("while she

believed everyone alive played a role in the resistance, [she said] 'It's much more likely that 30 or so people stayed in their seats while six or so guys ran down the aisle' "). It is perhaps something of a statement about the manner in which mythical narrative comes to be considered as obviously true that Bingham's mother is one of the hardline defenders of the selective vision of heroism, given the fact that, of the four central hero figures, Bingham is the only one who never mentioned an effort to take back the plane in his phone conversations and the evidence that he participated in a central role in the revolt is completely circumstantial.

12. A slightly different version of this same film was released under the title *Heroes of Flight 93.*

13. Longman, 2002, p. 208.

14. Ibid, p. 113.

15. See Richard Eicher, 2001, *The Longest Night: A Military History of the Civil War,* New York: Simon & Schuster, p. 657.

16. Ibid., p. 216, emphasis added.

CHAPTER 8. MYTH IN PRACTICE

1. Sather-Wagstaff, 2008.

2. Only a few months before I conducted these interviews, the Flight 93 Memorial Task Force was in negotiations with Mike Svonavec of Svonavec Inc., one of the local property owners, to purchase land needed for the permanent memorial. Svonavec proved a somewhat unwilling negotiator, and the Families of Flight 93 had written a letter to President Bush asking him to give the secretary of the interior authorization to take the land in dispute for use in the memorial (Bob Lentz, "A Request to Seize 9/11 land," *Philadelphia Inquirer,* December 29, 2008, p. B7).

3. Stark, 2008, pp. 56, 57, 126, 127.

4. He is perhaps referring here to the unfounded charge leveled by Alec Rawls and some other proponents of the memorial conspiracy theory, which I addressed in chapter five, that some of the unmarked wall segments are symbolically intended as covert acknowledgements of the hijackers.

CHAPTER 9. WHAT FLIGHT 93 TELLS US ABOUT AMERICA

1. Wright, 1977, p. 208.

2. Ibid., p. 212.

3. Haidt even cited Durkheim in using the term "effervescence."

4. *Inside 9-11: What Really Happened.* Reporters, Writers, and Editors of *Der Spiegel* Magazine. 2001. Translated by Paul De Angelis and Elisabeth Kaestner. New York: St. Martin's Press, pp. 22–24.

5. Bellah, 1975, p. viii.

REFERENCES

Albert, Jean-Pierre. 1999. "Du martyr à la star: les metamorphoses des héros nation-
aux." Pp. 11–32 in *La Fabrique des héros*, Pierre Centlivres, Daniel Fabre, and Fran-
çoise Zonabend, eds. Paris: Éditions de la Maison des Sciences de l'Homme.

Alexander, Jeffrey, Bernhard Giesen, and Jason Mast, eds. 2006. *Social Performance:
Symbolic Action, Cultural Pragmatics, and Ritual*. New York: Cambridge University
Press.

Amis, Martin. 2008. *The Second Plane: September 11: Terror and Boredom*. New York:
Alfred A. Knopf.

Anderson-Facile, Doreen. 2007. *Dueling Identities: The Christian Biker*. Lanham, MD:
Lexington.

Andrejevic, Mark. 2004. *Reality TV: The Work of Being Watched*. New York: Rowman
& Littlefield.

Ariès, Philippe. 1977. *L'Homme devant la mort*. Paris: Seuil.

Balzac, Honoré de. 1977 [1831]. *The Wild Ass's Skin*. Translated by Herbert Hunt. London: Penguin.

Barrett, Jon. 2002. *Hero of Flight 93: Mark Bingham*. Los Angeles: Advocate Books.

Barthes, Roland. 1972. *Mythologies*. Translated by Annette Lavers. New York: Farrar,
Straus, and Giroux.

Beamer, Lisa, and Ken Abraham. 2002. *Let's Roll! Ordinary People, Extraordinary Courage*. Wheaton, IL: Tyndale House.

Becker, Ernest. 1973. *The Denial of Death*. New York: Free Press.

Bellah, Robert. 1975. *The Broken Covenant: American Civil Religion in Time of Trial*.
New York: Seabury Press.

———. 1976. *Beyond Belief: Essays on Religion in a Post-Traditional World*. New York:
Harper & Row.

Britton, Dee. 2007. "Arlington's Cairn: Constructing the Commemorative Foundation
for United States' Terrorist Victims." *Journal of Political and Military Sociology*,
Volume 35, Number 1, pp. 17–38.

Brunsma, David, David Overfelt, and J. Steven Picou, eds. 2007. *The Sociology
of Katrina: Perspectives on a Modern Catastrophe*. Lanham, MD: Rowman &
Littlefield.

Burnett, Deena, and Anthony Giombetti. 2006. *Fighting Back: Living Life beyond Ourselves*. Altamonte Springs, FL: Advantage Inspirational Books.

Campbell, Joseph. 1949. *The Hero with a Thousand Faces*. Princeton, NJ: Princeton
University Press.

Chermak, Steven, Frankie Bailey, and Michelle Brown, eds. 2003. *Media Representations of September 11*. Westport, CT: Praeger.

Clavandier, Gaëlle. 2004. *La Mort collective. Pour une sociologie des catastrophes*. Paris: CNRS Éditions.

Collins, Randall. 2005. *Interaction Ritual Chains*. Princeton, NJ: Princeton University Press.

Czarnowski, Stefan. 1919. *Le Culte des héros et ses conditions sociales*. Paris: Alcan.

Dawson, Lorne. 1998. *Comprehending Cults*. Oxford: Oxford University Press.

DeLillo, Don. 2007. *Falling Man*. New York: Scribner.

Durand, Gilbert. 1999. *The Anthropological Structures of the Imaginary*. Brisbane: Boombana.

Durkheim, Émile. 1995. *The Elementary Forms of Religious Life*. Translated by Karen Fields. New York: Free Press.

Eliade, Mircea. 1988. *Aspects du mythe*. Paris: Gallimard.

Elias, Norbert. 1985 [1982]. *The Loneliness of the Dying*. Translated by Edmund Jephcott. New York: Basil Blackwell.

Fagan, Brian. 1984. *The Aztecs*. New York: W.H. Freeman and Co.

Fenster, Mark. 1999. *Conspiracy Theories: Secrecy and Power in American Culture*. Minneapolis: University of Minnesota Press.

Friedland, Roger. 2005. "Religious Terror and the Erotics of Exceptional Violence." *Anthropological Yearbook on European Cultures*, Volume 14, pp. 39–74.

Friend, David. 2006. *Watching the World Change: The Stories behind the Images of 9/11*. New York: Farrar, Straus and Giroux.

Giddens, Anthony. 1990. *The Consequences of Modernity*. Stanford: Stanford University Press.

Gitlin, Todd. 2006. *The Intellectuals and the Flag*. New York: Columbia University Press.

Glick, Lyz, and Dan Zegart. 2004. *Your Father's Voice: Letters for Emmy about Life with Jeremy—and without Him after 9/11*. New York: St. Martin's Press.

Goertzel, Ted. 1994. "Belief in Conspiracy Theories." *Political Psychology*, Volume 15, Number 4, pp. 731–42.

Goffman, Ervin. 1959. *The Presentation of Self in Everyday Life*. New York: Anchor.

Green, James. 2008. *Beyond the Good Death: The Anthropology of Modern Dying*. Philadelphia: University of Pennsylvania Press.

Griffin, David Ray. 2006. *Christian Faith and the Truth behind 9/11: A Call to Reflection and Action*. Louisville, KY: Westminster John Knox Press.

Halbwachs, Maurice. 1992. *On Collective Memory*. Edited and translated by Lewis Coser. Chicago: University of Chicago Press.

Heidegger, Martin. 1962. *Being and Time*. Translated by John Macquarrie and Edward Robinson. New York: Harper & Row.

Hunter, James. 1992. *Culture Wars: The Struggle to Control the Family, Art, Education, Law, and Politics in America*. New York: Basic Books.

Jefferson, Lisa, and Felicia Middlebrooks. 2006. *Called: "Hello, My Name Is Lisa*

Jefferson. I Understand Your Plane Is Being Hijacked . . ." 9:45 a.m., Flight 93, September 11, 2001. Chicago: Northfield Publishing.

Juergensmeyer, Mark. 2009. "Islam's 'Neglected Duty.'" Pp. 419–34 in *Psychology of Terrorism*, Jeff Victoroff and Arie Kruglanski, eds. New York: Psychology Press.

Kashurba, Glenn. 2002. *Courage after the Crash: Flight 93: Aftermath, an Oral and Pictorial Chronicle.* Somerset, PA: SAJ Publishing.

———. 2006. *Quiet Courage: The Definitive Account of Flight 93 and Its Aftermath.* Somerset, PA: SAJ Publishing.

Kaufman, Sharon. 2005. *. . . And a Time to Die: How American Hospitals Shape the End of Life.* Chicago: University of Chicago Press.

Kean, Thomas, and Lee Hamilton. 2004. *The 9/11 Commission Report: The National Commission on Terrorist Attacks upon the United States.* New York: St. Martin's Press.

Keen, Andrew. 2008. *The Cult of the Amateur.* New York: Doubleday.

King, Samantha. 2009. "Virtually Normal: Mark Bingham, the War on Terror, and the Sexual Politics of Sport." *Journal of Sport and Social Issues*, Volume 33, Number 1, pp. 5–24.

Lawton, Julia. 2000. *The Dying Process: Patients' Experience of Palliative Care.* Routledge: New York.

Lincoln, Bruce. 2003. *Holy Terrors: Thinking about Religion after September 11.* Chicago: University of Chicago Press.

Linenthal, Edward. 2001. *The Unfinished Bombing: Oklahoma City in American Memory.* New York: Oxford University Press.

Lofland, John, and Rodney Stark. 1965. "Becoming a World Saver: A Theory of Conversion to a Deviant Perspective." *American Sociological Review*, Volume 30, Number 6, pp. 862–75.

Lomnitz, Claudio. 2008. *Death and the Idea of Mexico.* New York: Zone Books.

Longman, Jere. 2002. *Among the Heroes: United Flight 93 and the Passengers and Crew Who Fought Back.* New York: HarperCollins.

Lyotard, Jean-François. 1984. *The Postmodern Condition: A Report on Knowledge.* Minneapolis: University of Minnesota Press.

Margry, Peter Jan, and Cristina Sánchez-Carretero. 2011. *Grassroots Memorials: The Politics of Memorializing Traumatic Death.* New York: Berghahn Books.

Marvin, Carolyn, and David Ingle. 1999. *Blood Sacrifice and the Nation: Totem Rituals and the American Flag.* New York: Cambridge University Press.

Marx, Leo. 1964. *The Machine in the Garden: Technology and the Pastoral Idea in America.* New York: Oxford University Press.

Mauksch, Hans. 1997. "The Organizational Context of Dying." Pp. 5–26 in *Death: The Final Stage of Growth*, Elisabeth Kübler-Ross. New York. Scribner.

Mauss, Marcel. 1969. "La Nation." Pp. 573–625 in *Œuvres*, Volume 3, Victor Karady, ed. Paris: Les Éditions de Minuit.

———. 1990. *The Gift.* New York: W. W. Norton and Co.

Mauss, Marcel, and Henri Hubert. 1981. *Sacrifice: Its Nature and Functions.* Chicago: University of Chicago Press.

Mauss, Marcel, Henri Hubert, and Robert Hertz. 2009. *Saints, Heroes, Myths, and Rites: Classical Durkheimian Studies of Religion and Society*. Translated by Alexander Riley, Sarah Daynes, and Cyril Isnart. Boulder, CO: Paradigm Publishers.

McDermott, Terry. 2005. *Perfect Soldiers: The Hijackers: Who They Were, Why They Did It*. New York: HarperCollins.

Monahan, Brian. 2010. *The Shock of the News: Media Coverage and the Making of 9/11*. New York: New York University Press.

Morgan, Rowland. 2006. *Flight 93 Revealed: What Really Happened on the 9/11 "Let's Roll" "Flight?* New York: Carroll & Graf.

Morin, Edgar. 1956. *Le Cinéma, ou l'homme imaginaire*. Paris: Éditions de Minuit.

———. 1971. *Rumour in Orléans*. New York: Pantheon.

———. 2002 [1970]. *L'Homme et la mort*. Paris: Éditions du Seuil.

Murphy, Dean. 2002. *September 11: An Oral History*. New York: Doubleday.

Patterson, Orlando. 1999. *Rituals of Blood: The Consequences of Slavery in Two American Centuries*. New York: Basic Books.

Paz, Octavio. 1993. *El laberinto de la soledad, Postdata, Vuelta a El laberinto de la soledad*. Mexico City: Fondo de Cultura Económica.

Picardie, Ruth. 1997. *Before I Say Goodbye*. London: Penguin.

Post, Jerrold, Ehud Sprinzak, and Laurita Denny. 2009. "The Terrorists in Their Own Words." Pp. 23–34 in *Psychology of Terrorism*, Jeff Victoroff and Arie Kruglanski, eds. New York: Psychology Press.

Prothero, Stephen. 2002. *Purified by Fire: A History of Cremation in America*. Berkeley: University of California Press.

Riley, Alexander. 2010. *Impure Play: Sacredness, Transgression, and the Tragic in Popular Culture*. Lanham, MD: Lexington Books.

Rosenblatt, Abram, Jeff Greenberg, Sheldon Solomon, Tom Pyszczynski, and Deborah Lyon. 1989. "Evidence for Terror Management Theory: The Effects of Mortality Salience on Reactions to Those Who Violate or Uphold Cultural Values." *Journal of Personality and Social Psychology*, Volume 57, Number 4, pp. 681–90.

Rozario, Kevin. 2007. *The Culture of Calamity: Disaster and the Making of Modern America*. Chicago: University of Chicago Press.

Santino, Jack, ed. 2006. *Spontaneous Shrines and the Public Memorialization of Death*. New York: Palgrave Macmillan.

Sather-Wagstaff, Joy. 2008. "Picturing Experience: A Tourist-Centered Perspective on Commemorative Historical Sites." *Tourist Studies*, Volume 8, Number 1, pp. 77–103.

Schudson, Michael. 1992. *Watergate in American Memory: How We Remember, Forget, and Reconstruct the Past*. New York: Basic Books.

Schuler, Rhoda. 2004. "Pilgrimage to Shanksville, Pennsylvania: Where Heaven and Earth Meet in American Civil Religion," paper presented at North American Academy of Liturgy Liturgical Theology Seminar.

Simons, Daniel, and Christopher Chabris. 2012. "Common (Mis)Beliefs about Memory: A Replication and Comparison of Telephone and Mechanical Turk Survey Methods." *PLos ONE*. Volume 7, Issue 12.

Simpson, David. 2006. *9/11: The Culture of Commemoration.* Chicago: University of Chicago Press.

Snodgrass, Richard. 2011. *An Uncommon Field: The Flight 93 Temporary Memorial.* Pittsburgh: Carnegie Mellon University Press.

Stannard, David. 1977. *The Puritan Way of Death: A Study in Religion, Culture, and Social Change.* New York: Oxford University Press.

Stark, Rodney. 2008. *What Americans Really Believe.* Waco, TX: Baylor University Press.

Stark, Rodney, and William Sims Bainbridge. 1986. *The Future of Religion: Secularization, Revival and Cult Formation.* Berkeley: University of California Press.

Sturken, Marita. 2004. "The Aesthetics of Absence: Rebuilding Ground Zero." *American Ethnologist,* Volume 31, Number 3, pp. 311–25.

———. 2007. *Tourists of History: Memory, Kitsch, and Consumerism from Oklahoma City to Ground Zero.* Durham, NC: Duke University Press.

Sudnow, David. 1967. *Passing On: The Social Organization of Dying.* Englewood Cliffs, NJ: Prentice-Hall.

Taylor, John. 1998. *Body Horror: Photojournalism, Catastrophe and War.* New York: New York University Press.

Taylor, Mark. 2009. *Field Notes from Elsewhere: Reflections on Dying and Living.* New York: Columbia University Press.

Vaughan, Diane. 2006. "The Social Shaping of Commission Reports," *Sociological Forum,* Volume 21, Number 2, pp. 291–306.

Wagner-Pacifici, Robin, and Barry Schwartz. 1991. "The Vietnam Veterans Memorial: Commemorating a Difficult Past." *American Journal of Sociology,* Volume 97, Number 2, pp. 376–420.

Wright, Will. 1977. *Sixguns and Society: A Structural Study of the Western.* Berkeley: University of California Press.

INDEX

ABOUT THE AUTHOR

Alexander T. Riley is Professor of Sociology and Anthropology at Bucknell University. His previous books include *Godless Intellectuals? The Intellectual Pursuit of the Sacred Reinvented* and *Impure Play: Sacredness, Transgression, and the Tragic in Popular Culture.*